CHRISTINA REID

Plays: 1

Tea in a China Cup
Did You Hear the One About the Irishman . . . ?
Joyriders
The Belle of the Belfast City
My Name, Shall I Tell You My Name?
Clowns

with an introduction by Maria M. Delgado

Methuen Drama

METHUEN CONTEMPORARY DRAMATISTS

This collection first published in Great Britain 1997
by Methuen Drama
an imprint of Reed International Books Ltd
Michelin House, 81 Fulham Road, London SW3 6RB
and Auckland, Melbourne, Singapore and Toronto

Joyriders and *Tea in a China Cup* first published as a Methuen Theatrescript in
1987

The Belle of the Belfast City and *Did You Hear the One About the Irishman . . . ?*
first published as a Methuen New Theatrescript in 1989.

Introduction copyright © 1997 by Maria M. Delgado
Collection copyright © 1997 by Christina Reid

The author has asserted her moral rights

ISBN 0 413 71220 6

A CIP catalogue record for this book is available at the British Library

The photograph on the cover is of the author's mother and Tommy the
Banjo-player, *circa* 1938

Typeset by Wilmaset Ltd, Birkenhead, Wirral
Printed and bound in Great Britain by Cox & Wyman Ltd, Reading,
Berkshire

Contents

Chronology

of first performances
of stage plays

Introduction

'Beyond the Troubles':
The political drama of Christina Reid

Although Irish drama has been largely perceived as a male-dominated phenomenon, since Lady Gregory at the turn of the century women have played an important role in the country's theatrical culture; a role often overlooked in histories of Irish theatre, which tend to focus on a male literary canon. Women's prominence as directors, designers and performers, both in the theatrical mainstream and in the alternative structures of music-hall, fringe, children's and community theatre, as well as theatre-in-education, has rarely been chronicled or commented on. Nevertheless, as women in Eire and Northern Ireland enjoy greater prominence in the varied areas of theatrical production, it is not surprising to note their growing visibility as dramatists.

Christina Reid is one of a number of women dramatists who emerged in the 1980s. Born in 1942 into a fiercely Protestant Belfast working-class family, Reid left school at fifteen, working in a range of menial and administrative jobs before returning to full-time education in her mid-thirties, as a married mother of three. She had already written *Did You Hear the One About the Irishman . . . ?* (1985)[1], winner of the UTV Drama Award in 1980, when she began a degree in English, Sociology and Russian Studies at Queen's University, Belfast. When *Tea in a China Cup* (1983) won her a Thames TV Award and a residency at Belfast's Lyric Theatre in 1983, Reid abandoned her studies to concentrate on her writing. Since then, she has proved herself a prolific dramatist, drawing on her own family experiences to provide a series of plays which have daringly interrogated issues of

---

[1] Dates are those of the first stage production and not previous television or radio productions or rehearsed readings.

nationalism and colonialism through a concentration on those whose experiences lie outside of 'official' history – particularly working-class women.

Contemporary Irish drama itself has defied and continues to defy easy categorization. Critics have avoided classification based on the North–South divide because so many Northern Irish writers have stated that they perceive themselves as Irish rather than British. The poet Derek Mahon, for example, a Belfast-born Protestant, thinks of Ireland, despite the border, as a single country.[2] Reid too states that she considers herself Irish. 'We don't speak English the same way,' she claims, 'our speech patterns are different, how we say things is different.'[3] As such, classification has taken place largely according to genre and subject matter, with certain dramatists like Tom Kilroy, Marie Jones and Marina Carr associated with a poetic, Beckettian or allegorical tradition, whilst others like Reid, Martin Lynch and Anne Devlin are too often pigeonholed rather pejoratively as 'political' dramatists, engaging in a pseudo-documentary, largely realist dialectic with the Troubles. As Reid's work, like that of Frank McGuinness and Brian Friel, indicates, such classification is fraught with problems. Political drama is not by definition dependent on simplistic agit-prop techniques. Genres have become anything but fixed, with dramatists drawing on both recent and distant cultural and political history to provide plays which destabilize any stable notion of what an Irish play is. Reid's work, as the plays in this volume clearly indicate, playfully deconstructs established genres, and cannot be easily attributed to a 'realist' or 'poetic' tradition. What her plays do constantly demonstrate, however, is the fact that political theatre can be witty, dynamic, challenging, formally inventive and wickedly humorous.

---

[2] See Jane Eisner, 'Using art to break down barriers', *The Philadelphia Inquirer*, 9 September 1986, pp. 1c, 5c.

[3] Quoted in Michael Herbert, 'Across the Great Divide', *The Irish Post*, 22 September 1990, p. 4.

Although plays about the sectarian struggles in the North of Ireland are by no means a recent phenomenon – St John Ervine's *Mixed Marriage*, for example, was written in 1911 – the 1980s saw a concerted attempt on the part of an emerging generation of dramatists to engage with the debate by presenting the multiple consequences of the entry of British troops into Northern Ireland in 1968. During the 1970s, works about the Civil War raging in the North of Ireland rarely reached the British stage. Rob Richie, former literary manager of the Royal Court Theatre, cites numerous reasons for this, writing of 'the stifling pressures that affected more general coverage and debate [of the subject] in the 1970s', the censoring of potentially controversial material by the BBC as well as a hesitancy on the part of fringe companies to deal with issues beyond the immediate isles.[4] Brian Friel's *The Freedom of the City*, produced in 1973, did provide a controversial reading of the Bloody Sunday massacre of 1972 where fourteen civilian civil rights marchers were killed in Derry by British paratroopers, but it was one of the few exceptions in a decade where the sectarian conflict stimulated only a limited dramatic response.

The 1980s and 1990s, however, have seen Northern Ireland become, in Christina Reid's words, 'flavour of the month'.[5] The traumatic Maze Prison hunger strikes of the early 1980s – Bobby Sands's funeral providing the largest mobilization of Northern Ireland's Roman Catholic population this century; the 'shoot to kill' policy allegedly in operation by the security forces; and the Government's restrictions over the broadcasting of interviews with members of Sinn Fein resulted in an interrogation of issues generated by the situation in Northern Ireland through drama: a medium perhaps perceived as less susceptible to censorship in the conservative political climate of the 1980s. Whilst Hollywood limited the scope of representation, reducing Belfast to a convenient battletorn backdrop for

[4] Rob Ritchie, 'Out of the North', *Rat in the Skull* (London: Methuen, 1984), pp. 3–4.
[5] Quoted in Jane Eisner, 'Using art to break down barriers', 1c.

thrillers, with IRA terrorists presented as aberrant and robotic villains, programmed to kill and synonymous with evil itself, dramatists such as Reid sought to question such simplistic portrayals by chronicling the support provided by the Catholic and Protestant communities for the paramilitaries, and discussing the supposed differences between the nationalist and loyalist communities. In addition, the steady increase in loyalist violence in the 1980s generated a number of textual explorations of loyalist paramilitary violence – conspicuously Reid's *The Belle of the Belfast City* (1989), which examines the tensions present when three generations of women in a Belfast Protestant family come together during the week of an anti-Anglo–Irish agreement rally in which the National Front displays an ominous presence. Also, as the British Government's broadcasting ban restricted the airing of views held by factions of the Catholic population, dramatists took up the challenge of representing the views of these communities. Not that dramatists like Devlin and Reid have limited themselves to dramatizing the concerns of their own communities, although both found initial recognition with such works: Devlin with *Ourselves Alone* (1985), and Reid with *Tea in a China Cup*, a work which like the later *The Belle of the Belfast City*, interrogates the traditions and loyalties which govern the behaviour of the city's fiercely Protestant working classes. Rather, both have gone on to deconstruct the problematic issues of identity and self-definition facing both Catholic and Protestant communities in Northern Ireland.

Christina Reid's plays are often centred around the domestic environment and the disenfranchised. Significantly, many of her protagonists are working-class women whose stories and memories form the backbone of the plays. In *The Belle of the Belfast City*, Dolly, the seventy-two-year-old grandmother who struggles to keep her fractured family together is a former music-hall star whose bawdy songs and unconventional antics conjure a magical Belfast far removed from that represented by her nephew Jack, a hardline loyalist politician. It is equally distant from the harsher puritanical ethos of her daughter Vi, and vastly different again from her black granddaughter Belle's incomprehension of a society which she has never visited. *Tea in a China Cup* focuses on the differing experiences of three generations of women in a working-class Belfast Protestant family, but here the tapestry of tales is linked by the presence of a single central character, Beth, torn between the influence of the particular traditions she has grown up within and the pull of a future away from the rhetoric of gentility and respectability to which her family has slavishly adhered. *Joyriders*, commissioned and produced by Paines Plough in 1986, grew out of the work Reid did with residents at the notorious Divis Flats estate while she was writer-in-residence at the Lyric Theatre, Belfast. The play is structured around the day-to-day activities of four Catholic teenagers on a youth training scheme running at a now-disused textile mill in Belfast. The four teenagers feel themselves to be on the periphery of a society which they regard as having already rejected them. At seventeen, they have no illusions about the future that awaits them and view their training as largely futile, offering little possibility of eventual employment. Cynicism prevails, as they read the scheme as a government joyride – a cheaper means than official imprisonment for the authorities to keep them off the streets and supposedly out of trouble. The joyriding motif is important, not simply in narrative terms or as a means of crystalizing the anarchy prevailing on the streets where 'speed' provides temporary power and prowess to the disenfranchised, but also as a comment on the British Government's position within Northern Ireland. They too are presented as joyriders, hijacking a country and ransacking it in the insatiable desire for imperialist speed – Britain 'driving the world', conducting those whom it perceives as primitive and/or incapable of ruling themselves and relegating them to the backseat of colonialist subjugation. All four teenagers, to varying degrees, organize a culture of resistance. Tommy's class analysis, although naïvely simplistic, does display an awareness of the carceral structures at work in society. In the opening scene of the play, Tommy comments on 'the fur coat brigade' (p. 106) in the theatre where the teenagers have just seen a production of O'Casey's *Shadow of a Gunman*. This functions not only as a clear reference to those who are the largely exclusive patrons of established theatre venues, but also to the class who employ Kate, the social worker in charge of the Youth Training Programme, and who have the right to come to the centre to observe and comment on the teenagers' work. Kate is perceived by Tommy and Sandra as a regulator, employed to monitor them. The teenagers function under her watchful glance and are all differentiated from her in a number of ways, most conspicuously through discourse: her eloquent language contrasted with their slang and colloquialisms. Tommy and Sandra attempt to steal food from the centre and drink from Kate's home. Arthur and Maureen believe that this is stealing from their own but Sandra and Tommy clearly associate Kate with the regimental regime, a regime Arthur and Maureen are increasingly sucked into. Observing and regulating Tommy and Sandra's behaviour, Arthur and Maureen function, in effect, as part of the watchful regime. As in *The Belle of the Belfast City*, where Janet's behaviour is vigorously observed by her brother Jack, systems of surveillance are shown to operate as a means of regulating and constraining behaviour. Tommy is even attacked by the IRA, those who purport to be on his side, for transgressing what they define as acceptable codes of behaviour. As Beth's position in *Tea in a China Cup* also indicates, all are to some degree or other, implicated in the subjugation that is witnessed. *Joyriders* is in many ways more daring than *Tea in a China Cup* for it indicates how imperialism, seeking to teach and modernize its subjects, relies on institutions like the YTS to continue that process: a process which Tommy notes begins in schools with a colonialist education that concentrates almost exclusively on the history of England whilst pertinently ignoring the history of Ireland. Irish history is inextricably bound up with the history of England, but to focus exclusively on England, as Reid recalls occurred at her school, negates the existence of an Irish history.[6]

[6] See Michael Herbert, 'Across the Great Divide', p. 4.

Colonialism, in the words of the critic Edward Said, disfigures the past. Only through the imagination, Said argues, can it be reappropriated and recovered.[7] Tommy espouses a recognition of the need to end the British claim to guide Northern Ireland but fails to acknowledge his own implication in this geographical violation.

This is also the case in *Did You Hear the One About the Irishman . . . ?*, where both nationalist and loyalist are shown to depend on each other. The perpetuation of the conflict necessitates an agreement of intransience on the part of both sides. Allison Clarke and Brian Rafferty, the play's protagonists, negate this agreement. Their annihilation is a gesture on the part of those whose existence is verified by a continuation of the sectarian dispute. The play's parallel structure – scenes with the Catholic Raffertys following those with the Protestant Clarkes – and pertinent doubling – the IRA and loyalist terrorists Joe Rafferty and Hughie Boyd are played by the same actor and quote similar messages in their respective conversations with Brian and Allison – comment on a crisis numerous factions have an interest in maintaining. In addition, the emphasis on doubling suggests the identities of Joe and Hughie as social constructs, shaped by the bigoted environment which Allison and Brian are attempting to overcome.

Empty rhetoric, as Joe and Hughie's diatribes indicate, can be seen to play a crucial part in perpetuating the crisis. In *The Belle of the Belfast City*, Jack, the Unionist politician, articulates a rigid rhetoric which celebrates misogynism, sexual repression – linked interestingly with sectarian hatred – and racism. In *Joyriders*, rhetoric sustains the characters' illusions. For Maureen, it is the rhetoric of romance which signifies stability and security, a magical land of Oz where she can live happily ever after with her student lover. For Tommy, it is the rhetoric of nationalism. He enjoys elaborating on his clandestine activities as a runner for 'the lads', i.e. the IRA, and articulates complex concepts which

[7] See Edward Said, *Orientalism: Western Conceptions of the Orient* (Harmondsworth: Penguin, 1995), pp. 352–53.

he simply fails to comprehend. Pertinently, *Joyriders* begins
with the closing speeches of Sean O'Casey's 1923 play *Shadow
of a Gunman*, the opening play of the Dublin trilogy. The
reference functions in a number of ways. Firstly it establishes
parallels between the Dublin slums of O'Casey's trilogy, and
the Divis Flats estate in which the teenagers of *Joyriders* live,
reputedly one of the worst housing estates in Western
Europe. The characters repeatedly comment on their poor
living conditions. As Tommy succinctly states, 'it would take
more than a licka paint to make any of them flats fit to live in'
(p. 114). Additionally, the opening reference to O'Casey's
play sets up several analogies with O'Casey's trilogy.
Maureen's mother, for example, was shot by a plastic bullet.
Maureen too is shot in the play's penultimate scene. This
circularity, the sense of events repeating themselves, negates
any sense of progress. The fate of generations seems
predetermined. Maureen is destined to repeat the fate of her
mother and that of Minnie Powell before her. Kate, in
describing herself as a 'shadow of a socialist' (p. 132) equates
herself with *Shadow of a Gunman*'s Donal Davoren – a
cowardly idealist. Arthur undercuts Tommy's pompous
comments by reducing the political to its sexual level; in this,
he echoes the irreverent Fluther Good in *The Plough and the
Stars* (1926). Tommy's hands are broken by the
paramilitaries, and so he falls victim to those who are
supposedly fighting to defend his own interests, the IRA. As
in all three plays of O'Casey's trilogy, dangers are faced from
within the community. Schisms exist as much within
communities as between them. *Tea in a China Cup*, *The Belle of
the Belfast City* and *My Name, Shall I Tell You My Name?* (1989)
all deal with the questioning of Protestant traditions by a
younger generation of women who refuse to accept the
intransigence and inflexibility of a particular masculine
loyalist ideology which would dictate their behaviour. All
these plays also link the construction of masculinity within
the family to sectarian politics. Too often it is a destructive
inflexible masculinity. All also draw sharp attention to the
imposition of domestic roles on women by both Protestant
and Catholic iconography. In Catholicism, we see woman as

angelic virgin figure reworked by the nationalist movement
into Mother Ireland; in Protestantism, woman as loyal
steadfast servicer and nurturer of men willing to die for
Queen and country. In *Tea in a China Cup* and *My Name, Shall
I Tell You My Name?*, Reid uses the Battle of the Somme
during World War I as a powerful symbol of loyalist
devotion to the Crown. Both plays, like Frank McGuinness's
Observe the Sons of Ulster, Marching Towards the Somme (1985),
present the incompetence of an officer class which led
Protestant servicemen to the widescale carnage that was the
Battle of the Somme. As with the Easter Rising of 1916 in *The
Plough and the Stars*, the loss of life is equated by male
characters with unimpeachable heroism; a holy crusade in
whose realization the women should be honoured their
husbands have died. Reid has argued on numerous occasions
that the Protestant and Roman Catholic hierarchies are
unified in their attitudes to women; that women are
primarily presented through objectionable and limiting
stereotypes, and are conspicuously absent from existing
histories of Ireland. 'The public faces of the Protestant and
Catholic paramilitaries,' Reid has stated, 'are all men. All
the people who talk about religion and the Church are all
men. The politicians are all men. Women are never the
leaders, the faces, the voices. Ian Paisley and the Pope are
basically in total agreement over what a woman's role in the
home should be.'[8] This is a view articulated by Rose, Dolly's
younger daughter in *The Belle of the Belfast City*. Reid's work,
whether dealing with Protestant or Catholic communities or
both, as in *Did You Hear the One About the Irishman . . . ?*,
presents Northern Ireland as a deeply patriarchal society
where women are unequivocally subordinated and
categorised into neat, compact categories – mothers, sisters,
wives. As Janet states in *The Belle of the Belfast City*, 'there are
no women in Ireland. Only mothers, sisters and wives'
(pp. 209–10). The myth of motherhood is exploited by both
the nationalist and loyalist communities to inspire
uncompromising devotion. As the intransigent grandfather,

[8] Quoted in Michael Herbert, 'Across the Great Divide', p. 4.

Andy, reflects in *My Name, Shall I Tell You My Name?*, 'The men go off to war, and the weemin' and the children stay behind and keep the home fires burnin' till the men get back' (p. 259). The feminization of Ireland into an idealized Mother Ireland who protects her sons from impending perils and/or is prepared to sacrifice all for the worthy cause is seen in Reid's plays to suit both colonizer and colonized. Through the character of Sandra in *Joyriders* and its sequel *Clowns* (1996), both currently being adapted by the author into a single screenplay, we are reminded that death is 'not lovely, an' its not romantic like in stupid friggin' plays' (p. 170). Romantic myths and glorified idealizations imprison rather than emancipate. By confining women to narrow constructed spheres of behaviour, stereotypes are perpetuated by each tribe in which men and women are segregated. Reid's plays portray a society in which women are disenfranchised; not that they reduce gender relations to a simple polarized view of woman as good and man as bad. Women comply with their own oppression, appropriating the standards of their oppressors, as demonstrated by Sarah in *Tea in a China Cup* and Vi in *The Belle of the Belfast City*. Equally men, often background figures in the plays, are not indiscriminately aggressive. Although the majority are presented as wayward fellows, easily led astray, falling prey to political whims, drunken, weak or unreliable, a number display instincts for non-violent means of communication – that which is traditionally read as being the realm of the feminine. Brian, for example, in *Did You Hear the One About the Irishman . . . ?* is patient, caring and understanding; he possesses a temperament habitually seen as passive, and his sense of humour equates him with many of the dynamic women characters who form the backbone of Reid's plays. Constantly aware of the difficulties inherent in affirming a 'female' identity, Reid's plays do deconstruct traditional dichotomies by concentrating on the plurality of women's experiences in Northern Ireland. Often this is articulated by the intersecting storylines merging past and present, dreams and memories, oral traditions and visual metaphors. Multiple tales are told in plays whose fluid structures mark a healthy move away from the conventions of the classic realist text.

Importantly, Reid's plays also present women in environments outside the domestic sphere. As such, they point to the societal institutions which perpetuate the strict gender divide. In *Joyriders*, the YTS scheme on which the teenagers are employed, situated in a disused linen mill where women were grievously exploited economically and regularly died of lead poisoning, encourages women to work on knitting machines while men train as mechanics. 'Weemin don't repair cars' (p. 109), Arthur argues when Sandra inquires as to the possibility of transferring to the mechanics' workshop. Equally, however, Arthur is aware of the problems surrounding his choice of career. 'Men don't cook in West Belfast,' he informs Kate (p. 123). All the characters, to a greater or lesser extent, are trapped within gender stereotypes; roles in which they have been cast by society. Sandra rejects the rhetoric of O'Casey's *Shadow of a Gunman* just as she rejects the dominant images of femininity society imposes on her. Equally, however, she sees those definitions reproduced in the socialist organisation Tommy is part of and thus his attempts to recruit her to the party are met with sharp retorts. 'What for?', she asks him, 'To end up typin' letters fer wankers like you?' (p. 138). Even in supposedly radical parties campaigning for a new utopia, women are still trapped within limiting roles clearly associated with nurturing and servicing the men who are on the frontline, so to speak. Sandra reads the possibilities for women of her class as offensively restrictive: 'A bride of Christ or forty years' hard labour . . . my mother thinks anything in between is a mortal sin' (p. 175). Kate, supposedly a liberal product of the struggles of 1968, recognizes the danger of the gap between bride and bride of Christ and fears it. The independent woman, like Arthur's single sister, is read as an 'old maid' – another social construct imposed on women who refuse to conform. In *Tea in a China Cup*, Beth's dilemmas are a dramatic realisation of this struggle between acquiescence and defiance. In a society where the feminine is too often perceived in essentially negative terms, Reid's plays attempt to undermine this ideology. *Tea in a China Cup* and *The Belle of the Belfast City* especially announce women as creative sources of energy. The humour displayed by many of the women in Reid's plays, especially when no longer under the watchful eye of prying men, is presented as subversive and challenging. Reid has spoken repeatedly of the radical potential that humour offers. 'Women', she has claimed, 'have humour and humour, of course, is what I think can ultimately destroy bigotry and prejudice.'[9] It's worth contrasting the phallocentric masculine humour of the comic in *Did You Hear the One About the Irishman . . . ?* with the feminine humour shared by the women in *The Belle of the Belfast City*. In *Clowns*, equally, Sandra's punchy stand-up routine as enacted by Maureen is a fierce antidote to that of the offensive comedian in *Did You Hear the One About the Irishman . . . ?* She daringly articulates a politics of reappropriation and blisteringly exposes a tradition of writers from Congreve to Wilde appropriated by the British: '. . . why should Bernard Manning and Jim Davidson make a living out of slagging off the Irish, when we can do it better for ourselves. And with more wit and style. That's the real joke. You forbade us to speak our own language. You forced us to speak yours and we took it and turned it into poetry' (p. 306).

Issues of gender surface in all of Reid's plays. They are, however, commented on in relation to the specific socio-political context in which Reid worked until 1987 before moving to London, where she lives today. Like Devlin, Lynch and Graham Reid (no relation), she interacts with her own traditions, traditions she finds both attractive and repulsive. *Did You Hear the One About the Irishman . . . ?* uses the device of the comic to interrogate our complicity in the Troubles: the audience's complicity in the laughter signals their involvement as part of an oppressive apparatus which fuels the conflict. As I mentioned earlier, the fiercely loyalist community in which Reid grew up provides the backdrop for numerous of her plays – notably *Tea in a China*

[9] Quoted in ibid., p. 4.

Cup, My Name, Shall I Tell You My Name? and *The Belle of the Belfast City*. Rather than idealizing such a community, these plays expose its fissures, often overlooked by simplistic readings of its united opposition to the threat of domination by a Roman Catholic Ireland. The Protestant and Catholic communities of Reid's plays are anything but united entities. Each is riven by contentious disputes, and oppositions of class and creed. *The Belle of the Belfast City* and *My Name, Shall I Tell You My Name?* especially provide a sharp critique of the conservativism of the Protestant ethos: a debilitating system of beliefs which allows no real possibilities for rational discussion with the republican movement. The dependency on Britain must be maintained unquestioningly and is preferable to any type of discussion with Irish nationalists. This single-minded view is expressed by the Protestant politicians Reid creates in her work. Uncle Henry in *Did You Hear the One About the Irishman . . . ?* and Jack in *The Belle of the Belfast City* are familiar types in Reid's work, gangsterish figures who exist outside the law, if you like – the maintenance of the Union with Britain read as a moral crusade which justifies all tactics, however lawless. Blame is not attributed solely onto these characters. *Did You Hear the One About the Irishman . . . ?*, *The Belle of the Belfast City* and *Tea in a China Cup* all cite the complicity of the middle classes in the current situation: those who run the factories and shops and employ a segregated workforce are clearly implicated in the perpetuation of the conflict. Reid has spoken in interviews of misunderstandings regarding the wealth of the Protestant community: 'People seem to think that all the Protestants are rich and all the Catholics are poor. But there is a massive Protestant working class who were a totally loyal workforce because they were always told that, if they went on strike, they would let the Nationalists in. It's a perfect example of divide and rule. So you had this Loyalist workforce who worked in appalling conditions in the mills and factories for bad wages'.[10] History is thus used to validate economic

---

[10] Quoted in ibid., p. 4.

exploitation. *Joyriders* also makes reference to the problems experienced by Protestants working in a Catholic area where if not faced by intimidation in the workplace, they leave because they are anxious of the dangers of working in a hostile environment.

Reid creates a strong sense of time and place in her plays. All are located in specific historical moments where the political is seen to impinge on the personal in a whole series of complex and vivid ways. In *My Name, Shall I Tell You My Name?*, set in 1986, the disputes at Greenham Common and racist attacks to which her partner is subjected are palpable presences in Andrea's politicization. In *Clowns*, Reid's most recent play, the Lagan Mill YTS centre has now metamorphosized into the Lagan Mill Shopping Centre. Eight years on, on the eve of the IRA ceasefire, Arthur is about to open his new café–bar. Sandra returns from London where, haunted by Maureen's ghost, she has been working as a stand-up comic, and confronts the society she left behind soon after Maureen's death. Debates on the ceasefire ensue as the characters come to terms with what the future may bring. For Molly, Arthur's mother, the death of her gambling husband brings a new lease of life, higher education and financial independence. Johnnie, Maureen's wayward brother is now a drug dealer: 'king of the only scene in Belfast that has nothing to do with religion, class or creed' (p. 330). For Sandra he is a manifestation of 'The ultimate joyride. You do the driving, and the passengers get killed' (p. 329). Although, as with *Tea in a China Cup*, the dramatic environments and situations depicted suggest parallels with Reid's own experiences, what strikes the reader is the manner in which the play skilfully captures the essences of a particular moment in contemporary Anglo–Irish relations without recourse to heavy-handed lecturing. Reid's stagecraft displays an effective use of dramatic imagery to express her concerns as a writer commenting on the complex ways in which larger political events affect the lives of those experiencing them. In *Joyriders*, the graffiti described in the introduction clearly situates the drama within a particular social mileau. The Royal Shakespeare Company production of *Did You Hear the One About the Irishman . . . ?* juxtaposed portraits of the Pope and the Queen as emblematic metaphors for the two communities: providing a clear indication of the civil strife which informs the play. Additionally, however, they are ambivalent symbols in that they are subject to simplification and can too often reduce the conflict to a series of clear cut binary oppositions. Binary oppositions provide a selective way of reading the conflict and as such are problematized and indeed systematically undermined by the play. In *Tea in a China Cup* too, Beth and Theresa laugh at the myths each have been told about the other's religion. Humour, so absent in the make-up of a substantial percentage of the characters in *Did You Hear the One About the Irishman . . . ?*, here works to deflate potential tension and ensures that both women reflect with a healthy distance on the fables promoted by their respective families. *Joyriders* too interrogates myths surrounding the representation of Ireland. The propaganda advertising a holiday scheme for Northern Irish children in America puts forward archetypal visions of Ireland as a rural backwater or a dark violent maelstrom – two sharp binary opposites: primitive rural idyll versus strife-torn urban metropolis. The limitations of both are systematically undermined by the characters' dialogue and behaviour.

Perhaps too often overlooked when examining Reid's work is the playful manner in which her plays are structured. *Tea in a China Cup* and *My Name, Shall I Tell You My Name?* both display a hearty awareness of the poetic possibilities of the stage; with scenes merging into one another in a fluid dreamlike manner. *Did You Hear the One About the Irishman . . . ?* too is not segregated into a traditional scene/act structure. Rather it consists of a series of juxtaposed episodes punctuated by the comedian's rude jokes. The cabaret format is also employed, although less rigorously in *Joyriders* and *Clowns*. In the former, the narrative is fractured by musical interludes which comment on the environment in which the play is set, the characters and the action witnessed. Each song (except the opening Belfast Street Song which serves to set the scene), has a clear association with the scene that precedes it. In *Clowns*, Sandra's abrasive routines seek to clarify her ambivalence to the environment to which she has returned. Equally in *Did You Hear the One About the Irishman . . . ?*, the context in which the comic performs affects our reading of his material. The significance of events, quotations, songs, gestures and symbols is thus subject to constant modification. Reid's work doesn't provide happy endings or produce easy answers to the questions it poses. Rather, it seeks to interrogate the conflicting and disparate ways in which a certain political situation affects those who function within it. What emerges is a body of work that constantly displays a humanity and understanding of people struggling to make sense of the ideologies within which they have to exist. Few dramatists have provided such compassionate or stimulating social studies of the post-1968 period or such enthralling theatre.[11]

Maria M. Delgado, October 1996

[11] This article is based on a lecture delivered at the University of Barcelona during my time as a visiting lecturer on an Erasmus exchange scheme in 1995. I am grateful to Henry Little and Jacqueline Roy for their comments on earlier drafts and to Christina Reid for her generous assistance with and support of my research.

Tea in a China Cup

*For Christina my mother
and my daughters Heidi, Tara and Siubhan*

Tea in a China Cup was first produced by the Lyric Players Theatre, Belfast on 9 November 1983, with the following cast:

Sarah	Stella McCusker
Beth, *Sarah's daughter*	Paula Hamilton
Theresa, *Beth's friend*	Frances Quinn
The Grandmother	Trudy Kelly
The Grandfather	Louis Rolston
Great Aunt Maisie	Sheila McGibbon
Samuel, *Sarah's brother*	
Sammy, *Sarah's son*	} Adrian Gordon
A Youth	
Council Clerk	
Fortune Teller	} Margaretta D'Arcy
Mrs Jamison	
Army Officer, *Second World War*	
Modern British Soldier	} John Hewitt
Valuer	

Note. In this production only, the valuer in the final scene was male and became female in subsequent productions following rewrites.

Director Leon Rubin
Set Designer Ken Harrison
Lighting Designer Trevor Dawson
Costume Designer Ivor C. Morrow
Wardrobe Jacqueline Berryman and Ivor C. Morrow
Set Construction Jim Carson
Stage Manager Rose Morris
Deputy Stage Manager Karen Kerr
Assistant Stage Manager Maggie Burge
Acting Assistant Stage Manager Adrian Gordon

The action of the play is set in Belfast and spans more than three decades (from 1939 to 1972) in the life of a Protestant family in Belfast.

A velvet sofa symbolizes Beth's elegant house.

A china cabinet plus three large framed photographs of: the grandfather in First World War uniform; his son Samuel in Second World War uniform; his grandson Sammy in modern army uniform, symbolize the little house that is occupied first of all by the grandparents and subsequently by Sarah.

Changes of lighting indicate changes of time and place.

Act One

The stage is in darkness. Offstage, in the distance is heard the sound of an Orange band playing 'Up Come the Man'. As the music increases in volume, stage left lightens to show a velvet sofa by a window. This is **Beth**'s *house in 1972.* **Beth**'s *mother,* **Sarah**, *a woman in her mid-fifties, walks slowly out of the darkened stage area and lies down on the velvet sofa. She is wearing a dressing gown, and is obviously very ill. She listens to and watches the Orange band as it passes by with great enjoyment. Offstage a crowd is heard singing and cheering 'Up come the man with the shovel in his hand, and he says boys go no farther, for we'll get a great big rope and we'll hang the bloody Pope, on the twelfth of July in the morning.' The music and singing increase as the band marches past.* **Sarah** *sinks back on the sofa and closes her eyes. She smiles and sings softly to herself 'Up comes the man with the shovel in his hand . . . and he says . . . boys go no farther . . .' The lights darken around* **Sarah** *and lighten on stage right where* **Beth** *is standing at a desk facing a female* **Council Clerk**.*

Beth (*nervously*) I want to buy a grave . . .

Clerk (*briskly*) It'll have to be in the new cemetery, the old one's full, you know.

Beth Yes, I know.

Clerk A single or a double?

Beth What?

Clerk Plot . . . a single or a double?

Beth A single . . . please . . .

Clerk When's the burial?

Beth The burial?

Clerk The time and date of the funeral?

Beth I don't know . . .

Clerk Today's Friday, this office closes at the weekend you know. If the interment is to be on Monday you'll have to arrange for the grave to be opened today.

Beth Oh, I don't want it opened . . . not now . . . not yet . . .

Clerk Oh, I see, you don't have a dear departed, you just want to buy a grave plot.

Beth Yes, that's right.

Clerk Right, then we won't need the blue form for the gravediggers, just a straightforward sale docket.

The **Clerk** *writes details on a form,* **Beth** *watches nervously.*

Beth It's my mother . . . she's . . . she's terminally ill . . . she insisted that I buy a grave now . . .

Clerk She wants to know where she's going to lie . . .

Beth Yes, that's exactly what she said . . .

Clerk That's very responsible of her. The older generation are more sensible about these things.

Beth We have a family plot in the old cemetery, but it's full.

Clerk Yes, they all are. The new cemetery's very nice though. The council are always being complimented on the flowering shrubs . . . something in bloom all the year round . . . does your mother like flowers?

Beth (*slightly startled*) Yes, yes, she does actually.

Clerk (*pleased*) Well, there you are then.

Beth Would it be possible to have a plot near the old cemetery wall . . . ? She wants to be as near her mother and father as possible . . .

Clerk Ah now, that depends . . .

Beth On what?

Clerk On whether you want a Protestant or a Catholic plot.

Beth You're joking.

Clerk Indeed not. The new cemetery is divided in two by a gravel path. Protestant graves are to the right, Catholic graves to the left. Now what side would your mother want?

Beth The right, definitely the right.

Clerk Ah good, you're in luck, the Protestant graves go right up to the old cemetery wall . . . now let me see . . . I can offer you a choice of two . . .

The **Clerk** *shows* **Beth** *the plan of the cemetery.* **Beth** *looks at it and then hands it back to the* **Clerk**.

Beth I can't . . . I just can't . . . you pick one for me.

Clerk There's a lovely hydrangea behind this one . . .

Beth That'll do . . .

Clerk Or this one has a forsythia . . . absolutely laden with yellow blossoms in the spring . . .

Beth The hydrangea will do nicely, thank you.

Clerk Yes, you're probably right, they have a much longer flowering period . . . now if you'll just sign here.

Beth *signs the docket.*

Clerk And your address here . . . You know, I wish there were more people like your mother.

Beth Dying?

Clerk Oh no no . . . organized . . . buying their final resting place in advance of the event. It saves the relative a lot of trouble when the call comes from above, makes it easier to organize the funeral. You've no idea how difficult it all is; if people go and die at the weekend and the family has no burial plot.

Beth I suppose you own a grave plot.

Clerk Oh indeed, yes, in the old cemetery. I bought one years ago when I saw how quickly it was filling up . . . (*She leans forward and speaks confidently in hushed tones to* **Beth**.) Laid

my Jack to rest there the year before last . . . my husband . . .
cancer . . . very nasty . . .

Beth Yes, it is.

Clerk Your mother? . . . Same thing?

Beth Yes.

The **Clerk** *pats* **Beth**'s *hand.*

Clerk I hope she doesn't linger too long.

Beth *pulls her hand away, angrily.*

Beth Oh, I do.

Clerk Oh no, my dear, take it from one who's been through
it . . . You won't want her to linger . . . my Jack lingered . . .
very nasty when they linger, for them and for you . . . is your
mother in the hospital?

Beth No, she's in my house.

Clerk A little bit of advice, dear . . . at the end . . . don't let
them take her into the hospital . . . all they do is drag it
out . . .

Beth I really must go, I don't like leaving her alone for too
long . . .

Clerk Now, this is only a sales docket. I'll post you out the
deeds to the bit of ground some time next week, all right?
That will be fifty pounds, dear. Just make the cheque
payable to the North Down District Council.

The **Clerk** *compares the cheque with the cheque card.*

Beth Tell me something . . . why is the new cemetery
segregated? The old one wasn't, was it?

Clerk Not officially, but the people sort of segregated it
themselves. If you walk around the old cemetery you'll see
what I mean. There's clumps of Catholics and clumps of
Protestants. The odd one buried among the wrong crowd
stands out like a sore thumb.

Beth So the council decided to make it official in the new cemetery?

Clerk They did, makes it easer for everybody.

Beth What happens in a mixed marriage . . . do you bury them under the gravel path?

The **Clerk** *is not at all amused by this sort of levity.*

Sorry . . . it was only a joke . . .

Clerk Is your family mixed . . . will the segregation bother your mother?

Beth Bother my mother? . . . She'll be tickled pink when I tell her.

Beth *moves out of the council office to the street outside. She takes a deep breath, relieved that the episode is over.* **Theresa** *approaches.* **Beth** *doesn't see her.*

Theresa Excuse me, missus, could you direct me to Sandy Row? I've a date with a big sexy Orangeman.

Beth Theresa . . . I thought you weren't coming home from London till next weekend.

Theresa I said I'd *see* you next weekend. I'm going to Dublin this week for our Danny's wedding. Pay attention when you're reading my letters.

Beth I forgot . . . God, I'm so confused . . .

Theresa So what else is new? Beth, are you all right? . . . You look . . . strange. What were you doing in there?

Beth You'd never believe me if I told you. Theresa, come and see me as soon as you get back to Belfast . . . I need to talk to you.

Theresa Let's go and get a cup of coffee and talk now.

Beth I can't . . . I've got to get back to my mother.

Theresa How is she?

Beth Surviving . . . Theresa, I'm sorry . . . I'll have to go. I'll see you soon.

Theresa I'll phone you the minute I get back. Give my love to your mother.

Beth *walks to where* **Sarah** *lies on the sofa.*

Beth You promised to stay in bed till I got back.

Sarah The bands have been out practisin' for the twelfth, came right past the house, so they did. You should have heard those boyos play.

Beth You could have fallen.

Sarah I took it slowly.

Beth You've exhausted yourself, your face is all flushed.

Sarah It's the sound of the flute bands . . . always gets the oul Protestant blood going. I tell you, a daily dose of the True Blue Defenders would do me more good than them hateful transfusions they give me up at the hospital . . . how long is it now till the twelfth?

Beth Ten days.

Sarah I'll see it one more time before I go, if God spares me.

Beth You'll have a ringside seat at that window.

Sarah If I'm well enough on the day will you take me down to the end of the driveway in the car? I want to sit with the windows rolled down and be a proper part of it one last time.

Beth It's a wonder you don't want me to drive you to the Field at Finaghy.

Sarah If I thought I could manage it, I would. But sure what's the point of kiddin' myself. I'll be lucky if I can make it to the gate, even in the car.

Beth You'll make it.

Sarah God willing . . . Did you get that wee bit of business done for me?

Beth Yes.

Sarah And were you able to get a plot near the old cemetery?

Beth Right at the wall . . . do you know if you'd been a Catholic, you'd have been out of luck.

Sarah How do you mean?

Beth The new cemetery is segregated. Prods to the right, Fenians to the left. The Protestant graves are alongside the old cemetery.

Sarah *finds this very funny. She laughs delightedly.*

Sarah God, isn't it great to know that you'll be lying among your own.

Beth*'s face contorts and she turns her head away.*

Sarah Ach now, child, I didn't mean to upset you . . . don't look like that. You have to face up to these things. I'm sorry I had to ask you to go to that place for me. If I'd been fit enough I would have gone myself.

Beth I'm all right, honestly, I'm all right.

Sarah And now my mind's at rest knowing it's done and we don't need to think about it or talk about it any more . . . I think I'll go back to bed for a wee while . . . hearing the oul bands has took more out of me than I thought.

Beth Would you like a cup of tea?

Sarah I would love a cup of tea.

Beth and Sarah (*together*) In a china cup.

They both laugh. **Beth** *helps* **Sarah** *to her feet.*

Sarah You're a good child. I don't know what I'd do without you.

Beth What am *I* going to do without *you*?

Sarah Grow up . . . change, the way everybody does when their mother dies . . . now you go and make the tea, I'll go to bed myself.

Beth I'll help you in first.

Sarah No, I want to manage myself for as long as I can.

Beth *watches* **Sarah** *as she walks slowly towards the darkened part of the stage. At the edge of the light* **Sarah** *turns around.*

You know, if I'm well enough on the twelfth of July, we will go to the Field, you and me. I'd like to stand there with you beside me, one more time, just like when you were a child. I carried you to the Field at Finaghy when you were a few months old, do you know that?

Beth (*smiling*) Yes, I know that.

Sarah You mind it now, you mind all the old family stories, tell them to your children after I'm gone.

Sarah *turns and steps into the darkness.* **Beth** *makes an involuntary gesture as if to stop her from leaving.* **Beth** *walks forward and addresses the audience.*

Beth She carried me to the Field when I was four months old. She was sitting on the grass, her back to a hedge, giving me a bottle, when a gentleman in a clerical collar came up and patted us both on the head. 'I'm proud of you, daughter,' he said to my mother, 'coming all this way with a young baby. Women like you are the backbone of Ulster.' She knew he was a gentleman, because apart from the clerical collar, he had a hard hat and white gloves. The upper-class Orangemen always wear a hard hat and white gloves. She was very proud that a man like that had stopped to pay the likes of her such a compliment. I have an image in my mind of that day . . . the hedge littered with empty bottles and bits of red, white and blue paper, my mother feeding me as she sang along with the Orange bands. I couldn't possibly remember it, I was only an infant, but I've heard that story and all the other family stories so often that I can remember and see clearly things that happened even before I was born . . . like the day my mother's brother Samuel went off to fight for King and Country.

The centre of the stage lightens to show the home of the grandparents, **Sam** *and* **Annie** *in the year 1939. An enlarged sepia photo of the grandfather in First World War uniform hangs in an ornate frame on the back wall. The* **Grandmother** *and* **Sarah** *(aged about twenty-*

three) are sitting looking miserable. Offstage an Orange band is playing and people are singing 'On the green grassy slopes of the Boyne, Where King Billy and his men went to war, we will fight for our glorious deliverence . . . Where? . . . on the green grassy slopes of the Boyne.' The **Grandfather** *comes dancing in, highly excited.*

Grandfather Man, they're going to see the lads off in great style, so they are. Are the two of yous not comin' out?

Sarah Where's my wee Sammy? Where's the chile?

Grandfather I left him playin' with the childer next door. He's all right, he'll come to no harm. You fuss too much about that wain . . . Women!

Grandmother I suppose you think I fuss too much about *our* Samuel?

Grandfather Our Samuel's not a wain any more, he's one of the King's men now.

Grandmother He's still only a child. This is all your doin', filling his head full of nonsense abut the great times you had with the lads in France during the First World War.

Grandfather It'll make a man of him.

Grandmother He's only eighteen. I want him to grow into a man here, in his own street with his own ones all around him, not in some stinkin' hole in the ground in France among strangers.

Grandfather I was in the trenches in France when I was little more than a lad. It never did me no harm.

Grandmother Oh aye, I suppose you were born with that bit of shrapnel in your leg.

Grandfather I'd do it again gladly, if they'd have me, for my King and Country.

Grandmother But they won't have you, will they, because your oul chest is still full of gas from the last great war.

She says the word 'great' with contempt. **Sarah** *goes and looks outside.*

Grandfather My son will represent me. You should be proud of him, not sittin' here mopin'.

Grandmother You're on oul fool, you always were.

Sarah He's comin' up the street. Now don't be arguing, you two, you don't want to upset him. God knows when we'll all be together again.

Offstage there is cheering from the crowd. **Samuel** *comes in dressed in Second World War uniform.*

Samuel The band's marching with us to the boat. I've never seen anything like it. It's like the twelfth of July out there.

Grandfather Don't yous all deserve it? The young men of this road are doing Ulster proud.

Grandmother I've made you some sandwiches, son, in case you get hungry.

Samuel Ach mammy, I can't go off to war with a packet of sandwiches in my hand. Do you want me to be a laughin' stock?

Grandfather Take a bit of advice from an old campaigner, son. Put them sandwiches in your pocket. Army life's grand, but you'll not get the good food you're used to at home.

Samuel *puts the sandwiches in his pocket.*

Samuel I'll probably get my pay docked for ruining the line of my uniform.

Grandmother The line of your uniform'll be well ruined after a night sleepin' rough in thon oul boat.

Offstage there is more cheering from the crowd.

Samuel I'll have to go. They're lining up . . .

Grandfather Good luck, son.

Samuel Thanks, father.

They shake hands awkwardly. The **Grandfather** *turns away, overcome with emotion. To hide this, he blows his nose noisily. The* **Grandmother** *embraces her son.*

It won't be for long . . . I'll be back before you know it, with a string of medals on my chest.

Grandmother Never you mind the medals, Samuel. You just keep your head down, and come home in one piece.

Grandfather And go easy on the oul French water son, it's not like the good clean stuff you get here. They're awful clarty people the French . . . Catholics, you know . . .

Sarah *embraces her brother.*

Sarah Now, you take care of yourself, do you hear? No heroics.

Samuel And you take care of mother.

Sarah I will.

Samuel Where's my namesake?

Sarah He's next door, playin' . . .

Grandfather I'll go and get him. He'll have to see his uncle off . . .

As the **Grandfather** *goes out, the* **Grandmother**'s *sister* **Maisie** *rushes in.*

Maisie They're linin' up, ready to go. Ach, boys a dear, don't you look great? . . . How's about a big kiss for your aunt before you get stuck intil them Germans.

She hugs **Samuel** *exuberantly.*

God bless you, love. You show them Germans what the Ulster Protestant boys are made of. Here's a wee something for you from your Aunt Maisie.

She puts some money into his hand. **Samuel** *is embarrassed.*

Samuel There's no need . . .

Maisie You put it in your pocket. Always have a wee roughness of money about you when you're away from home . . . for emergencies.

*The **Grandmother** removes her wedding ring and places it on **Samuel**'s finger.*

Grandmother Don't take it off, no matter what. It'll guard you, bring you home safe.

Samuel *kisses her and moves away. He is close to tears.*

Sarah Don't forget to write . . .

As he goes out the crowds outside cheer and the band begins to play.

Maisie Come on, the pair of you, we have to see him off . . .

Maisie *rushes out.* **Sarah** *puts her arms around her mother and walks her to the door. The sounds of the bands are replaced by the sounds of war.* **Sarah** *comes back on stage reading a letter from* **Samuel**. *At one side of the stage the lights brighten on* **Samuel**. *He is in an army billet somewhere in France sitting on the floor, leaning on his kitbag, writing the letter that* **Sarah** *is reading. They read the letter together.*

Sarah and Samuel My darling sister, this is to let you know I have arrived safe and well. We got here late as the boat was held up for days because of fog, and we had our Christmas dinner in the middle of the English Channel. My father was right when he said that the food's not what we're used to at home, but then nobody can cook a dinner like my mother. The drink here is dirt cheap, best rum about 1/6 for a ten-glass bottle. If it was that price at home, the men on our road would never sober up. It's just as well that I don't drink, not that I could afford to set the town on fire even if I wanted to. They only give us thirty francs a week while we're here, that's roughly 3/6. It means that I'm saving about seven bob a week, so that by the time I get leave, I hope round the beginning of June, I'll have a nice wee bit put by to bring home to my mother. The life here is okay. The locals are nice but funny, you know, different from us. We are billeted in an old chapel, which is dry and quite comfortable, although, mind you, I don't think the Pope would be too happy if he got to hear about the Orange sash rolled up inside my kitbag. I brought it with me for luck. If you see anybody from the lodge, tell them that the Ulster boys in France are thinking about them and I hope they're praying for us when they meet at the Orange Hall. Your loving brother, Samuel.

Sarah *exits reading* **Samuel**'s *letter. The sounds of war increase then fade into the sound of a typewriter. A British Army* **Officer** *walks on and faces the audience. He stands very erect, hands behind his back, dictating an official letter to an unseen secretary in the background. The* **Grandmother** *walks on (from where* **Sarah** *has exited) reading this buff-coloured official communication.*

Officer Form B104 stroke 81 stroke AS. RA Records. CD and AA Branch. Footscray. Sidcup. Kent. Third June 1940. Sir or Madam . . .

Grandmother I regret to have to inform you that a report has been received by the War Office to the effect that . . .

Officer Number 1473529 . . .

Grandmother Gunner Samuel Bell . . .

Officer Eleven stroke Third Signal Regiment, Royal Artillery . . .

Grandmother Has been wounded and was admitted to Saint Luke's Emergency Hospital, Bradford, on the first day of June 1940 . . .

Officer The nature of the wound . . .

Grandmother Gunshot wounds in the chest . . .

Officer I am to express to you the sympathy of the Army Council. Any further information received as to his condition will be at once notified to you. Yours faithfully . . .

Grandmother Lieutenant Colonel . . . Cromie? . . . Crowe? . . . Croft? . . . Officer in charge of records.

Officer Important! Any change of address should be notified immediately to this office.

The **Grandmother** *holds the letter to her face and exits, weeping. As she leaves, the* **Officer** *intones impassively.*

Officer   If replying, please quote number ED stroke CAS stroke N.

He exits. **Beth** *walks on and addresses the audience.*

Beth   My Great Aunt Maisie looked after my brother Sammy while my mother and my grandmother went to Bradford to visit Samuel in St Luke's hospital. I went too, barely formed inside my mother's womb. It was a beautiful day, the day we arrived. The wounded lay on stretchers outside on the grass, their bandages removed. Seemingly, there was some desperate hope that exposure to the sun's rays could stop the spread of gangrene. The smell was indescribable. Luckily the weather turned cold, so the doomed soldiers were allowed indoors to die. We stayed for two weeks, and Samuel, although he didn't get any better, at least appeared not to get any worse. As soon as we got back to Belfast, my Great Aunt Maisie took my grandmother to consult a fortune teller.

The stage lightens on the **Fortune Teller**. *The* **Grandmother** *is sitting facing her.* **Sarah** *and* **Maisie** *watch and listen.*

Fortune Teller   You must cross my palm with silver, for luck.

The **Grandmother** *puts a coin into the* **Fortune Teller**'s *hand. She holds out her hand for more, the* **Grandmother** *gives it, the* **Fortune Teller** *pockets the coins.*

Sarah   She's worse than the money lender.

Maisie   She's worth every penny, listen.

Fortune Teller   You have great trouble, great sorrow . . .

Grandmother   Yes.

Fortune Teller   Somebody you love is very ill . . .

Grandmother   Yes.

Fortune Teller I see soldiers . . . running . . . falling . . . guns firing . . . not here, on foreign soil.

Grandmother France.

Fortune Teller A young man is wounded . . . an artillery gunner . . . dark haired . . . very young . . . your son.

Maisie (*to* **Sarah**) Didn't I tell you she was good?

Sarah She could have got all that from the paper. There was a photo of Samuel along with the write-up about him being wounded.

Maisie I'm telling you, she has the gift.

Sarah Aye, of the gab . . .

Fortune Teller (*angrily*) Shush!

Maisie Sorry, missus.

Grandmother Can you see into the future as well as the past?

Fortune Teller What is it you want to know?

Grandmother My son that's wounded . . . will he be all right?

Fortune Teller He'll come home to you.

Grandmother Are you sure?

Fortune Teller I'm sure your son will return to Belfast from Bradford.

Maisie Now how did she know that, eh? There was no mention of Bradford in the paper.

Sarah She could have heard about it on the road. Everybody knows we were in Bradford.

Grandmother God bless you, missus.

The **Fortune Teller** *nods impassively. The* **Grandmother** *gets to her feet. She is very emotional.* **Maisie** *goes to her, puts her arm around her and leads her off.* **Sarah** *looks at the* **Fortune Teller** *sceptically and turns to follow them.*

Fortune Teller Wait . . . I want to have a word with you
. . . sit down.

Sarah *sits down slowly, warily.*

Fortune Teller You're her daughter?

Sarah Yes.

Fortune Teller Do you live with her?

Sarah I thought you knew everything.

Fortune Teller (*coldly*) Make sure your mother isn't alone
at any time over the next few days. She'll be getting the
telegram.

Sarah But you said . . . you told her he'd come home . . .

Fortune Teller An Army coffin is what he's comin' home
in.

Sarah You're an evil old woman!

Fortune Teller I don't decide what happens, I only see.

Sarah You see nothin', you make it up as you go along . . .
or you tell gullible people what any fool with ears and eyes
could hear on the road or read in the papers.

Fortune Teller He's dyin' . . . he won't last the week.

Sarah You're a liar . . . you're a fake . . . you do it for the
money . . . you take money from poor, desperate people and
tell them . . . tell them . . . I don't believe you . . . he won't
die . . . you know nothin' . . . nothin' . . .

Distraught, **Sarah** *is now standing accusing the* **Fortune Teller**,
who remains impassive, cold.

Fortune Teller Give me your hand.

Sarah *stares at her as if mesmerized.*

Sit down and give me your hand.

Sarah *sits down slowly and stares at the* **Fortune Teller**. *The*
Fortune Teller *holds out her hand and* **Sarah** *slowly places her
hand on top.*

You have a three-year-old son. He has the same name as the wounded soldier.

Sarah That's common knowledge.

Fortune Teller You're expecting again . . . is that common knowledge?

Sarah, *startled, looks down at her abdomen.*

Fortune Teller It doesn't show. I can see the two heartbeats.

Sarah I've only just missed a month.

Fortune Teller And you've told nobody, not even that waster you married . . . so you can't say I heard about that on the road, or read it in the papers.

Sarah Please . . . please . . . tell me he's not going to die.

Fortune Teller I told you, I don't decide, I only see.

Sarah *gets wearily to her feet. The* **Fortune Teller** *holds out her hand.* **Sarah** *gives her a silver coin. The* **Fortune Teller** *still holds out her hand.*

Sarah I don't have any more.

Fortune Teller Lost it all on the horses again, did he?

Sarah The dog track.

She walks away. The **Fortune Teller** *pockets the coin and shrugs. She calls after* **Sarah**.

Fortune Teller And it'll be a girl . . . and neither of yous will have your sorrows to seek . . .

The lights darken around her, and lighten on the other side of the stage to show the Army **Officer** *reciting the telegram. As he reads, the centre of the stage lightens to show the* **Grandfather** *hanging an enlarged tinted photo of* **Samuel** *in Second World War uniform beside the sepia photo of himself in First World War uniform. The* **Grandmother** *sits listening as* **Sarah** *reads the newspaper report of* **Samuel**'s *death.*

Officer Deeply regret to inform you 1473529 Samuel Bell, 113 Signal Regiment died from gunshot wounds 17.40 hours. RA Records.

Sarah Death of Belfast Gunner . . . Result of war wounds . . . Prominent in Orange Order . . . Gunner Samuel Bell . . . son of . . . son of . . . Gunner Bell was with the BEF at Dunkirk . . . A prominent figure in the Orange and Black Orders, he personified the bravery and loyalty of the sons of Ulster . . . four of his cousins are at present serving their country overseas . . . his father served with the Royal Ulster Rifles in the last great war . . . there's a photo with his name underneath . . .

Grandmother Cut it out, I'll put it away with the telegram and the letters.

Grandfather There'll be money to come, you know . . .

*The **Grandmother** looks at him with contempt.*

I'm only sayin' . . . we're entitled . . .

*The **Grandmother** continues to stare at him silently.*

I'm only sayin' . . .

Sarah Father, just leave it . . . leave it.

*The **Grandmother** takes some money from her purse and hands it to the **Grandfather**.*

Grandmother Here, away down to the pub and give my head peace.

*The **Grandfather** takes the money. He looks as if he wants to say something but is put off by his wife's cold stare. He walks to the door and turns.*

Grandfather He was my son too, you know.

*The lights darken on the centre of the stage and lighten on **Beth** at one side. She addresses the audience.*

Beth Eventually the Army sorted out how much Samuel had saved while he was in France. They added up all the seven shillingses and deducted an amount to cover the cost of the kit he'd lost on the beaches of Dunkirk. There was no pension. He was not considered old enough to have any dependent relatives. The Army did provide, free of charge, a war grave in a Belfast cemetery. My grandmother scrubbed boards in a bakery to pay for the white marble headstone and surround. For the rest of her life she forbade her family to buy anything that was German-made. After the war, an American cousin married a German. As far as my grandmother was concerned, that particular branch of the family tree ceased to exist.

The lights rise on the **Grandparents**' *house in March 1941.* **Sarah**, *very pregnant, is saying goodbye to her Mother.*

Grandmother Now you put your feet up when you get home, Sarah, you're done in. Let your man put the wee lad to bed.

Sarah I'll see you tomorrow.

Grandmother I'll come and see you tomorrow, save you walkin' round.

Sarah All right.

They embrace and **Sarah** *walks towards the door.*

Grandmother Sarah?

Sarah What?

Grandmother Is everything all right at home?

Sarah Yes, everything's all right.

Grandmother I'll see you tomorrow, then.

Sarah See you tomorrow.

As she reaches the door, **Sarah** *suddenly doubles forward.*

Oh, dear God.

Grandmother What is it?

Sarah Oh no, I think I'm startin' . . . oh dear God . . .

Grandmother Come in and shut that door, don't be makin' an exhibition of yourself in front of the neighbours.

Come back and sit down for a minute, it might be a false alarm, you remember the way you were with Sammy . . . stoppin' and startin'.

As she is talking she gets **Sarah** *to the chair. Immediately there is another contraction, and* **Sarah** *gasps with the pain.*

Sarah I can feel the child movin' down.

Grandmother We'd better get you to the hospital. Now don't you move, I'll get our Maisie.

Sarah *yells as wave after wave of pain engulfs her.*

Sarah There's something wrong . . . it doesn't feel right . . .

Grandmother You can't go on the bus in that state . . . I'll run to the shop and ask them to phone for a taxi.

Sarah I've no money for a taxi . . . I've no money for anything . . . he hasn't been home for two days . . . not since he lifted his wages . . .

Grandmother Gods curse him . . . I'll get the money somewhere . . . you hold on . . . Maisie'll know what to do . . . keep your knees together till I get back . . .

She rushes out. The lights darken. **Beth** *addresses the audience.*

Beth I was born breech on March the eighth, a jaundiced, sickly, underweight child. My mother was advised by the ward sister to take me home and love me, because I was delicate and probably wouldn't last long. She was also advised by the Grand Master of the local Orange Lodge that I wouldn't die as the eighth of March was the anniversary of the death of William, Prince of Orange, and this was a good omen. God works in mysterious ways and, as he and King Billy had obviously sent me as a replacement for my heroic Uncle Samuel I should be called Mary after the Good King's wife. I didn't die, but I wasn't called Mary either. It's a very Catholic sort of name in Northern Ireland, despite King Billy's wife, and my mother didn't fancy it at all. She compromised by calling me Elizabeth, after the heir to the throne.

July 1952. Sounds of Orange bands playing 'The Sash My Father Wore'. The **Grandmother**, **Maisie** *and* **Beth** *as a child of eleven come dancing into the* **Grandmother**'s *house, singing and giggling. They all fall laughing on to the sofa.*
Sarah *comes in from the other side of the stage carrying a tray of tea in china cups.*

Sarah Beth, look at the state of you, your face is black.

Grandmother Ach, leave the child alone, you can't expect her to be neat and tidy all the time.

Sarah She looks like one of them wee street urchins from the Catholic quarter.

Maisie *spits on a handkerchief and cleans* **Beth**'s *face.* **Beth** *finds this unpleasant and struggles.*

Grandmother Is Sammy still sleepin'?

Sarah He is, he must be sickenin' for somethin'. His face is awful hot.

Maisie (*to* **Beth**) Keep still, child . . . there now, that's a bit more Protestant-lookin'.

Beth Are all the Catholic children dirty?

Maisie I never seen a clean one yet.

Beth Why are they dirty?

Grandmother It's just the way they are. They're not like us.

Maisie They never scrub their front steps nor black-lead their fires nor nothin'. They're clarty and poor.

Beth Are we not poor?

Grandmother There's poor and poor. We keep our houses nice, always dress clean and respectable. There's no shame in a neat darn or a patch as long as a body is well washed.

Maisie And we don't go about cryin' poverty and puttin' a poor mouth on ourselves the way they do neither. Did you hear thon oul nationalist politician on the wireless the other day? Tellin' the world about goin' to school bare-fut in his da's cut-down trousers? I would cut my tongue out before I'd demean my family like that.

Beth Mammy made this dress out of one of her old skirts.

Sarah Don't you ever go sayin' that to strangers.

Beth Why?

Sarah Because you just don't, that's why. I don't know where I got her at all. She hasn't the sense she was born with.

Grandmother Why don't you go and lie down, Sarah, you look awful tired.

Sarah I've had no sleep for two nights with our Sammy, up and down gettin' drinks of water. I think it must be the flu he has.

Grandmother Away upstairs and take the weight off your feet for an hour or two. Sure the men won't be back till the pubs close.

Sarah I think I will. Now you behave yourself, Beth, and give your granny and Aunt Maisie peace.

She goes out. The **Grandmother** *and* **Maisie** *sip their tea contentedly.* **Beth** *sits looking miserable.*

Maisie There's nothin' like a drop of tea in a china cup . . . what's up with her? (*Nodding towards* **Beth**.)

Grandmother I don't know. What's wrong child?

Beth When I want a drink of water in the night she shouts at me, she never shouts at our Sammy.

Grandmother You're easily bothered.

Maisie Is that all?

Beth I don't see why my mammy was so annoyed with me. I like this dress.

Grandmother Of course you do, it's lovely.

Maisie Your mammy was always very clever with a needle and thread, so she was.

Beth Well, what's wrong with saying she made it out of her old skirt?

Grandmother It's all right to say it in front of us, your own family, it's strangers you don't say that sort of thing to.

Beth Why?

Maisie Why? *Why*? I swear to God, that wain was born askin' questions.

Grandmother Because it's family business and it's private. No matter how hard times are, you don't let yourself down in front of the neighbours.

Maisie Because if you do, you bring yourself down to the level of the Catholics, whining and complainin' and puttin' a poor mouth on yourself.

Grandmother No matter how poor we are, child, we work hard and keep ourselves and our homes clean and respectable, and we always have a bit of fine bone china and good table linen by us.

Maisie If the new Queen herself, God bless her, was to call here for her tea, we could do her proud. None of your old dirt here.

Beth Mammy had to sell our china cabinet to pay the rentman.

The **Grandmother** *and* **Maisie** *look at each other. This is obviously news to them.*

Grandmother Who did she sell it to?

Beth Mrs Duffy, Theresa's mammy.

Grandmother And all the stuff in it?

Beth Yes . . . except for one china cup and saucer. She took that out before Mrs Duffy came, and afterwards she made herself a cup of tea in it and she cried and she said she'd never forgive my daddy as long as she lived.

Grandmother That child sees and hears more than's good for her.

Maisie A fine state of affairs when a God-fearin' hard-working Protestant has to sell her good china to a Fenian to make ends meet.

Grandmother Don't you ever go tellin' all that to anybody else, do you hear me, Beth?

Beth Yes, granny.

The lights darken on this scene. At one side of the stage we see **Theresa Duffy**, *a child of eleven, skipping. She sings 'On the hill there stands a lady, who she is I do not know, all she wants is gold and silver, all she wants is a nice young man.'* **Beth** *arrives and they skip together and sing the song again. They sit down, breathlessly.*

Beth Theresa?

Theresa What?

Beth You know the way your mammy bought my mammy's china cabinet and all the stuff in it?

Theresa Yes.

Beth Well, sure you won't tell anybody about it?

Theresa Why not?

Beth Because it's private and my granny says nobody's to know.

Theresa All right . . . I think it's rotten-looking anyway.

Beth My mammy loved it. She used to polish it every day.

Theresa My daddy says it's daft having all those cups and saucers and things just for looking at.

Beth That's what my daddy said too.

Theresa Have you got your new uniform for the grammar school yet?

Beth Not yet, my mammy's still saving up to pay for it.

Theresa I got mine last week. You want to see it. Everything's dark green, even the knickers.

Beth Our uniform's navy blue.

Theresa Are the knickers navy blue too?

Beth Yes.

Theresa Do you know what that big lad down the street says those sort of knickers are called?

Beth What?

Theresa Passion killers.

Beth What does that mean?

Theresa I don't know. I asked my mammy and she hit me and made me go to confession.

They sit and ponder this for a moment.

Beth Aren't your teachers all nuns?

Theresa Some of them are. They'll all be nuns when I go to the convent grammar school.

Beth Is it true that they always go around in pairs because one of them's really a man?

Theresa Who told you that?

Beth My Great Aunt Maisie.

Theresa Nuns are women. The men are called monks. Your aunt's having you on.

Beth She read it in a book that was written by a girl who escaped from a convent.

Theresa My granny has a book about a rich Protestant landowner, and all these young Catholic girls worked in his big house and they all got babies, so they did.

Beth Were they married?

Theresa No, they weren't.

Beth Your granny's head's cut. You have to be married to get a baby.

Theresa I have a cousin who's not married and she got a baby.

Beth How?

Theresa I don't know. I asked my mammy about that too, and she hit me again.

The lights darken on the two puzzled children. **Beth** *as an adult addresses the audience.*

Beth We knew nothing. We found it impossible to get an accurate answer to anything relating to bodily functions. Babies were a gift from God to married women. I asked my Great Aunt Maisie why God gives more gifts to the Catholics if the Protestants of Ulster were his chosen people. She said it was because the Catholics were greedy. They were always looking for something for nothing. My mother did attempt to have a serious talk with me once. It was very confusing and embarrassing for both of us.

At the other side of the stage **Beth** *aged eleven is sitting in a chair reading a comic.* **Sarah** *is ironing, her back is to* **Beth**.

Sarah Beth?

Beth What?

Sarah Don't say what, say pardon.

Beth Pardon.

Sarah That's better . . . I want to explain something to you . . . you're growing up and there's things you have to be told . . . are you listening?

Embarrassed, she keeps her back firmly to **Beth**.

Beth Yes, mammy.

Sarah Some time . . . in the next year or two . . . there's a thing that happens to girls of your age . . . it happens once a month . . . you know where you go to the toilet . . . down there . . .

Beth Yes.

Sarah Well, once a month . . . when you start to grow up . . . to become a young woman . . . you get . . . you get . . . a drop of blood comes out of there . . .

Beth (*startled*) Blood?

Sarah Now there's nothing to worry about. It happens to all women . . . it's just a part of growing up . . . it doesn't do you any harm . . . it comes for a few days and then it goes away again . . . until the next month. When it happens, you tell me, you don't go telling your father or our Sammy, do you hear?

Beth Do my daddy and Sammy not know about it?

Sarah You don't talk to men about that sort of thing, it's not nice.

Beth Why does it happen . . . what's it for?

Sarah It's just one of those things women have to put up with . . . there's a lot of things in life that women have to put up with, you'll find that out as you get older . . . and another thing, Beth, when you do get older and maybe go out with boys . . . don't ever let them do anything that's not nice . . . always remember, your private parts are your own . . . do you understand that, now?

Beth (*uncertainly*) Yes, mammy.

Sarah That's a good girl.

Relieved that the talk is over, **Sarah** *folds up the ironing board and carries it off without looking at* **Beth**. **Beth** *sits with a puzzled look on her face. She looks down at herself, shrugs and continues reading her comic. Lights darken on* **Beth**. *At the other side of the stage the eleven-year-old* **Theresa** *appears in green convent uniform. She is carrying a schoolbag. She waves and calls towards the darkened part of the stage.*

Theresa Beth! Beth!

Beth *steps into the light. She is not in a uniform, just a dress and cardigan. She also is carrying a schoolbag.*

Theresa Mine started, last night, just when I was getting ready for bed.

Beth Now we're both grown up.

Theresa Yes.

Beth Did your mammy cry?

Theresa No. But she told me I wasn't to wash my hair while I had it or put my feet in cold water, or the blood would all rush to my head and I'd die. Did your mammy cry?

Beth A wee bit. She said, 'God help you, child, this is the start of all your troubles.'

Theresa My mammy calls it the curse.

Beth I wish somebody would tell us what it's all about. I mean, if it's going to bring us some sort of trouble, do you not think we should know?

Theresa Sure they never tell you anything.

Beth I like your uniform. It's lovely.

Theresa Why are you not going to the grammar school, Beth?

Beth My mammy can't afford the uniform, but don't be telling anybody, because I'm not allowed to say.

Theresa All right.

They walk off together. The stage lightens on the **Grandmother**'s *house, where* **Sarah**, **Maisie** *and the* **Grandmother** *are talking.*

Grandmother You should have let me buy the uniform, Sarah. It's a cryin' shame, a clever child like that missin' her chance.

Sarah It's not just the uniform, it's all the other expenses over the years . . . books, games equipment, trips, extras . . . I can't depend on him for the money. At least at the secondary school she'll be as good as the rest of them, better even because she's so bright, in the grammar school she'd have been like a poor relation.

Maisie You can get help with the uniform you know.

Sarah I'm not runnin' to the assistance pleadin' poverty.

Grandmother It's a disgrace. If they pass the exam the government should pay for the lot, not expect workin' people to fork out for the extras.

Maisie They say this Butler Education Act is a great thing for the workin'-class children. Me eye it is. What I want to know is why kids like Theresa Duffy can get their fees paid to go to a Fenian grammar school, and one of ours has to miss out.

Sarah The Duffy's have always had a wee roughness of money about them . . . and I don't begrudge Theresa her chance, she passed the exam, she deserves it.

Maisie Not as much as our Beth, she doesn't. No good'll come of this subsidized education, you mark my words. The Catholics will beg, borrow and steal the money to get their kids a fancy education. This country'll suffer for it in years to come when well-qualified Catholics start to pour out of our Queen's University expecting the top jobs, wantin' a say in the runnin' of the country.

She points to **Samuel***'s photo.*

Is that what him and all the others died for, eh? To educate the Catholics so that they can take over Ulster? By God, he's well out of it. He must be turnin' in his grave this day.

Grandmother He'd be thirty now if he'd lived. Sometimes I try to picture him as a man, married maybe, with a family of his own, but I can only see him as a lad of nineteen.

Maisie He never needed any woman while he had you two. He always said he'd never marry.

Grandmother Ach, they all say that when they're young.

Beth (*to audience*) He remained in their hearts forever young, forever true, a perfect son and brother, a perfect man. If he had survived the war, I wonder would he have lived up to all their expectations. No one will ever know. Perhaps the Germans, without realizing it, killed the only truly honest Ulsterman who ever lived.

Act Two

Offstage, sounds of Orange bands. **Sarah** *lies on the velvet sofa in* **Beth**'s *house enjoying the sights and sounds.* **Beth** *comes in with a tray of tea. The music dies away.*

Sarah Only five more days till the twelfth.

Beth If they have any more practice runs, they'll be worn out before the actual event.

Sarah Not at all. They get better every day.

Beth *blows her nose.*

Beth I don't think my nose is ever going to stop streaming.

Sarah Summer colds are always the worst to shift. Did you put a drop of butter on the bridge of your nose like I told you?

Beth No, I did not.

Sarah Well, you've only yourself to blame then.

Beth My skin's greasy enough without putting butter on it.

Sarah Just a wee drop, between the eyes, and I'm tellin' you, this time tomorrow your cold'll be gone.

Beth Old wives' tales.

Sarah They work. Butter for colds and burns, everybody knows that.

Beth A penny on the forehead for nosebleeds, docken leaves for nettle stings, a wedding ring to charm away warts . . .

Sarah Don't scoff at the old remedies. Without them you wouldn't have survived your first year.

Beth Drink your tea, it'll get cold.

She addresses the audience.

I took whooping cough when I was eight months old. My grandmother wrapped me in a blanket and carried me to the gas-works, where she held me over the waste gas outlet until I'd choked and spluttered and coughed up all the infection. It's one of the family legends, how I was at death's door until the Belfast Corporation Gasworks saved my life.

Sarah I'm tellin' you, if it wasn't for the Belfast Corporation Gasworks you'd be dead . . . I wonder, could they do anything for me? . . . Ach child, don't look away like that, you have to face death.

Beth I can't . . .

Sarah You must . . . you'll do things proper for me, won't you?

Beth You know I will.

Sarah Promise.

Beth I promise.

Sarah With a proper sit-down tea afterwards.

Beth With a proper sit-down tea . . . afterwards.

Sarah It's a pity your granny and your Aunt Maisie are gone, they knew the right way of these things.

Beth Well, they'd plenty of practice, hadn't they?

Sarah Aye, they did that . . . do you remember the day oul Granda Jamison died?

Beth I'll never forget it as long as I live.

Sarah It was your own fault. Aunt Maisie and my mother warned you you'd be scared, but you insisted on goin' with them.

Beth I wasn't scared at the begining, just curious to find out why they were always sent for when somebody in the street died.

Sarah *laughs.*

Sarah Well, you found out that day and no mistake.

There is the sound of bands offstage. **Sarah** *looks out the window again. The lights darken around* **Beth**'s *house and lighten on the other side of the stage. A dead man (* **Granda Jamison** *) lies on a bed. Offstage the bands are still playing. As the sounds of the bands recede,* **Maisie** *and* **Grandmother** *come in, followed by the child* **Beth**. **Beth** *looks apprehensive. The* **Grandmother** *looks at her and grins at* **Maisie**.

Grandmother Now are you sure you want to stay, Beth? You can still change your mind . . .

Beth I want to stay.

Grandmother Well, on your own head be it now.

Maisie She looks a bit green round the gills to me.

Beth I'm not.

Grandmother You never know, Maisie, she might have a taste for it. Maybe after you're gone, she'll take over the laying out of the dead in this street.

Maisie The young ones have no stomach for it.

Grandmother You never know, it could be in her blood, like you and old Aunt Sarah before you.

Maisie *goes over to the corpse.* **Beth** *stays close to her* **Grandmother**, *who is taking white starched linen covers out of a bag.*

Maisie (*to corpse*) So, you're dead at last, you oul bugger. By God, there'll be a quare wake on the road this night.

Grandmother Typical of him to die on the twelfth.

Maisie He done it on purpose. Sure he always took a great delight in being as much trouble as he could.

The **Grandmother** *is covering mirrors with the white covers.*

Beth Why are you doing that, granny?

Grandmother You must always cover the mirrors when somebody dies, or their soul can be reflected away by evil spirits.

Maisie A bit late in the day for him. I reckon oul Granda Jamison's soul was took away by evil spirits the day he was born.

Grandmother Aye, you could be right, but we'll give him the benefit of the doubt, just in case.

Beth Was he a bad man?

Maisie He was a vindictive oul bastard all his life, treated his wife and childer like dogs, so he did.

Mrs Jamison *comes in with a tray of tea. She hands it to the* **Grandmother** *and goes over to the corpse and looks at him.*

Mrs Jamison All the same, Maisie, he looks quare and well, doesn't he?

Maisie He does indeed, Mrs Jamison, he does indeed.

She makes a face at the **Grandmother** *behind* **Mrs Jamison**'s *back.* **Mrs Jamison** *stands looking tearfully at the corpse.*

Now you go on downstairs, Mrs Jamison, we'll call you when he's nicely laid out.

She steers **Mrs Jamison** *firmly towards the door.* **Mrs Jamison** *turns and looks back at the corpse.*

Mrs Jamison I'll miss him so I will . . .

She goes out.

Maisie (*imitating her*) I'll miss him so I will . . . like a hole in the head she'll miss him.

Grandmother Ach now, they were married a long time.

Maisie And this is the first good turn he's done her since the day and hour they got married.

Beth What did he do that was bad?

Maisie What did he not do? He was the sort of man that liked nothin' better than annoyin' people. Always lookin' out for somebody he could do a bad turn to.

The **Grandmother** *grins, nudges* **Beth** *and speaks slyly.*

Grandmother In his heyday, one of his favourite tricks was pickin' an argument with somebody and then takin' out a summons against them when they retaliated.

Beth What's retaliated?

Maisie Givin' him a dig in the gub, that's what retaliated is. By God, it was worth every penny of the ten-shillin' fine to see him lyin' on the pavement.

She lifts up the corpse by the hair and speaks with a mixture of fury and glee.

Do you hear me, you skittery ghost? Worth every penny. This time it's you who's gettin' the summons . . . from your maker.

Beth *runs out, panic-stricken.* **Maisie** *releases the corpse and laughs.*

Take after me and old Aunt Sarah? Some chance. I told you, the young ones have no stomach for it. Come on, Annie, let's get this oul sinner laid out and then we'll go down the road and see the Orangemen.

The lights darken on the death scene and lighten on **Sarah** *and* **Beth** *in* **Beth**'s *house.*

Sarah It was the biggest wake the road had ever seen. They came from miles around to make sure that oul Granda Jamison was really dead . . . I wonder . . .

Beth What?

Sarah I wonder will there be a big turn-out for me . . .

Beth Don't talk like that.

Sarah Child, I'm not afraid of dying. Don't you understand? I'm tired, I want to go . . . I've wanted to go for a long time now.

Beth Don't say that.

Sarah You wouldn't want me to be dreadin' it, would you?

Beth I want you to fight it . . . for once in your life, put up a fight. Stop accepting that everything awful has to be, that it's all part of some meaningful eternal plan. People who fight live longer.

Sarah I don't want to live any longer.

Beth Not even for me?

Sarah Particularly not for you. You have a husband in America, you should be there with him, not here nursing me.

Beth You know Stephen doesn't like me going on business trips with him.

Sarah You spend too much time apart, you two . . . is everything all right between the two of you?

Beth Yes, of course it is.

Sarah He hasn't written for a while now.

Beth He's travelling about a lot.

Sarah Maybe when he gets back you'll think about startin' a family . . . you're thirty, you don't want to leave it too late.

Beth There's plenty of time.

Sarah That's my one regret . . .

Beth What?

Sarah That I'll not be alive to see my grandchildren makin' their way in the world . . . Still, if it's not to be, it's not to be, and I'll watch over you all from heaven.

Beth If it's okay with you and God, I'd rather you watched over me from a bit nearer at hand.

Sarah You get more like your Great Aunt Maisie every day.

Beth Do you want more tea?

Sarah No, I think I'll have a wee doze.

Beth Come on, I'll help you into bed.

Sarah No, I'll just doze here, it's comfortable and . . .

Beth And you'll not miss the bands if they come past again.

Sarah Do you think there'll be bands in heaven?

Beth I'd say there's a fair chance that my granny and Aunt Maisie will have it well organized by now.

Sarah I'm looking forward to seeing them all again, my mother and father, Aunt Maisie . . . and Samuel . . . most of all, Samuel.

Beth And what about my father . . . or do you think they didn't let him in?

Sarah Of course they let him in! What a thing to say. He wasn't a bad man your father, just weak, easily led, he loved us all you know, especially you. You were his pride and joy.

Beth He'd a funny way of showing it.

Sarah Now, you mustn't speak ill of the dead, especially your own flesh and blood . . . he could have been worse . . . he never lifted a finger to any of us in his life, he just had a weakness for the drink and the bettin' . . . he couldn't help it, he was only a man, God help him.

Beth Next thing you'll be saying it was all your fault.

Sarah I sometimes think if I'd been a stronger sort of person, you know, took him in hand a bit more, that he'd of turned out all right. I was always too soft.

Beth You *do* blame yourself.

Sarah A bit . . . mostly I blame his mother and his sisters for the way they spoilt him . . . What are you smiling at?

Beth You, and all the other women like you. No matter what a man does wrong it's always some woman's fault, isn't it?

Sarah Men need lookin's after, like children, sure they never grow up.

Beth Oh, go to sleep before I lose my temper with you.

She kisses **Sarah** *and tucks a blanket around her.*

Did I tell you Theresa's home from London?

Sarah Is she? Is she coming over to see us?

Beth Tomorrow.

Sarah Ach, that'll be nice. I always liked Theresa, a bit flighty maybe, but a good soul at heart.

Beth (*grinning*) Not a bad sort . . . for a Catholic.

Sarah Like I said, you get more like your Aunt Maisie every day.

Lights darken on **Beth** *and* **Sarah** *and lighten on* **Theresa** *as a girl of eighteen. She is sitting on a chair, waiting to be interviewed for a job in the Northern Ireland Civil Service.* **Beth** *aged eighteen comes in.*

Beth Theresa, what are you doing here?

Theresa Same as you, I expect. Job interview? God, life's hilarious, isn't it? When you think of all the fuss there was about grammar schools and secondary schools, and here we both are, eighteen years old, waiting to be interviewed for boring jobs in the Northern Ireland Civil Service.

Beth It couldn't be more boring than the job I'm in at the moment. We all sit in rows typing invoices in front of a crabby old man in a glass booth. He taps the window if he sees anyone talking and times us when we go to the toilet.

Theresa Sounds just like the convent grammar school, only we weren't even lucky enough to have a crabby old man to look at.

Beth You never liked it, did you?

Theresa I hated it . . . spent half my time in the sin room.

Beth The what?

Theresa The sin room . . . it's where girls got sent for bad behaviour. One of the nuns told me that even when I wasn't behaving immodestly I looked as if I'd like to.

Beth I wouldn't have thought that there would have been much chance of behaving immodestly in a crowd of girls and nuns.

Theresa Don't you believe it. They saw sin everywhere.
During my life sentence there, they decided that it was
unhealthy the way some of the girls walked around the
playground with their hands in their skirt pockets. We had to
sew the pockets up to remove temptation.

Beth You're making it up.

Theresa I am not. They expelled a girl last year for having
a dirty book in her locker.

Beth What dirty book?

Theresa *The Invisible Man.*

Beth You'll never last in the Northern Ireland Civil
Service, Theresa Duffy, you never take anything seriously.

Theresa You know, I reckon I've as good as got one of the
three jobs that's going here today.

Beth How do you make that out?

Theresa Well, I was here early, I've seen all the other
candidates going in, and they were all definitely Prods. I'm
the only Tague here.

Beth How would you know what they were?

Theresa By the look of them. Your eyes are closer set. Did
nobody ever tell you that?

Beth I was always told that the Catholics are the ones with
the close-set eyes.

Theresa Aw don't be telling me that. I've it all worked out.
If I'm the only Tague being interviewed, and there are three
jobs going, I'm bound to get one of them.

Beth Why?

Theresa Why? Because low-grade positions in the
Northern Ireland Civil Service are allocated on a strict
population basis, two-thirds to the Prods, one-third to the
Catholics.

Beth You're joking again.

Theresa I'm not. It's to prove to the big wide world that they don't discriminate. Mind you, the Catholic third haven't a hope in hell of being promoted to the top grades. They're allowed so far and then it stops, but at least they employ us.

Beth The firm I'm with doesn't employ Catholics, at least not in their offices. There are a few in the factory.

Theresa Aye, and if they could get enough Protestants to fill the factory they'd do that too.

Beth I'm sorry.

Theresa Don't be daft, it's nothing to do with you, and anyway, they say it works the other way round in the South.

Beth Even if it does, you live here.

Theresa Not for long, kid. I'm just going to work here for a while to get some experience, and then I'm off to London.

Beth London?

Theresa Aye, London. I'm not stopping here to end up marrying some boozy Catholic layabout who'll give me a baby a year and little else . . . My God, Beth, do you remember all those confused talks we used to have about sex?

Beth You thought you were pregnant because Joe Maguire put his hand up your skirt.

Theresa And you told me that I couldn't be pregnant because Joe Maguire had pimples, and boys could only make babies after their spots cleared up. Where did you hear a yarn like that?

Beth In the school playground, from a wee girl called Iris Agnew.

Theresa Well, if you ever run into Iris Agnew, you can tell her from me that her theory presented me with a bit of a problem. You see, my da always had spots on his face, they never cleared up, yet my mother kept on producing a baby every other year. I thought she must be an immoral woman who was making babies with somebody else.

Beth Do you ever wonder what it's like?

Theresa All the time. When my eldest sister got married, I thought she'd tell me all about it, we were very close.

Beth And did she not?

Theresa She came back from the honeymoon with such a stunned look on her face that I hadn't the nerve to ask her . . . Do you ever notice the way women giggle a lot before they're married but they don't giggle much afterwards? I wonder why?

Beth I suppose we'll find out some day.

Theresa That's why I'm going to London . . . to find out without my mother watching me like a hawk. The only way to find out here is to get married, and I'd like to sample it first before I commit myself, just in case it really is a fate worse than death . . . Why don't you come to London with me, and we'll lead a life of delicious sin and debauchery.

Beth My mother'd never let me go to London. Nobody in our family ever leaves home except to get married.

Theresa Or to join the British Army.

Beth The only reason my mother gave in and let our Sammy join the Army was because he couldn't get a decent job here. I think she was worried that if Sammy sat about the house much longer, he'd end up drinking himself to death like my father.

Theresa I'm sure she misses him.

Beth Oh yes, you know what my mother's like about Sammy. She consoles herself with the thought that he's learning a good trade.

Theresa Killing people?

Beth Motor mechanic.

Theresa Oh . . . how's he getting on, does he like it?

Beth He's been posted to Germany. He leaves this afternoon. He can't wait to go. My grandfather says it's only natural, coming from a long line of fighting men the way he does. He was called after an uncle who died in the Second World War, you know.

Theresa I was called after a saint.

The lights darken on the two girls and lighten on the **Grandmother**'s *house. The* **Grandfather** *is hanging a large framed photo of* **Sammy** *in Army uniform beside the two photos of himself and* **Samuel**. *The* **Grandmother**, **Maisie**, **Sarah** *and* **Sammy** *in Army uniform sit drinking tea. The* **Grandfather** *steps back and looks at the three photos with pride.*

Grandfather Boys, oh dear, isn't that a sight to make a family proud? Three generations for King and Country.

Grandmother It's Queen and Country now, you oul fool.

The **Grandfather** *ignores her and shakes hands with* **Sammy**.

Grandfather I'm proud of you, lad, proud.

Beth *comes rushing in.*

Beth Oh, I thought I'd missed you . . .

Sarah What kept you?

Beth The interviews ran late, I don't know what the hold-up was.

Grandfather Bloody civil servants, probably drinkin' tea. They don't know they're livin', that lot.

Sarah How did you get on?

Beth All right, I don't think I did too badly. Theresa was there too.

Grandmother Theresa Duffy?

Beth Yes.

Maisie I thought she was goin' to the university.

Beth She changed her mind.

Maisie Isn't it a great state of affairs when the Catholics can pick and choose like the gentry? I don't know why you

knock about with her anyway. Do you not know any
Protestant girls?

Beth I don't knock about with Theresa, in fact today's the
first time I've seen her in ages.

Maisie Ah, yous were always very pally.

Beth She's a friend. I like her.

Maisie Will you still like her if she gets a cushy job in the
civil service and you don't?

Beth Yes, I will.

Maisie You've no sense, you, trustin' the Catholics.
They're after all our jobs, they're after takin' over.

A car horn sounds offstage. **Sammy** *stands up.*

Sammy That's me. Time to go.

The rest of the scene is almost a re-enactment of **Samuel**'s *departure
for war.*

Cheer up everybody, I've been away before.

Grandmother Aye, but this time you're goin' overseas.

Sarah Here, son, I've made you a few sandwiches. It's a
long journey.

Sammy Mother, they give us a travel allowance, I don't
need sandwiches.

Grandfather They look after them well in the modern
Army. When I was in transit with the regiment, we were
lucky to get a drink of water, so we were.

Grandmother Don't you start reminiscin' about winnin'
World War One, or he'll miss the boat.

She hands **Sammy** *some money in an envelope.*

Here, love, you put that away safe, it's from me and
Maisie.

He is embarrassed and is about to protest.

Maisie Take it. Always have a wee roughness of money about you when you're away from home, for emergencies.

Sammy *smiles, accepts the money and embraces* **Maisie** *and the* **Grandmother**.

Grandfather Good luck, lad.

Sammy Thanks, granda.

They shake hands. The **Grandfather** *blows his nose to hide his emotions.* **Sammy** *embraces his mother,* **Sarah**.

Sarah Now, you take care of yourself, do you hear?

Sammy I'll be home on leave in no time at all.

Sarah Of course you will.

Grandfather You do us proud, son.

Sammy I'll come home with a string of medals on my chest.

They all fall silent and look at **Sammy** *and then at the photo of* **Samuel**. *The* **Grandmother** *begins to cry.*

Grandmother Don't say that, Sammy.

Sammy What did I say?

Sarah Nothin' . . . nothin', son, it's all right.

The car horn hoots offstage again.

Sammy I'll have to go . . . goodbye Beth.

Beth Goodbye big brother, take care.

Sammy You take care of mother.

Beth I will.

Sammy *leaves.* **Beth** *calls after him.*

Beth Don't forget to write . . .

They all wave from the door as the car drives off, then the women sit down in silence. The **Grandfather** *looks proudly at the photos.*

Grandfather There's no doubt about it, you can't keep a good family down. Another Samuel gone overseas to sort out the Germans.

Grandmother He's not away to fight the Germans, he's away to protect them from the Russians. The Germans are our allies now, remember?

Grandfather Just as long as he doesn't turn his back on them . . .

He stops as he realizes what he has said. **Sarah** *sniffs tearfully. The* **Grandfather** *looks impatiently at the sad women.*

I'm away to the pub for a bit of cheerful company.

Grandmother You're late today. Your oul stomach's probably beginnin' to wonder if your throat's cut.

Beth I'll walk down the road with you, granda, I'm going to get my hair done.

Sarah Will you be home for your tea?

Beth No. Stephen's taking me out for a meal.

She leaves with the **Grandfather** *and returns to watch (unseen) the three women.*

Maisie Is that the Stephen with the car that lives in the big house up the Lisburn Road?

Sarah It is.

Grandmother He's awful well-to-do, Maisie. It could be a quare good match for our Beth, if she plays her cards right.

Sarah The house belongs to his old aunt, you know. She reared him; his parents died young.

Grandmother She has neither chick nor chile of her own. He stands to inherit the lot when she goes.

Maisie I hadn't heard him mentioned for a while, I thought it was all off.

Sarah He's been away in England on business. He goes away a lot on business, but he always gets in touch with our Beth the minute he gets back.

Maisie What does he do for a livin'?

Sarah I'm not sure, but he must make a bit of money at it. He's always well turned out and runs a nice car.

Grandmother Tell Maisie about the tea-set, Sarah.

Sarah Stephen took our Beth up to the house to meet the old aunt, and she stayed for her tea. Our Beth says the house is full of lovely old furniture and good ornaments, and they had their tea out of china that was so fine, our Beth was afraid she'd take a bite out of it.

Maisie And why should she feel like that. We've always had a bit of good china about us. Beth's had a cup of tea in a china cup before this.

Sarah Of course she has, but this was the really old stuff, you know, very very fine.

Grandmother Will you tell her about the tea-set?

Sarah I'm coming to the tea-set . . . after they had their tea the old aunt showed Beth round the house, and apart from all the other nice stuff, do you know what she has?

Maisie What?

Grandmother A real Belleek tea-set.

Sarah The real McCoy.

Maisie I was never all that struck on Belleek. Do you not think it's awful Fenian-looking?

Sarah It's over a hundred years old, it must be worth a fortune.

Maisie Oh, I'm sure it is, but I still say you can't beat the fine English bone china.

Sarah Well, I like it, it's really elegant. The old aunt said it belonged to her grandmother.

Grandmother The old aunt has taken a real shine to our Beth from what I can make out.

Maisie You'd better start savin', Sarah. It looks as if there might be a weddin' in the offin'.

Sarah Oh, I started puttin' a bit by for that years ago. When our Beth gets married it's all going to be done proper.

The lights darken on scene and lighten on one side of the stage where **Beth** *on the eve of her wedding is sitting, looking at herself in the mirror. She lifts a wedding veil and head-dress out of a box and sets it on her head. She stares at herself in the mirror. Her expression is sad, pensive. She removes the head-dress and puts it back in the box.* **Theresa** *comes bounding in to the bedroom, singing 'Here Comes the Bride'.* **Beth** *is delighted to see her.*

Beth Theresa, when did you get back?

Theresa This afternoon.

They hug each other delightedly.

The whole road's talking about you. (*She folds her arms over her chest and puts on an exaggerated Belfast accent.*) 'Here, all the same Mrs Jannsen, she's done quare an' well for herself, that wee girl, so she has. A businessman with his own house an' all up the posh end of the Lisburn Road. Fully furnished and wall-to-wall carpet. She'll want for nathin' . . . nathin' . . .'

Beth You never change, you. I suppose my mother took you on a conducted tour of the wedding presents.

Theresa As soon as I came in through the door. My God, Beth, you could open a wee shop. How many china tea-sets did you get? I lost count.

Beth Six.

Theresa Six? In my flat in London there are five beakers, two of them chipped, and an assortment of plates and bowls that I picked up cheap in a jumble sale. As the woman down the road said, 'You don't know yer livin'.'

Beth I'd give you the lot, Theresa, if I could do it without offending anybody. Stephen's house is already coming down with china that belonged to his family.

Theresa Including a complete set of Belleek, you mother tells me.

Beth She tells everybody. Some day, I'm going to give her that Belleek tea-set.

Theresa Don't you like it?

Beth It's really beautiful, but it symbolizes a lot more to my mother than it ever will to me. Do you know, one day we were up at the house and she was gazing at it, and I offered to make a drop of tea and serve it to her in one of the Belleek cups and saucers. She nearly had a fit at the very idea. 'That's for looking at not drinking out of,' she said . . . I sometimes think that about Stephen . . .

Theresa Think what?

Beth That he's for looking at, for . . . show, not for everyday use . . .

There is a silence. **Theresa** *looks at* **Beth** *curiously and then puts her arm around her.*

Theresa Come on now . . . I think this is called wedding eve jitters . . . you do love him?

Beth Oh yes . . . at least . . . I think so . . . I'm not sure what love is . . .

Theresa Ask youself, would you still love him if he was a welder in the shipyard?

Beth Then he wouldn't be Stephen.

Theresa You're quite right, that was a daft thing to say . . . go on, admit it, you're marrying him for the Belleek tea-set, aren't you?

Beth Oh Theresa, I hope not.

Theresa Beth . . . you don't have to get married . . . do you?

Beth No, nothing like that . . . Stephen is very . . . respectable.

Theresa There's still time to change your mind.

Beth Do you want me to break my mother's heart? She adores him.

Theresa Do you adore him?

Beth Oh, this is silly, you're quite right, it's just an attack of wedding eve jitters . . . I've been sitting up here too long on my own. Let's go downstairs and have a drink, eh?

Theresa Why have you been sitting up here on your own?

Beth I just sat down for a while, and got to thinking . . . I'm getting married tomorrow, I'm moving from my mother's house to Stephen's house . . . I've been my mother's daughter, and now I'm going to be Stephen's wife . . . I've never been just me. I've never made a decision in my life, Theresa.

Theresa You decided to get married.

Beth After Stephen's aunt died, he suddenly said to me one day, 'Let's get married, I'm lonely in that big old house all by myself.' I don't even remember saying yes . . . I wonder what would have happened to me if I'd gone to London with you?

Theresa Do you want to hear what happened to me?

Beth I know what happened to you, your mother told me. You have a lovely flat of your own, a fantastic job, independence, and in spite of countless offers, you prefer to be single . . .

Theresa So that's what she's been saying? Beth, I have two rooms in a depressing house in a seedy London suburb. I have a boring job in the city which I can't leave because I need the money . . . I also have a three-year-old child.

Beth What?

Theresa That's why I can't leave the boring job. It pays well, and the hours fit in with Shauna's day nursery.

Beth Shauna?

Theresa My daughter . . . This is all top secret, Beth. For God's sake don't tell a soul. I promised my mother I wouldn't disgrace her in front of the neighbours.

Beth You're not married, then?

Theresa Married! I told him I was pregnant on a Tuesday, by Thursday he was gone. I just heard recently that he got married . . . probably to some nice, clever, well-brought-up girl who made him wait until she'd got a wedding ring safely on her finger.

Beth Does he know he has a daughter?

Theresa Oh, I'm sure he does, there's a flourishing grapevine within the Irish community in London . . . just like home.

Beth He's Irish?

Theresa Yes, hilarious, isn't it? I go to London to get away from all this, and I'm hardly off the boat before I fall hook, line and sinker for a sweet-talking, good-looking Catholic boy from Dublin.

Beth My Great Aunt Maisie always said that them Southern Tagues are the worst.

Theresa I never thought I'd see the day when I'd be agreeing with your Aunt Maisie.

Beth How do you manage, alone . . .

Theresa I cope. It's amazing what you can do if you have to. My mother wanted me to get her adopted, but I wouldn't, and I'm glad. I love her, even if the sight of her scares off prospective husbands. There only seem to be two types of men about. The ones who run away, and the ones who think, 'Wey hey, I'm on to a good thing here' . . . but I live in hope. One day my prince will come.

Beth So the streets weren't paved with gold after all?

Theresa They weren't even gilded.

Beth We're going to London for the honeymoon.

Theresa For how long?

Beth About two weeks. Stephen has a couple of business appointments there at the end of the month, we'll be coming back home after that, on the twenty-ninth.

Theresa That's the day I go back. We'll just miss each other.

Sarah *comes in.*

Sarah Beth, could you come down for a minute? Mrs McMullan from up the street is here with a present for you and she can only stop for a minute.

Beth Okay, I'll not be long . . .

Beth *leaves.* **Sarah** *turns to* **Theresa**.

Sarah The neighbours have been awful good. They've bought her some lovely stuff.

Theresa They have indeed.

Sarah No sign of you taking the plunge, Theresa?

Theresa I'm a career girl. Did my mother not tell you?

Sarah *is stroking the head-dress and is not really listening.*

Sarah Just think, this time tomorrow our Beth will be in a private suite in a big London hotel . . . Mrs Stephen Martin. She's done quare and well for herself, hasn't she, Theresa?

Theresa She's certainly done better than I did.

Sarah *pats* **Theresa**'*s hand comfortingly.*

Sarah Your time will come, Theresa, you wait and see. A good-lookin' girl like you won't stay single for long.

Theresa I'm not so sure I want to get married.

Sarah 'Course you do! You wouldn't want to end up an oul maid, would you? It's not natural for a woman to stay single.

Lights darken on **Theresa** *and* **Sarah** *and lighten on* **Beth** *sitting alone beside a telephone in a hotel bedroom in London. She looks at the shiny new wedding ring on her finger and turns it round. She looks at the phone, then at her watch, then at the phone again. She moves to lift the receiver, changes her mind and opens her handbag. She removes a sprig*

*of white heather. The stem is wrapped in silver foil. She removes some
confetti from it, holds the confetti between her fingers and lets it fall to
the floor. The phone rings.*

Beth Hallo? . . . Stephen . . . you said five or ten minutes
. . . yes . . . yes . . . I see, no, no I'd rather not come down, I
. . . Stephen, I don't really want a drink, . . . and anyway,
there's a bottle of champagne here, compliments of the
management . . . well, if it's business and it's important,
you'd better buy them another drink . . . no I won't . . . I
think I'll have a bath . . . it's been a long day . . . yes . . . yes
of course I do . . .

*She replaces the receiver. She sits very still for a moment, then moves to
close her handbag. She stops, looks puzzled, puts her hand in the bag and
removes a book. She looks at the title and grins. She phones* **Theresa**.

Beth Hallo, is that you, Theresa? It's me . . . Beth, I just
thought I'd give you a quick ring . . . Stephen? . . . no, he's
not here, I mean he's here in the hotel, but he's downstairs at
the moment . . . when we arrived there were some business
colleagues of Stephen's in the foyer . . . we couldn't get away
from them . . . Stephen's buying them a drink to get rid of
them . . . no, no, not long, just a few minutes ago . . . Is it
really? (*She looks at her watch.*) . . . We were late arriving, the
plane was held up . . . (*Desperately.*) Theresa? (*Pause, then
calmly.*) . . . I'm ringing to say I've just this minute opened
my handbag and found the book . . . very funny! Of course I
knew it was you, who else would it be . . . Yes, I do remember
. . . Do you know, I've never actually read it? (*She listens and
laughs.*) Oh, I am glad I phoned you, I feel better already . . .
No, no of course there's nothing wrong . . . Listen, I'd better
go . . . there's a waiter here with champagne . . . Stephen
must have ordered it at the bar . . . he'll be here any minute
. . . thanks . . . I will. (*She replaces the receiver and looks at the book
title.*) *The Invisible Man* . . . Oh, Theresa, if only you knew . . .

*She sits, turning the wedding ring round on her finger. Quietly, in the
distance is heard the sound of* **Beth** *and* **Theresa** *as children singing
'On the hill there stands a lady, who she is I do not know, all she wants
is gold and silver, all she wants is a nice young man.'*

The lights darken. The stage stays dark for a few moments to mark the passing of time. The children's singing merges with radio reports of the 'Troubles' in the North. There is the sound of gunfire. The stage lightens to show **Sarah** *in the house that once belonged to the* **Grandparents**. *Below the three photos of the* **Grandmother**, **Samuel** *and* **Sammy** *is a china cabinet. A large photo of* **Beth** *and* **Stephen** *on their wedding day is on top of the cabinet. The year is 1971.*

Sarah *is very nervous. She is dusting the china cabinet and keeps looking out of the window at each sound of disturbance. She turns apprehensively as she hears the front door open.* **Beth** *rushes in.*

Sarah Beth, what are you doing out in the middle of all this?

Beth I've been worried sick about you. Your phone's dead, do you know that?

Sarah I know . . . the electricity's been goin' off and on too . . . You shouldn't have come away over here, there's been shootin' and an explosion . . . is Stephen with you?

Beth He's abroad on business.

Sarah You mean you came the whole way here all by yourself? You could have been killed . . . Oh, but I am glad to see you . . . you've no idea what it's been like since the internment started . . . bin lids bangin' and riots in the streets . . . and . . .

She begins to cry. **Beth** *puts her arms around her.*

Beth You can't stay here alone. You have got to come home with me.

Sarah I can't leave my house.

Beth You'll have to . . .

Sarah I won't . . . it's all I've got . . .

Beth You've got me . . .

Sarah I'm not abandoning this house . . .

Beth Mum, you have no idea how bad it is out there. It's not only shooting and rioting . . . people are leaving their houses, Protestants and Catholics. Some of the houses at the bottom of this road are ablaze. They're burning the houses as they leave.

Sarah Who are?

Beth Both sides. Frightened, desperate people are burning their own houses to stop other frightened desperate people from moving in.

Sarah And you're askin' me to leave?

Beth Please, please come home with me.

Sarah *looks at the photos and touches the china cabinet.*

Sarah No . . . no, this is my home.

There is a loud banging on the door and shouts. The two women look scared. **Beth** *walks slowly towards the door.*

Sarah Beth, be careful . . .

Beth *opens the door and returns with a* **Youth.**

Youth We're evacuating the street, missus, you have to get out.

Sarah And who are you when you're at home?

Youth We're your local defence committee.

Sarah Well, clear away off and defend us then.

Youth There are too many Catholics in this street. A lot of the Protestants have already been intimidated out. We've orders to move the rest of yous to safety.

Sarah I moved into this house after my mother and father died. Three generations of my family have lived here, three generations. No IRA gunman is goin' to intimidate me out . . . no, nor no Protestant defence committee neither.

Beth *puts her arms around* **Sarah.**

Beth Mum, please, let's just go.

Sarah No.

Youth We've orders to burn these houses.

Sarah *moves defensively in front of the china cabinet.*

Sarah Over my dead body . . .

Beth Mum, please . . .

Sarah You'll not burn my house, nor all the stuff in it. We worked hard all our lives for what's here. It may not be much but it's mine and nobody's goin' to set fire to it . . .

Youth We have orders . . .

Sarah From who? To hell with your orders . . . Get out of my house . . . get out . . .

She moves as if to attack the **Youth**. *There is the sound of a heavy vehicle outside. The* **Youth** *looks out of the window.*

Youth It's the fuckin' Army. They're liftin' everybody in sight. Prods or Fenians, it makes no difference to them bastards.

He exits by the rear door of the house shouting threateningly as he goes.

I'll go out the back way. I'm warnin' you two – get out of here and quick – if we don't come back the IRA will . . . Either way, your house is goin' to burn.

He runs out.

Beth Mum, I'm not asking you any more, I'm telling you, we have to go . . .

Sarah *looks around the room at the china cabinet and the photos.*

Sarah I'm not leavin' my wee house, I won't abandon them . . .

Beth We can bring the pictures with us . . .

Sarah It's not just the pictures . . .

Beth Look, I'll put all the china, linen, anything you want into the car . . .

Sarah My mother worked her fingers to the bone to buy that new devon grate . . .

Beth The cooker, the kitchen sink, anything you want . . .

Sarah I remember the day the men came to put it in. She was that pleased, no more black leadin' . . . that was when she started to buy the brass ornaments, one every nigh and again when she could afford it . . .

Beth Mum, they're only . . . things . . . bits and pieces . . . they can all be replaced . . .

Sarah They're my life!

There is silence for a moment. An **Army Sergeant** *enters.*

Sergeant A man was seen entering these premises. Does he live here?

Beth *glances towards the back door. The* **Sergeant** *moves towards this.*

Sarah You'd be wastin' your time. You wouldn't know the way of the entries.

Sergeant Have you been threatened? (*The two women don't reply. He looks with interest at the photos.*) I see you're on our side anyway.

Sarah Aye, but whose side are you on?

Sergeant We're here to keep law and order.

Sarah Law and order. That's a laugh . . . three generations of my family have fought in your army, and for what? That's my father, gassed in the First World War, that's my brother, killed in the Second, and that's my son, my only son, and he can't even come home on leave any more in case he gets a bullet in his back. The IRA shot an oul lad in the next street the other day, an ex-serviceman. He was goin' to the British Legion for a reunion dinner. Wearin' all his medals, he was, proud as punch. If they'll do the like of that to a harmless old man, what they could do to my Sammy doesn't bear thinkin' about.

Sergeant Do the two of you live here alone?

Beth I'm her married daughter, I live across town.

Sergeant Perhaps you should go there. This is a very tense situation tonight. I'm not sure we'll be able to contain it. And she's probably at special risk with a serving soldier in the family.

Beth She won't leave.

Sergeant Think over what I've said. We haven't enough troops to protect every house.

Sarah I'm not leavin'.

The **Sergeant** *moves towards the door followed by* **Beth**.

Sergeant Try to persuade her, will you?

Beth I'll try.

Sergeant Where's your brother stationed?

Beth Cyprus.

Sergeant Cyprus. I fought there . . . at least there you could recognize the enemy. Here they all look the same.

Beth You can tell the Catholics by their close-set eyes. Did nobody ever tell you that?

Sergeant No, but I'll bear it in mind. Good night.

Beth Good night.

The **Sergeant** *leaves.* **Beth** *looks at* **Sarah** *who is caressing the china cabinet.*

Sarah I'm not leaving, so you needn't bother trying to persuade me.

Beth All right, I'll stay here with you then . . . God, I almost wish they would burn this house down, then you'd have to leave, you'd have no choice . . .

Sarah That's a terrible thing to say, Beth.

Beth (*tiredly*) I'll make a cup of tea.

The lights darken. **Beth** *steps out of the darkness and addresses the audience.*

Beth The Army managed to contain the violence, and there were no more houses burned that night. The family house, plus a few others, stood forlornly, defiantly amid the blackened ruins of what the media called 'people's little palaces'. The rattle of the bin-lid had challenged the supremacy of the Lambeg drum. From that night onwards my mother began to die. The doctor's diagnosis was depression. It would pass, he said, it was just her age. It was his standard diagnosis for all his female patients no matter what age they were. The Troubles couldn't shift her, but undetected cancer did within the year.

Beth *crosses the stage abruptly and sits down in the empty sofa.* **Theresa** *comes in. She has been visiting* **Sarah** *in the bedroom.*

Theresa She was talking away, and suddenly she fell asleep in mid-sentence.

Beth Yes, it happens all the time now, more and more often, it's all the drugs.

Theresa Well, at least she's not in bad pain (**Beth** *looks up sharply.*) . . . because of the drugs, I mean . . .

Beth We must all be thankful for small mercies . . . God's good, as my grandmother used to say.

Theresa *stares at her.* **Beth** *looks away.*

Theresa You shouldn't be coping with this all on your own, Beth.

Beth It's amazing what you can do if you have to.

Theresa Can't Sammy get compassionate leave from the Army?

Beth Sammy doesn't know how ill she is. She's afraid that if he comes home he might get shot by the IRA. 'There's nothing he can do here,' she said, 'and one dead hero's enough for any family.'

Theresa You should tell him anyway.

Beth A bit late in the day, don't you think, for me to start defying my mother?

Theresa And what about Stephen?

Beth What about Stephen?

Theresa When's he coming home from America?

Beth He's not.

Theresa Oh . . . I see . . .

Beth (*sarcastically*) Do you?

Theresa (*levelly*) No, I don't actually.

Beth . . . My father gambled in half-crowns and ten-shilling notes. Stephen gambles in thousands of pounds and bits of paper called stocks and shares. When my father had blown his entire pay packet at the dog track, and was too ashamed to come home, he used to hide out with one of his married sisters. When Stephen's creditors began to hammer on the door, he fled to his aunt in America. She's a wealthy widow and she has no son.

Theresa Why didn't you ever mention any of this in your letters?

Beth I come from a long line of respectable women, who never let themselves down in front of the neighbours.

Theresa I was never one of the neighbours.

Beth No, you're the one that got away.

Theresa Why are you angry with me?

Beth I'm not angry with you . . . I'm just angry.

Theresa Why?

Beth Because it's all a lie . . . and I want to tell *her* about it . . . and I can't. My marriage has been the one big success of her life, and I can't spoil it for her, not now. I can't tell her that I faithfully repeated all her mistakes, that if you take away the velvet sofas and the china cabinets . . . there's nothing there . . . it's all a lie . . .

Theresa So, what are you going to do about it?

Beth I can't do anything about it.

Theresa Why not?

Beth Because I have to look after her.

Theresa And what about afterwards?

Beth Afterwards?

Theresa After she dies.

Beth I don't want to talk about this.

Theresa Will you stay on here?

Beth I . . . I don't know . . .

Theresa Will you go back to your mother's old house?

Beth It's not her house. Her family rented it for three generations. I'm the first one who ever owned a house, that's another reason for her pride in me.

Theresa You could come to London, stay with me and Shauna for a while.

Beth I'll think about it.

Theresa Don't just think about it. Do something about it.

Beth Don't you tell me what I should do! All my life people have been telling me what I should do!

Theresa Maybe because all your life you have let them!

Beth (*stiffly*) You'd better go. You've to meet your mother in town. You'll be late.

Theresa Shall I come to see you tomorrow?

Beth If you like.

There is an awkward silence.

Theresa Beth . . . I didn't mean to . . .

Beth (*tiredly*) It's all right . . . it's all right . . . you didn't tell me anything I didn't already know . . . I'm scared, Theresa . . . my mother's dying and very soon for the first time in my life I am going to be alone . . . and I'm scared . . . my head is full of other people's memories. I don't know who *I* am . . . what *I* am . . .

Theresa That's all right. I'm nearly thirty, and I still don't know what I want to be when I grow up.

Beth (*smiling*) Oh, Theresa . . .

Theresa That's better. I'll come and see you tomorrow, and I'll tell you about my grotty flat in London and my mad teenage daughter. Then you'll definitely not want to come.

They exit. **Sarah** *enters, slowly, painfully. She lies down on the velvet sofa.* **Beth** *returns.*

Sarah Has Theresa gone?

Beth She had to meet her mother in town. She'll be back to see us tomorrow . . . why won't you stay in bed?

Sarah Because I love being in this room . . . all the same, Beth, you have to admit I'm going out in quare style . . . velvet sofas and fine bone china and the Orangemen paradin' past the window . . .

Beth's *face contorts as if she doesn't know whether to laugh or cry.*

Beth Would you like a cup of tea?

Sarah In a minute.

She takes two wedding rings off her finger and holds them out to **Beth**.

Here, I want you to wear these.

Beth Why?

Sarah They'll guard you after I'm gone, my wedding ring and your granny's. They'll keep you safe, put them on, child.

Beth Why now?

Sarah Because I know you. If I die with them on you'll never wear them . . . and I want you to wear them, for luck. Wedding rings are charms, you know.

She puts the rings on **Beth**'s *right hand.*

Now I'll have that cup of tea you were offerin'.

Beth Do you know what I'm going to do?

Sarah What?

Beth I'm going to get one of those Belleek cups and saucers out of that cabinet in the dining-room and serve you tea in it.

Sarah You can't do that.

Beth I can if I want . . .

Sarah I suppose you can, it belongs to you . . .

Beth That's right . . . wouldn't you like to be the very first person to have actually had a drink out of that set?

Sarah Don't tempt me.

Beth That's exactly what I'm going to do, I won't be a minute.

She goes to get the Belleek. **Sarah** *sits back, smiling in anticipation. Her dead brother,* **Samuel,** *appears in Second World War uniform.*

Sarah Oh, Samuel. I thought you were never coming.

Beth *returns with the Belleek cup and saucer in her hand. She thinks that* **Sarah** *is asleep again, but slowly realises that she is dead. She sets the cup and saucer down and strokes* **Sarah**'s *hair. The stage darkens.* **Beth** *walks out of the darkness and addresses the audience.*

Beth I had a long time to prepare myself for her death. I used to sit and watch her sleeping and find myself wondering what I would do first, when it happened. Would I phone Sammy, send for a minister, a doctor, an undertaker? I did all of those things later, but first of all I covered the mirrors in the house with white starched linen cloths, just as my grandmother had shown me, so that the evil spirits could not reflect away her soul.

The whole stage lightens on the family house and **Beth**'s *house. (* **Sarah** *is no longer on the velvet sofa.)* **Beth** *walks to the three photos of the family soldiers and takes them off the wall. She carries them to the velvet sofa and sets them in a row. A woman (a* **Valuer** *from an auction house) comes in with a list of the contents of* **Beth**'s *house on a clipboard.*

Valuer I've put an approximate valuation on everything in the house. 'Course, with auctions, you never know, you might get more, you might get less. Do you want a reserve price on anything?

Beth No, just sell the lot for whatever you can get.

Valuer Whatever you say.

Beth You'll be here when they come to pack it all up?

Valuer Oh, I'll be here. You have some valuable pieces. We don't want any of it broken.

Beth You'll need the house keys.

She hands her the keys.

Valuer What'll I do with the keys after?

Beth Pass them on to the solicitor, with the money.

Valuer I'm sure you'll be sorry to leave this lovely house.

Beth I won't be sorry at all.

Valuer If I'd the money I'd buy it myself.

Beth Is your list complete now?

Valuer It is . . . Pity about the Belleek tea-set.

Beth What?

Valuer The Belleek tea-set, there's a cup and saucer missing. Didn't you know?

Beth Oh yes . . . I did . . . they got broken, a long time ago.

Valuer Pity about that. It's still worth a bit of money of course, but if the set had been complete, it would have fetched maybe three or four times as much.

She peers at the Army photos on the velvet sofa.

Beth They were my mother's. They're not part of this house.

Valuer They're not worth anything anyway. Old wartime photos, cheap frames . . . there's a lot of them about.

Beth Yes, I'm sure there are.

Valuer Well, I'd better be off. It was a real pleasure valuing your stuff, Mrs Martin, a real pleasure. Lovely, some of it, lovely . . . pity about the Belleek tea-set though.

She leaves. **Beth** *smiles after her. She opens her handbag and takes out a small tissue-wrapped parcel. She removes the tissue paper, looks at the Belleek cup and saucer, and smiles. She sings quietly to herself 'On the hill there stands a lady, who she is I do not know . . .' As she sings she wraps up the Belleek cup and saucer and carefully replaces it in her handbag. She walks off the stage, still singing.*

Did You Hear the One About the Irishman . . . ?

A Love Story

For Richard Howard

Did You Hear the One About the Irishman . . . ? was first produced and directed by Brigid Larmour during a Royal Shakespeare Company tour of America in 1985. This revised version was performed at the King's Head Theatre, London in 1987 with the following cast:

Allison Clarke	Janet Behan
Brian Rafferty	John Keegan
The Comedian	Richard Howard
Mrs Boyd	
Mrs Clarke	Jane Lowe
Bernie Cassidy	
Mr Clarke	
The Irishman/Newsreader	Ultan Ely O'Carroll
Hughie Boyd	
Joe Rafferty	Billy Clarke
Marie Rafferty	Mandy McIlwaine

Directed by Caroline Sharman
Designed by Angus Campbell
Lighting Design Steve O'Brien
Stage Manager Mark Jones
Production Assistant Lauren Emmerson

Belfast 1987

Irishman (*reading from a list*) Her Majesty's Prison, Maze, Lisburn, Northern Ireland, 1987. Permitted Christmas Parcels for H/Blocks. 25 small cigars (cigarette size) or 100 cigarettes or 4 and a half oz. tobacco.
2lb. chocolates or sweets. 2lb. cake, quartered.
2lb. loose biscuits.
One unstuffed chicken, boned and quartered.
1lb. sliced cooked meat.
4lb. fresh fruit – no bananas or pears.

Spotlight on the **Comedian**. *He tells jokes directly to the audience as if he is performing in a club. The* **Irishman** *stops reading the list as his voice is drowned by the* **Comedian**'s *voice. He watches the comedy routine impassively.*

Comedian Good morning everyone. This is your captain speaking. We are now approaching the city of Belfast. Will all passengers please fasten their seatbelts and turn their watches back three hundred years.
The time is seven a.m. And if there are any Irish passengers on board, that means that the big hand is at twelve and the little hand is at seven.
Did you hear the one about the Irishman whose plane ran out of peat? He radioed for help. Mayday! Mayday!
'Cleared to land,' answered Control. 'Can you give us your height and position?'
'Certainly,' said the Irishman, 'I'm five foot two and I'm sitting at the front of the plane.'
Then there was the Irish terrorist whose first assignment was to hijack an aeroplane. It turned out to be his last assignment. As soon as the plane took off, he lit the fuse, put the bomb under his seat, and told the captain that everybody had three minutes to get out.
Little Paddy heard the story and it made him very nervous about flying. So he always carried a bomb in his suitcase

every time he had to travel by plane. He figured that the chances of two people on the same flight carrying a bomb were practically nil.

The **Comedian** *pauses to drink some beer.*

Irishman   Individual Christmas parcels. Maze Prison. Compound Seventeen. 400 cigarettes or 12 oz. tobacco or 25 small cigars
6 mince pies.
One fruit loaf – 1lb.
6 pastries.
6 baps.
1lb. chocolates.
2lb. sweets.
3lb. Christmas cake with no marzipan.

The Rafferty House. 7 a.m.

Brian Rafferty *and his sister* **Marie** *are packing a food parcel for their brother* **Joe** *who is in the Maze Prison.*

Brian   You know, a committee of grown men must have sat round a table and compiled these lists and decided that marzipan was a threat to national security.

Marie   Where are you going?

Brian   I'm going to phone Allison.

Marie   You'll finish this first!

Brian   I'll finish it when I've phoned Allison.

He goes to the phone.

Marie   She'll be the finish of you, that one.

Comedian   An Irish telephonist answered an international call. It's a long distance from America, said the operator. Sure any fool knows that, said the Irish telephonist, and hung up.

Irishman Bulk Christmas Parcels. Maze Prison.
Compound 17.
2 large tins of coffee.
5 turkeys cooked and stuffed.
8lb. sausages, cooked.
2 mince pies per prisoner.
2 pastries per prisoner – small bun size.
8 cakes not over 2lb. each.
12 Christmas puddings not over 2lb. each.
3 Christmas trees maximum 4ft 6 inches.
No decorations. Prisoners to buy them from the tuck shop.
All parcels to be signed.

Comedian (*to the* **Irishman**) Have you heard the latest
Irish joke?

Irishman I'm warning you. I'm an Irishman myself.

Comedian That's all right, Paddy. I'll tell it nice and
slowly for you.

The Clarke House 7 a.m.

Allison *sitting waiting for* **Brian** *to call. The phone rings. She
smiles and lifts the receiver.*

Brian It's 7 a.m. and this is your early morning obscene
telephone call. You have three minutes to get aroused.

Mrs Clarke, **Allison**'s *mother, enters.*

Allison I'm sorry, caller. Security are here to check the
bugging device. Please call later. (*She replaces the receiver.*)
Good morning, mother.

Mrs Clarke Who was that on the phone?

Allison (*smiling*) The Divis Flats heavy breather.

Mrs Clarke Oh really, Allison. Can't you be serious about
anything!

Allison You know very well who it was, mother. And yes,
I'm serious about a lot of things, but you don't want to know
about them. Particularly at seven o'clock on a Saturday

morning. What are you doing out of bed this early anyway? Is there a bomb scare in our select suburb?

Mrs Clarke That's not funny, Allison.

Allison No, it's not.

Mrs Clarke Susan phoned last night when you were out. She left a message for you.

Allison She's emigrating.

Mrs Clarke I do wish you two could be friends.

Allison Mother, it is a legal fact that when Susan married your beloved son, I acquired a sister-in-law. There is no law says I have to like her.

Mrs Clarke She's such a lovely, likeable girl. A good wife and mother. A considerate daughter-in-law.

Allison A lousy daughter.

Mrs Clarke Susan is very generous to her own mother.

Allison Then this message is not what I suspect it is?

Mrs Clarke Susan can't take Mrs Boyd to . . . that place . . . today.

Allison That place is called Long Kesh. The Maze Prison. And Susan's brother Hughie is one of its most notorious inmates. What's today's excuse for not giving her mother a lift there in the nice new car you bought her for Christmas?

Mrs Clarke Susan has a cold.

Allison In her feet, no doubt.

Mrs Clarke She wanted to know if you would give Mrs Boyd a lift, as it's your morning for voluntary work.

Allison Voluntary work? Is that what you tell your friends I do at the camp?

Mrs Clarke Well, it is what you do.

Allison I make tea.

Mrs Clarke Well, there you are then.

Allison It's not like the Women's Institute, mother. It's a drafty hut where the relatives of the prisoners hang around waiting for security clearance before they're bused up the road to the main camp. Voluntary work! Do you know what Susan calls it? Doing my middle-class bit. Mingling with the lower orders, the undeserving poor, from behind the safety of a tea urn on a counter. And she's right. That's what galls me. In her own nasty little way, she's right. But she has no right to judge me. Her only brother has been remanded there for over a year, and she has been to see him once.

Mrs Clarke She doesn't know what to say to Hughie.

Allison No. She's married into the middle classes; got herself out of those mean back streets; and his arrest has forced her to look back to what she came from.

Mrs Clarke She is not responsible for her brother.

Allison She could care a little more about her mother.

Mrs Clarke You're very hard on poor Susan. I think she's coped wonderfully well under the circumstances. It hasn't been easy for her.

Allison It hasn't been easy for her mother either. Have you any idea what it's like for a quiet, gentle little woman like Mrs Boyd to go to that place alone. To face the searches, the questions, the police guard while you try to talk to your only son?

The phone rings again. **Allison** *lifts the receiver.*

Brian I've thought it over, and I've decided to give you a second chance.

Allison To do what?

Brian To tell me how madly you love me.

Allison Love you? Are you mad? You're a working-class Catholic.

Brian I'm a very sexy working-class Catholic.

Allison Are you going to make an honest woman of me?

Brian Not until you've told me why you hung up on me.

Allison I got distracted by a message from your cousin, the lovely Susan.

Brian Ah, let me guess . . . She's broken her leg and can't drive to Long Kesh today.

Allison Congratulations, contestant. You have won first prize in our 'spot-the-lame-excuse' competition.

Brian No stamina, these middle-class prods.

Allison Common Catholics are not permitted to speak ill of the Protestant Ascendancy. It's written into the Constitution.

Brian I didn't know that.

Allison It's in the small print. Now, if I were your wife, I couldn't be called to give evidence against you.

Brian If you were my wife. I'd be part of the Protestant Ascendancy.

Allison Well, if you don't want to become a handsome prince, I'll become a frog. I'm not proud.

Brian You never give up, do you?

Allison Never.

Brian If I let you take me out tonight and get me drunk, will you promise not to take advantage of me.

Allison No.

Brian Nine o'clock?

Allison Nine o'clock.

Brian And will you drive Aunt Isa to the camp to see Hughie?

Allison You know I will.

Brian You know, you're not a bad sort . . . for a Protestant.

Allison I love you.

Brian I know.

Allison *replaces the receiver*.

Mrs Clarke Allison . . .

Allison Not now mother. I have to pick up Mrs Boyd and be at the camp by nine.

Mrs Clarke We have got to have a serious talk sometime soon.

Allison Mother, I am over eighteen and I don't need your permission to do anything.

Mrs Clarke You're not serious about this person, are you?

Allison He has a name, mother. Brian Rafferty. He was here only last week. Remember? Eye-patch. Wooden leg. Parrot on his shoulder.

Mrs Clarke He is most unsuitable.

Allison Why?

Mrs Clarke His background . . .

Allison Is exactly the same as Susan's.

Mrs Clarke His family . . .

Allison Is Catholic, and Susan's is not.

Mrs Clarke His brother is a terrorist.

Allison So is Susan's. Or are there terrorists and terrorists, mother? Theirs and ours?

Mrs Clarke Henry is very concerned about this whole affair.

Allison You are not to discuss my affairs with Uncle Henry.

Mrs Clarke A marriage of this sort could have detrimental effect on your Uncle Henry's career.

Allison Mother, if I thought for one moment that me marrying a Catholic could put a stop to Uncle Henry's career, as you call it, I'd marry the first Catholic who'd have me.

Mrs Clarke My brother is a very important man.

Allison Your brother is a well-bred gangster.

Mrs Clarke He says he will not permit this.

Allison How's he planning to stop us?

Mrs Clarke *looks uncomfortable and moves away.*

Mother! What did he say!

The Rafferty House.

Brian *returns to help* **Marie** *pack* **Joe***'s parcel.*

Marie And how is little miss wonderful this morning?
Nobody's put a bullet through her head yet, I take it?

Brian Marie, some day that mouth of yours is going to get
your nose broke.

Marie Or better still, maybe somebody'll put a bullet
through her Uncle Henry's head.

Brian Stop it, Marie.

Marie I don't understand how you can go about with the
likes of her. It's her kind are responsible for our Joe being
where he is. You should be concentrating on getting him out
of that place. Not knocking about with well-to-do Prods
from up the Malone Road.

Brian I'm sorry to be such a disappointment to you and
your friends, Marie. I tell you what. As soon as I get my
Rambo Outfit back from the cleaners, I'll scale the wire and
carry our Joe out on my back.

Mrs Clarke Long Kesh is no joking matter.

Brian No it's not. (*Pause.*) Wouldn't it be a laugh though, if
that camp was what united the Irish, once and for all.

Marie What are you blethering on about now.

Brian Where else do you know of in Northern Ireland
where the Prods and the Fenians meet on common ground?

Marie Let's all say a wee prayer together? Our church this
week, their church next week?

Brian I said Prods and Fenians, Marie. Not well-meaning moderates.

Marie The camp, like the country, is segregated.

Brian I'm not talking about the prisoners. I'm talking about their families. Drinking tea in the waiting area. Together. Standing in line checking in food parcels. Together. Sharing the same bus to the main camp to visit their sons, fathers, husbands, brothers, lovers. Together.

Marie They don't visit together. They go their separate ways to segregated blocks. Prods to the right. Fenians to the left.

Brian But before that they've sat together and talked. Without fighting. Which is more than can be said about their so-called political leaders. Maybe we should put all the politicians on the Long Kesh bus, and drive them round and round the camp till they've reached an agreement.

Marie There'll be no agreement here as long as there are H Blocks and men on the blanket.

Brian There are Protestants in the prison as well, Marie.

Marie One or two.

Brian Well the pair of them must have a hell of a lot of visitors, that's all I can say.

Marie All right. All right. So there are Protestants in jail too. So what?

Brian So, where else in Northern Ireland can a Provie wife and a UDA wife take a long look at each other and realise that they're both on board the same sinking ship. Common ground. Common enemy. And there's nothing like a common enemy for resolving a family feud.

Marie It's too late Brian.

Brian It's never too late to hold out your hand.

Marie You're a dreamer. They'd tie your hands behind your back and shoot you. You finish Joe's box. I'll take Mum up a cup of tea.

Brian How is she the day?

Marie Same as usual. Full of life and hope. Chatting away, ten to the dozen.

Brian Don't, Marie.

Marie What do you want me to say? You know how she is. You still believe there'll be a miraculous cure, don't you? That some morning she won't be lying in that bed staring blankly at the cracks in the ceiling. How is she the day! She's the same as she's been every day since some Protestant hero crept up behind daddy and fired a bullet into the back of his head.

Brian We don't know who killed him, Marie.

Marie Maybe he shot himself.

The Clarke House

Allison's *father,* **Mr Clarke** *comes in.*

Mr Clarke What are you doing up at this hour on a Saturday morning?

Allison It's my Saturday for making tea at the Maze. What's your excuse?

Mr Clarke Didn't your mother tell you? We're going to Enniskillen for the weekend. Your Uncle Henry is having one of his do's.

Allison Oh daddy. Why don't you just refuse to go?

Mr Clarke Your mother would sulk for a fortnight. Besides, I like to keep on friendly terms with Henry. If we ever get our parliament back, he could be our new leader.

Allison God forbid.

Mr Clarke He was born with the gift of the gab.

Allison I wonder how many people have died as a result of his clever speeches.

Mr Clarke What's the matter, love?

Allison It's been one of those mornings. Susan's leaving her mother to face the camp alone again. And mother's been going on about Brian. How unsuitable he is, wrong class, wrong religion . . . Do you disapprove of Brian?

Mr Clarke If I left you into a family secret, will you promise never to tell your mother that I told you? My grandmother was Catholic. A native Irish speaker from Donegal. I think your mother is very worried that it might be a hereditary complaint coming out in you.

Allison Dad, I get enough jokes from Brian. Don't you start.

Mr Clarke No joke, love. Just the unspoken truth. It was an important clause in the marriage contract that it should never be mentioned. I think over the years, your mother has convinced herself that my grandmother was a senile old woman who only imagined she was born a Catholic.

Allison You wouldn't object then, if I married Brian?

Mr Clarke You're over eighteen.

Allison That's not an answer.

Mr Clarke It would . . . worry me.

Allison Why?

Mr Clarke I don't care one way or the other about religion. You know that. I'm all for people leaving each other alone. But unfortunately, there are too many people here who do care. I don't want to see you getting hurt.

Allison Bigoted opinions don't bother me.

Mr Clarke It's not what they'd say, Allison. It's what they might do.

Allison Oh come on daddy. Brian and I aren't that important.

Mr Clarke   Whether you like it or not, you are the niece of a loyalist politician. You marry a Catholic and it will be headline news. Especially when word gets out that the groom's brother is Joe Rafferty.

Allison   You do disapprove.

Mr Clarke   No. I like Brian. He's witty, articulate, good education, good job. In any other time and place, the perfect son-in-law. But not here, Allison, not now.

Allison   I was prepared for objections from every side. His family. Mother's family. All comers. But not you. Not my nice easy-going, middle of-the-road dad.

Mr Clarke   Listen to me, love.

Allison   Don't waste your breath trying to talk me out of it.

Mr Clarke   Let me tell you another family story from way back. Your grandfather, my father, had a stroke and I found myself suddenly in charge of the factory. There was . . . an arrangement . . . about the workforce. There wasn't a Catholic employed in the place. Protestants all. From the managing director to the old man who swept the floors. I'd always known about it, but I'd never really given it much thought until I became the boss. I'd been away from Ireland a lot. Educated in England. Travels abroad. I considered myself a liberal thinker. I was naïve enough to believe that good intentions could change the world. Your Brian is like that. I was wrong, of course. When word got around the factory that I'd shortlisted a Catholic woman for canteen manageress, I received a delegation from the men. The message was very clear. Don't even consider it or we shut down the plant. The same day, I was summoned to my father's bedside. He was propped up with pillows. Half paralysed. But *his* message was also very clear. One more stunt like that and he'd bring my cousin George in as head of the family business. Whatever damn fool ideas I'd picked up in Oxford, I could forget them.

Allison   So you forgot them.

Mr Clarke I'd like to claim a great crisis of conscience. But I'm afraid I can't. I was an indolent young man. I had a sports car. An expensive social life, here and abroad. All paid for by my father's factory with its loyal Protestant workforce. I wasn't about to rock that gilt-edged boat for lost causes.

Allison You've never deliberately harmed anyone. Not like Uncle Henry.

Mr Clarke I've never gone out of my way to help anyone either. What is happening now in this country has come about not just because of greedy politicians, but because of people like me. Influential people of my generation who knew it was wrong, but did nothing to change it. The sins of the fathers shall be visited on the children. As my father was threatening me in his sick slurred voice, the face of his beautiful Catholic mother was smiling down at us from over the fireplace in his bedroom. He loved her. But when she was dying and asked for a priest, in Irish, he pretended not to understand what she was saying. Perhaps the child of a mixed marriage has more to prove than most.

Allison Is that what's worrying you? My children?

Mr Clarke What's really worrying me is that you might not live long enough to have any children.

Pause.

Allison I'm going to marry him.

Mr Clarke When?

Allison As soon as he'll have me. He keeps turning me down, you see. Says he can't afford to keep me in the style to which I am accustomed.

The Rafferty house.

Sounds of coughing offstage. **Brian** *grins as* **Bernie Cassidy** *enters.*

Brian Morning, Bernie. You're coughing better. I thought the doctor said you were to give up the fegs.

Bernie Ach, bugger him. You're a long time dead. Have you any spare seats in the minibus the day?

Brian I thought your Peter got out last week?

Bernie Oh he did. But I'm takin' a parcel down for young Declan Reilly. His mother's in bed with her stomach again.

Brian I think you like going down to The Maze, Bernie.

Bernie When you've been goin' down twice a week for two years, it's hard to give up. Like the fegs.

Brian And how's your Peter coping with the big wide world?

Bernie Oh he's all right. I'm the one that's sufferin'.

Brian Ah now, two years is a long time, Mrs Cassidy. They say it can make an animal of a man.

Bernie You're an awful wee boy, Brian. I'm not talkin' about that. Jeesus, I wish I was.

Brian Well, what are you talking about then?

Bernie Well to tell you the truth Brian, I never had such a good time in all my married life as I did when he got lifted. 'Ach Mrs Cassidy, sorry to hear about your wee bit of trouble. Can I get you a drink?' Jeesus it was stickin' out, while it lasted. But you see now he's out? My tongue could be hangin' out to my knees for all the notice anybody takes of me. Nobody's bought me as much as a packet of crisps in the last fortnight. You see, when your man's put away? You're a star. You see when he gets out? You're nuthin'.

Marie *enters.*

Marie Everybody's in the minibus, ready to go.
Hello Bernie.

Bernie Hello Marie, love.

Brian Well, I'd better get my driving gloves on, for the mystery tour.

Bernie Any prizes for guessin' where we're goin'?

Brian First prize, one week in Long Kesh. Second prize?

Bernie Two weeks in Long Kesh.

Brian Third prize, indefinite internment.

Bernie God, you're a tonic, Brian. Here, these fegs'll never see me through the day. Hang on. I'll not be a minute. Don't be goin' without me now.

Bernie *rushes out. There is a slight pause.*

Marie Brian . . . I'm sorry about this morning. I just get angry. Every morning I go into her room and I think, this is the day it's going to be all right. She's going to be back to normal. Sitting up. Smiling. But she never is.

Brian Allison's not responsible for what happened to mum.

Marie I said I'm sorry.

Brian You know, when you take off your black beret and dark glasses and stop mouthing political slogans, you're not a bad-looking girl at all. If you weren't my sister, I'd ask you out.

Marie Are you ever serious about anything?

Brian Only the increasing shortage of good pubs since the bombing started.

Spotlight on the **Comedian**.

Comedian Did you hear about the Irishman who was arrested for shoplifting? He lifted the shop three feet off the ground. What happened to the Irishman who tried to blow up a bus? He burned his lips on the exhaust pipe.
A Belfast businessman rushed into an insurance office and asked, 'How much to insure my car against fire?' 'Thirty pounds, sir,' said the clerk, 'but for only ten pounds extra you can insure it against theft as well.'
'Don't talk daft,' said the businessman. 'Sure, who'd want to steal a burning car.'

Irishman Clothing permitted for remand prisoners.
1 pair of shoes. Trainers are allowed but no shoes with steel tips.
3 pairs of socks. 3 sets of underwear.

3 pairs of trousers – jeans accepted. 3 shirts.
No pure white, black, blue or green colours are allowed for
any article of clothing.

Comedian What do you do if an Irishman throws a pin at
you? Run like hell. He's probably got a grenade between his
teeth.
Did you hear the one about the Irishman whose library was
burned down? Both books were destroyed. And worse still,
one of them hadn't even been coloured in.
Belfast City Hall was bombed and the Lord Mayor phoned
the Fire Brigade. 'Have you taken any steps to quench the
blaze?' asked the fire chief. 'My staff are pouring buckets of
water on it,' said the Lord Mayor.
'Well, there's no point in us coming over,' said the fire chief,
'sure that's all we'd be doing too.'

Irishman 2 pairs of pyjamas. Only type with elastic
waistbands are acceptable.
3 jumpers. No slogans allowed except manufacturer's trade
mark – for example, Adidas.

Comedian Mick and Paddy were planting a bomb, and
Mick said, 'Hey Paddy, hold that wire.' And then Mick put
his fingers in his ears. A couple of minutes later he took them
out again and said, 'What happened?' 'Nothing,' said
Paddy. 'Thank God for that,' said Mick, 'it must be the other
wire that triggers the explosion.' He must be the same
Irishman who read a poster that said: Man wanted for
bombing and murder. So he went in and applied for the job.
What's the fastest sport in the world? Pass the parcel in an
Irish pub.
An Irish pub was bombed and the landlord rushed to the
nearest telephone box. 'Hello, is that 999?' 'No, this is 998.'
'Well, would you ever nip next door and tell them me pub's
on fire?'
He was the same barman who thought that Vat 69 was the
Pope's telephone number.

Irishman One outdoor jacket. Not hooded.
One indoor jacket. Not leather or imitation leather.
Bomber jackets not allowed.

The Maze Prison. 9 a.m.

Brian *and* **Marie** *in the waiting room.*

Allison *enters with their aunt,* **Mrs Boyd**.

Brian Hello, Aunt Isa.

Mrs Boyd Hello, Brian love. (*Slight pause.*) Hello, Marie.

Marie *takes* **Joe**'s *parcel from* **Brian**.

Marie I'll go and sign our Joe's parcel in.

She exits. There is a small awkward silence.

Brian Give me Hughie's parcel, Allison. I'll sign it in. You
get the tea urn going.

Allison *hands him* **Hughie**'s *parcel and leaves* **Brian** *alone with*
Mrs Boyd.

Brian I'm sorry about Marie.

Mrs Boyd She was very close to your dad.

Brian We all were. Including you. He used to tease my
mother, you know. Say it was a close thing whether he
married her or you. (*Hurriedly, because* **Mrs Boyd** *looks as if she
might cry.*) Here, these are for Hughie. I called round with
them yesterday, but you weren't in.

He puts a packet of cigarettes into **Hughie**'s *box.* **Allison** *returns.*

Allison Tea'll be ready in about five minutes.

Brian I'll go and check the parcel in. You haven't hidden a
file or anything in the baps, have you Aunt Isa?

Mrs Boyd I'll do it, Brian.

Brian No, I want to do it. Joe Rafferty's brother checking
in a parcel for the Protestant compound? The computer'll do
its nut.

He exits.

Mrs Boyd He's a good boy. Always was. I remember him when he was a little child. Always laughing.

Allison He still is.

Mrs Boyd Are the two of you still going out together?

Allison Yes. You're not going to give me a lecture, are you? I get enough of those from my mother.

Mrs Boyd Do you go to his house?

Allison Not very often.

Mrs Boyd We used to go there every Sunday for our tea. Me and Hughie and Susan. After my Sammy died. It all seems such a long time ago.

Allison Why don't you go and see her? She just lies in her bed, day in day out, staring, seeing God knows what.

Mrs Boyd I remember the day she married Paddy Rafferty. Lovely she was. Dark blue suit. Kid gloves. I bought her the gloves. Mother and father refused to go to the wedding. But we went. Sammy and me. My Sammy gave her away. Paddy was his mate. They were in the Union together. Thought they were going to change the world. Afterwards, in the pub, we all promised one another that no matter what happened, we'd always be close. Nothing in the world would ever drive us apart. We're twins, Molly and me. Did you know that? She was the oldest by half an hour. I used to be jealous of that when we were kids.

Allison Let me take you to see her.

Mrs Boyd Then the Troubles broke out, and Paddy got shot. I suppose they'd have shot my Sammy too, if the cancer hadn't got him first.

Allison She might respond to you.

Mrs Boyd We went to Paddy's funeral, our Hughie and Susan and me. There was a big crowd outside in the street. A woman spat in my face. I went a few times after that. And then the threatening letters came. I was scared. There were a lot of sectarian murders that year. Anyway, our Molly didn't know me any more. Didn't know anybody. So I stopped going. One night our Hughie got beaten up on his way home from the pictures. He said Joe was there. Did nothing to help him. I couldn't believe it. Next thing I hear the police are looking for Joe in connection with an explosion in a pub in Belfast. Two people were killed. Then our Hughie took to stopping out late. By this time, Susan was married to your brother John, and the baby was on the way. I didn't want to worry her. I used to sit on my own, waiting for Hughie to come home. But when he did come back, in the small hours of the morning, I never could ask him where he'd been. What he'd been doing. I suppose I knew. Didn't want to know. And now he's locked up here. And so is Joe. They were like brothers when they were kids. We used to share a house near the sea, every summer. I don't understand why all this has happened to us. Paddy and Sammy must be turning over in their graves.

Allison Brian still keeps in touch with you.

Mrs Boyd Allison, I want you to tell Brian to stop visiting me. There's been talk in the street. I've tried to tell him, but he won't listen. Just laughs, makes jokes, tells me not to be so daft. I care about that wee boy like he was one of my own. I don't what to see him getting hurt.

Allison Why would anyone want to hurt Brian? He's the most gentle, caring man I've ever known.

Mrs Boyd So was his father. (*Pause.*) You'd better go and help with the tea. They'll be wondering what's keeping you.

Allison They've got more helpers than they need today. So, I'm going in to the camp with you to visit Hughie. Your Susan says I've no idea what it's like in there. Maybe it's about time I found out.

Spotlight on the **Comedian**.

Comedian Of course two-thirds of the Irish people don't know what the other half is doing. Maggie Thatcher was in

Rome to talk to the Pope about the Northern Ireland situation, and she discovered that the Pope had a direct line to God. So she asked His Holiness if she could make the call. 'Certainly,' said the Holy Father, 'but it's very expensive. About fifty million lire.' Now Maggie had used up all her traveller's cheques, so she couldn't afford to make the call. But next time she was in Belfast she noticed that Ian Paisley *also* had a hotline to God, so she asked *him* if she could make the call.

'Certainly,' said Big Ian. 'It'll cost you 10p.' '10p!' said Maggie. 'Do you know that it costs fifty million lire to phone God from the Vatican? Why is it so cheap from Belfast?' 'Because it's a local call,' said Ian.

Of course it was dear old Uncle Ian who said that all Irish people should link hands and go their separate ways.

Grow your own dope. Plant an Irishman. (*He reads from a copy of the Sun.*) Have you seen the paper today? It says here that the Irish attempt on Everest has failed. They've run out of scaffolding. Mind you, it also says that Mrs Murphy has moved her house two feet forward to take up the slack in her clothes-line. And Mr Murphy's not much better. He was given two weeks to live. So he said, 'I'll take one in June and one in September.'

Allo! The Irish daredevil Evil O'Kneivel has failed in his attempt to jump over twenty-three motorbikes in a bus.

He puts the paper aside.

What happened to the Irish jellyfish? It set! How do you tell an Irish pirate? He wears an eye-patch over both eyes. And what about the Irish Godfather who made an offer he couldn't remember?

The Protestant compound.

Allison, **Mrs Boyd** *and* **Hughie**.

Mrs Boyd There's a lovely bit of cooked ham in your parcel, son. Ellie Wilson sent it.

Hughie (*to* **Allison**) Ellie Wilson nicks it out of Jamieson's shop.

Mrs Boyd She does not, Hughie.

Hughie She does so. (*To* **Allison**.) Ever since oul Johnnie Jamieson refused to make a decent contribution to the Prisoner's Defence Fund, Ellie's been feeding half the inmates here at Johnnie's expense, without him knowing it. (*Pause.*) Thanks for bringing my mother down, Allison. You're more like a daughter to her than our Susan ever was.

Allison Brian sent you some cigarettes.

Hughie Allison, I have to talk to you. Now listen, and listen carefully. There's been a lot of talk in here about you and Brian. Not very nice talk.

Mrs Boyd There's been talk in the street too.

Hughie I know. The word is that Brian's not just visiting his aunt. That he's in our street to collect information for the other side.

Allison You can't believe that.

Hughie I've known Brian all his life. I know there's no harm in him. But they don't know that.

Allison Well, you tell them.

Hughie Why should they believe me? I'm his cousin. And now they've found out that he's going about with you. They think he's a spy, sent to get information about your Uncle Henry.

Allison That's the daftest thing I ever heard.

Hughie Not half as daft as him ignoring the danger he's in. Now I can't stop him going out with you, but you're to tell him, and make sure he heeds, that he's not to visit my mother any more. Brian thinks he can joke his way out of anything. But his sense of humour won't save him if some joker decides to put a bullet through his head.

Spotlight on the **Comedian**.

Comedian Sean was confessing his sins to Father O'Reilly. 'Forgive me Father, for I have sinned. I've been to bed with a Protestant.'

'What Protestant?' roared the priest.

'Oh, I couldn't tell you that, Father,' said Sean. 'It wouldn't be honourable.'

'Was it Margaret Stewart from the fruit shop?'

'No, Father.'

'Was it that schoolteacher, Fiona Wilson?'

'No, Father.'

'Well, who was it then?'

'Forgive me, Father. But a gentleman never reveals a lady's name. Even if she is a Protestant.'

'You'll either confess her name, or do a penance of ten Hail Marys,' threatened the priest.

'I'll do the penance Father,' said Sean, and went outside to meet his friend Paddy.

'How did you get on?' asked Paddy.

'Great,' said Sean. 'Ten Hail Marys, and a couple of dead certs for the night.'

The Catholic compound.

Brian, **Marie** *and* **Joe**.

Brian Allison's not really a Prod, you know. Rumour has it that her oul granda was Jewish on his mother's side.

Joe The time for silly jokes is over, Brian. Stop seeing her. The boys don't like it.

Brian The boys aren't gettin' it. Aw come on, Joe. It wasn't one of my best, but you might manage a little smile. You used to have a great sense of fun, in the old days.

Joe The old days are over.

Marie Her uncle is a leading loyalist politician, committed to Protestant supremacy in the North.

Brian Is that a quote from the Sinn Fein Handbook, Marie? Henry Sinclair doesn't give a damn about religion. What he worships is money and power. Allison can't stand him.

Joe We've only your word for that, Brian.

Brian What's with the 'we', Joe? Do I take it, if somebody has a pot-shot at me some dark night, that you might be behind it?

Joe Don't talk stupid Brian. I'm your brother, and I've been told to tell you.

Brian So now you've told me.

Joe Will you stop seeing her?

Brian No.

Joe You don't understand.

Brian Oh, I understand all right.

Joe Listen to me.

Brian No. You listen to me. You've been here so long, Joe, that you think nothing else matters but the Troubles. Well, you're wrong. Outside of here, in the real world, fellas and girls still go out together. To the pubs, the parks, the pictures. Normal life goes on, Joe, outside these wire fences. And that's all Allison and me are. Just a couple of normal people who fancy each other rotten . . .

Joe Listen!

Brian No! You listen! I'm going to marry Allison Clarke. And some cowboy threatening to blow my head off is not going to stop me.

Joe If you care about her that much, then give her up. It's not your head they're threatening to blow off. It's hers.

Spotlight on the **Comedian**.

Comedian It's not widely known that God at first intended to have his Only Son born in Belfast. But he couldn't find Three Wise Men. Or a virgin.
What do you call a pregnant Irishwoman? A dope carrier. They're all thick, the Irish. That's why it says 'Open other end' on the bottom of all the Guinness bottles.
Paddy was having a pint one night, when Mick came into the pub with a big sack over his shoulder. 'What's in the sack?'

asked Paddy. 'Ducks,' said Mick. Now Paddy was a bit of a
punter, so he said to Mick, 'If I guess how many ducks there
are in the sack, will you give me one of them?' 'If you guess
how many ducks there are in the bag,' said Mick, 'I'll give
you both of them.'

'Eh . . . five,' said Paddy.

Later that evening.

Brian *and* **Allison** *in a lounge bar in Belfast.*

Brian   I hate plastic pubs. And piped music.

Allison   Well what do you fancy? A sing-song at the UDA
club? Or you could take me to a real Irish pub up the Falls. I
hear the music's great.

Brian   Aye, and the drink's half the price. I'm not surprised
they're so short on customers here.

Allison   It's early yet. The place'll fill up later.

Brian   It's nearly half past nine.

Allison   You've got your watch back.

Brian   One of the kids came up to me in school yesterday.
'Here's your watch, sir,' he said. 'And my big brother says to
tell you if you ever have anything else pinched, just let him
know.' How do I explain to a nine-year-old boy who's never
known anything better, that I don't want his big brother
threatening to knee-cap some other little boy if he doesn't
give the teacher back his watch? How does anybody explain
anything about law and order and individual rights to a
child whose earliest memory is of his mother screaming when
armed soldiers broke down the door at four o'clock in the
morning, and dragged his father out of bed and into a Land
Rover. Why should that child respect the law that allows the
army and the police to terrorize in the name of catching
terrorists. His father was interrogated for two days simply
because he was the secretary of a Gaelic Football team, and
made regular trips across the border to arrange matches in
the South. And after his release, when he tried to sue them for
wrongful arrest, they harrassed his wife and children until he

dropped the case. Now his oldest son organizes big league games for the IRA and the nine-year-old can't wait until he's old enough to shoot a man in a uniform. The British never learn, do they? Men with guns create other men with guns. And that child learned very early on that the men with the most guns win. And he's right.

Allison What's up doc?

Brian I have to have a serious talk with you, Allison.

Allison God, it must be the time of year. Everybody wants to talk seriously to me these days. You haven't finally made up your mind to propose to me, have you? My stars today said I would find myself in an unusual situation.

Brian I think maybe we should . . . ease off for a while . . . not see so much of each other . . . give ourselves time to think.

Allison Go on.

Brian I don't want to settle down. The world's full of women I've never met.

Allison It won't work, Brian.

Brian Oh, I don't know. If I started tomorrow, I might work my way round half of them anyway, before I'm too old to enjoy it.

Allison Somebody's threatened me. They have, haven't they?

Brian I'm not in love with you.

Allison Look at me when you're talking to me.

Brian There's a group of hard men in Long Kesh who think that you're spying for Uncle Henry.

Allison Funny you should mention that. There's a second group of hard men in Long Kesh who think that you're spying for the first group.

They stare at each other for a moment and then laugh.

Brian You know, if we get shot, we won't even have the satisfaction of knowing who pulled the trigger.

Allison Don't!

Brian Joke, love.

Allison Sometimes I think it's all a very sick joke and we're destined to die laughing. A great life we'd have together. Drawing the curtains before dark. Jumping every time a car stops outside the house.

Brian We could always emigrate. There must be more Irishmen than kangaroos in Australia by now.

Allison I don't want to live in Australia. I want to live here. I want rain in the summer and snow at Easter. I want grey skies and green grass. I want a baby. I want you.

Brian Then we'll stay and prove them all wrong. We'll open the curtains and the front door. And we'll laugh. Show the world that it's all just a silly Irish joke.

Allison Are you asking me to marry you?

Brian Will you, Allison Clarke, promise to have a baby a year and bring them all up to be good little Catholics, and give them ethnic names like Maraid, Sinead, Fergus and Finbar?

Allison Will you, Brian Rafferty, promise to wear an orange sash on the twelfth of July, and beat a big drum in a kick-the-Pope band?

Brian You know something? When you and me get together, Ulster will never know what hit it. We'll be on the Gloria Hunniford show. Co-founders of the Apathetic Party for people who just don't want to know. We won't have a manifesto.

Allison We'll be too apathetic to write one.

Brian We won't have any members.

Allison They'll be too apathetic to join.

Brian We won't have a cause.

Allison Apathetic people don't have causes.

Brian They tell great jokes though.

Allison I love you.

Brian I know.

Allison My parents are away for the weekend.

Brian Well, what are we doing sitting here, when we could be lying in a big Protestant ascendancy bed up the Malone road?

Allison If we do that, you might have to marry me.

Brian And would you?

Allison You askin'?

Brian I'm askin'.

Allison Yes.

Brian Yes.

Spotlight on the **Comedian**.

Comedian How do you recognize the bride and groom at an Irish wedding? She's the one in the white wellies. He's the one in the flared wellies.
Did you hear about the girl who wanted to marry an Irishman, but her parents refused to give their consent. So the lovers decided to commit suicide by jumping off the Lagan Bridge. The girl hit the water all right. But the Irishman got lost on the way down.
What do you call an Irishman who marries a gorilla? A social climber.

Brian I love you.

Allison I know.

They exit, arms around each other.

The **Irishman** *walks on and reads a news bulletin.*

Irishman The two bodies discovered early this morning near the Cave Hill on the outskirts of Belfast, have been

identified as twenty-five-year-old Allison Clarke and
twenty-nine-year-old Brian Rafferty.
Miss Clarke was the niece of the Unionist politician Mr
Henry Sinclair, who today claimed that the IRA were
responsible, and called on the Secretary of State for
Northern Ireland to order more troops into the province for
the protection of its British citizens. However, a police
spokesman said today that Brian Rafferty comes from a
family with known Republican sympathies. His brother
Joseph is serving a life sentence in the Maze Prison for
terrorist offences including bombing and murder. Police say
that they are keeping an open mind as to the identity of the
killers, and have appealed for information. The bodies were
discovered at 6.00 a.m. by an army patrol . . .

Comedian It was reported in the American newspapers
today that there was a Belfast-type shooting in Chicago.
'Isn't it funny,' said the Irishman, who was reading the death
notices in the Belfast Telegraph, 'how people always seem to
die in alphabetical order.'
Did you hear about the Irishman standing in front of the
firing squad, who was asked if he'd like a last cigarette? 'No
thanks,' he said, 'I'm trying to give them up.'
An Irishman and an Irish girl were pushed off the top of the
Cave Hill. Who hit the ground first? Who cares, so long as
they're both Irish.
How do you save an Irishman from dying? You don't know?
Good.

The **Irishman** *tears the news bulletin into shreds.*

Comedian Hallo, Paddy. You still here? (*He walks to the*
Irishman.) Have you heard the Irish knock-knock joke?
You haven't? Right, you start.

Irishman (*expressionlessly*) Knock. Knock.

Comedian Who's there?

He laughs and begins to walk away.

Irishman (*quietly*) What do you call an Irishman with a
machine-gun?

Comedian I don't know, Paddy. What *do* you call an Irishman with a machine-gun?

Irishman (*wearily*) You call him sir.

Blackout.

Joyriders

For Jim and Jean & John and Aileen

Joyriders takes place mainly in the former Lagan Linen Mill where the Youth Training Programme now operates. There is one scene in a Belfast theatre, one in Kate's house, one in the Arts Council Gallery, Belfast.

The walls of the linen mill are decorated with the teenagers' paintings of Belfast street life and samples of the work produced on the knitting machines. There is a lot of graffiti, mainly in the form of abbreviations:

FTP	FUCK THE POPE
FTQ	FUCK THE QUEEN
UTH	UP THE HOODS
IRA	IRISH REPUBLICAN ARMY
INLA	IRISH NATIONAL LIBERATION FRONT
UDA	ULSTER DEFENCE ASSOCIATION
UVF	ULSTER VOLUNTEER FORCE
LPW	LOYALIST PRISONERS OF WAR
LFC	LINFIELD FOOTBALL CLUB
CFC	CELTIC FOOTBALL CLUB
GFC	GLENTORAN FOOTBALL CLUB

There are also some slogans:

No Pope Here – No friggin' wonder
Fuck 1690. We want a re-run
The Pope is a Para – Paisley for Pope
God save Ulster/The Queen/The Pope/Us
God Love Big Sandra
Jesus saves with the Abbey National
Give us a job. What's a job?
Is there a life before death?
Snuff is high-class glue.
Joyriders live. Joyriders die.

The mixture of Protestant/Catholic graffiti is due mainly to jokers, but also because there will be a small number of Protestant teenagers among the predominantly Catholic teenagers on the course.

This particular training programme is mainly peopled by young offenders on probation or suspended sentence for petty crime and joyriding.

Acknowledgement

The extract from *Shadows of a Gunman* by Sean O'Casey was taken from *Sean O'Casey – Collected Plays Vol. 1* and is reproduced by kind permission of Macmillan Ltd, London & Basingstoke. With special thanks also to Eileen O'Casey.

Cast

Sandra, *aged 16–17*. Tough, cynical, intelligent. Protects herself by refusing to believe in or aspire to anything.

Maureen, *aged 16–17*. Hopeful, dreamy. Lives alone with and constantly worried about her 12-year-old brother Johnnie who is a compulsive joyrider and glue-sniffer.

Arthur, *aged 17–18*. A skinhead by accident rather than choice. Was accidentally shot by the army. His injuries have left him with a shaven head, a scarred face and a limp. He looks dangerous/ menacing, but is in general a cheerful joker.

Tommy, *aged 17–18*. Slight physical signs of possible mixed racial parentage. Interested in politics. Steals for himself and for others.

Kate, *aged 34*. A social worker in charge of the Youth Training Programme that the four teenagers are attending. Middle-class, concerned, committed. Frustrated by the futility of the scheme. Tries to interest the teenagers in theatre, art, and so on.

Joyriders was commissioned and produced by Paines Plough, The Writers Company, and opened at the Tricycle Theatre on 13 February 1986, prior to a nationwide tour with the following cast.

Sandra	Michelle Fairley
Maureen	Clare Cathcart
Arthur	Gerard O'Hare
Tommy	Fabian Cartwright
Kate	Veronica Duffy

Voice-overs in *Shadow of a Gunman*

Mrs Grigson	Sheila Hancock
Donal Davoren	Stephen Rea
Seamus Shields	John Thaw

Director Pip Broughton
Designer Ellen Cairns
Lighting Designer Jim Simmons
Assistant Director Jeremy Raison
Stage Managers Margaret Sutherland, Robin Nash and Imogen Bertin

The songs in *Joyriders* were written and first performed by residents of Divis Flats working with Clair Chapman. For information on where to obtain musical scores, etc., apply to Alan Brodie Representation, 211 Piccadilly, London W1V 9LD. Tel. 0171 917 2871, Fax. 0171 917 2872.

In November 1985, the Divis Residents Association and the Town and Country Planning Association, London, held an exhibition of photographs of the Divis Flats complex in Belfast, which was described as the worst housing development in Western Europe. These flats provide the background for *Joyriders*.

The action of the play takes place between February and May 1986.

PROLOGUE

Belfast Street Song

First Voice	Everywhere we go
Second Voice	Everywhere we go
First Voice	People always ask us
Second Voice	People always ask us
First Voice	Who we are
Second Voice	Who we are
First Voice	And where do we come from
Second Voice	And where do we come from
First Voice	And we always tell them
Second Voice	And we always tell them
First Voice	We're from Belfast
Second Voice	We're from Belfast
First Voice	Mighty mighty mighty mighty mighty mighty Belfast
Second Voice	Mighty mighty mighty mighty mighty mighty Belfast
First Voice	And if they can't hear us
Second Voice	And if they can't hear us
First Voice	We shout a little louder
Second Voice	We shout a little louder

(Repeat song louder, and an octave higher. End with:
'And if they can't hear us, they must be deaf')

Act One

Mid-February 1986.

A theatre in Belfast. **Kate**, **Sandra**, **Maureen**, **Arthur** *and* **Tommy** *watching the end of Sean O'Casey's play* Shadow of a Gunman. **Kate** *and* **Tommy** *both watch intently.* **Arthur** *is grinning.* **Sandra** *is bored.* **Maureen** *is in tears. Sound of explosion, gunfire, then voice over.*

Scene One

Voice over (*Mrs Grigson*) What's goin' to happen next? Oh, Mr Davoren, isn't it terrible? Isn't it terrible? Minnie Powell, poor little Minnie Powell's been shot dead! They were raidin' a house a few doors down, an' had just got up in their lorries to go away, when they was ambushed. You never heard such shootin'. An' in the thick of it, poor Minnie went to jump off the lorry she was on, an' she was shot through the bozzum. (**Arthur** *grins at the word bozzom, nudges* **Sandra**.) Oh it was horrible to see the blood pourin' out, an' Minnie moanin'. They found some paper in her breast (**Arthur** *nudges* **Sandra** *again.*) with Minnie written on it, an' some other name they couldn't make out with the blood; the officer kep' it. The ambulance is bringin' her to the hospital, but what good's that when she's dead? Poor little Minnie, poor little Minnie Powell, to think of you full of a life a few minutes ago, an' now she's dead!

Voice over (*Donal Davoren*) Ah me, alas! Pain, pain, pain ever for ever. It's terrible to think that poor little Minnie is dead, but it's still more terrible to think that Davoren and Shields are alive! Oh, Donal Davoren, shame is your portion now till the silver cord is loosened and the golden bowl be broken. Oh Davoren, Donal Davoren, poet and poltroon, poltroon and poet!

Voice over (*Seamas Shields*) I knew something ud come of the tappin' on the wall.

Sounds of audience applause. **Kate** *and* **Maureen** *applaud.* **Tommy** *and* **Sandra** *do not applaud.* **Arthur** *gives a slow handclap, whistles.*

Arthur *and* **Sandra** *go to get up.*

Kate We might as well sit here until the crowd clears.

Tommy What for? Are we not good enough to mingle with the fur-coat brigade in the foyer?

Arthur You know what they say Sandra? Fur coat, no knickers.

Sandra *takes out a cigarette.*

Kate Sandra, I've already told you, no smoking in the auditorium.

Arthur Are you allowed to piss in the auditorium? Only, I need to go now.

Kate Arthur, you went four times during the play. You couldn't need to go again.

Arthur I've got a damaged bladder.

Kate No you haven't. You were injured in the head and legs. All the parts in between are in perfect working order.

Arthur (*leering at* **Sandra**) That's true.

Sandra Piss off, Arthur.

Arthur Are you all right Maureen?

Maureen You're rotten. Laughin' when the girl got shot.

Arthur How could ye feel sorry for a girl called Minnie?

Sandra She was pathetic. Gettin' killed to save him.

Maureen She was brave. It was lovely.

Tommy It wasn't lovely. (*He speaks slowly as if quoting from a political textbook.*) It was a comment on what happens to people what are kep' down by the yoke of British imperialism.

Arthur Is that what it was? I thought he just wanted to screw her, but he hadn't the nerve.

Sandra All talk, like you, Arthur.

Arthur Come roun' the back an' talk to me then.

Maureen Minnie loved him, that's why she died for him.

Sandra He wouldn't die for her though, would he? Some hero. All mouth, no action.

Kate That's why O'Casey called him the Shadow of a Gunman.

Arthur He was a five-star wanker.

Maureen He was a poet.

Sandra He was a shite.

Tommy He was a nuthin'. People like him what sit on the political fence live on while the innocent die.

Sandra Tommy, you must be the most borin' person on God's earth.

Arthur He's the one what's all talk, like him in the play . . . whadyecallhim . . .

Kate Davoren, Donal Davoren.

Tommy Whadye mean?

Arthur All his big ideas come from books. So do yours.

Tommy I don't just read about it. I know a few of the lads.

Sandra We all know a few of the lads. They live in the same rotten housin' on the same rotten road we do.

Tommy I've done them a few small favours.

Arthur Like what?

Tommy Nothin' I can talk about.

Arthur Because you've got nuthin' to talk about, that's why. Yer all mouth.

Maureen Donal really loved Minnie.

Sandra Aye, enough to let her die. You're as soft as she was. Kate, can we go now, I'm dyin' fer a feg.

Arthur An' my willie's bustin'.

Sandra Arthur, do you never think of nuthin' else? You think you're God's gift.

Arthur When I get my compensation fer the accident, you'll all be after my body.

Sandra Arthur, I wouldn't have ye if ye were studded with diamonds.

Arthur You'd have me, wouldn't ye, Maureen?

Sandra Maureen's in love with Nik Kershaw.

Maureen I like his records.

Sandra (*sings mockingly*) Wouldn't it be good to be in your shoes, even if it was for just one day . . .

Tommy, Sandra, Arthur (*sing*) Wouldn't it be good if we could wish our cares away . . .

Kate Well, as the philosophical discussion on the play appears to be over, I'll go and get the car. You wait here. It's still raining. No point in us all getting soaked. I'll see you in the foyer in about five minutes.

Arthur You givin' us all a lift home, Kate?

Kate Right to your front door. That way you'll get to bed early and be in on time in the morning.

Sandra Any word of me gettin' off them stupid knittin' machines and onto car maintenance?

Kate I've already had a word with the project leader. I've to see him again at the end of the week.

Sandra He doesn't want me there, does he?

Kate He thinks you wouldn't be strong enough to handle a lot of the work.

Sandra I'm bigger than half them wee lads doin' it.

Arthur Weemin don't repair cars.

Sandra If you can do caterin' I can change a sparkin' plug.

Arthur All the greatest chefs is men.

Sandra Aye, because women get landed with the cookin' jobs that pay buttons, or nuthin' at all.

Kate I'll get the car.

She exits.

Maureen It must be lovely to have yer own car. Drive out till the country an' all.

Sandra Get your Johnnie to steal one for ye.

Maureen Johnnie doesn't do that no more.

Sandra You mean he hasn't got caught for a while.

Maureen He's stopped. He's working hard at school.

Sandra Tell that to the probation officer.

Arthur Maybe I'll buy a car out of my compensation.

Tommy You haven't a hope in hell of gettin' compensation.

Arthur My solicitor says we have a good case.

Tommy The British Army have the best case goin'. The courts is on their side. No judge here is gonna convict a soldier of attempted murder.

Arthur It's not that sort of case. Nobody's on trial. Nobody has to get convicted of nuthin'. All my solicitor has to prove is that the Brits opened fire on a joyrider an' I got hit by accident. He has to prove that I wasn't doin' nuthin'.

Tommy Maureen's ma wasn't doin' nuthin'. She didn't get no compensation.

*There is a silence at the mention of **Maureen**'s mother.*

Sandra Shut up Tommy. Come on Maureen and we'll have a smoke.

Maureen I haven't got no fegs.

Sandra We'll share one.

The girls exit.

Arthur We'll all go to the bar, share a pint before Kate gets back.

Tommy They won't serve us.

Arthur They won't know we're under age.

Tommy I don't mean that. Did ye see the way they looked at us when we come in? This is a middle-class theatre. Not for the likes of us.

Arthur My money's as good as anybody else's.

Tommy How much have ye got left out of Maggie Thatcher's twenty-seven poun' thirty pence?

Arthur Enough to buy a pint.

Tommy I bet ye a poun' they won't serve ye.

Arthur Yer on. Here, if they don't serve us, how'll we know why?

Tommy By the way they look at ye.

Song: 'Children of Divis Flats'

We are the children of Divis Flats
And it's for houses that we're fighting
                              Repeat

A place to live a place to play
A place for health and happiness
                              Repeat

They took our houses they gave us flats
How much longer must we live here?
                              Repeat

We are the children of Divis Flats
And it's for houses that we're fighting
                    Repeat

Among the rats, among the clocks[1]
And breathing in asbestos
                    Repeat

We are the children of Divis Flats
And it's for houses that we're fighting
                    Repeat

Scene Two

The Lagan Mill. The following morning. **Tommy** *comes in, looks around to make sure no one is about. Lifts a catering bag of teabags, tosses it to someone offstage. Lifts a catering tin of coffee, tosses it to someone offstage. Goes to a clock card machine. Clocks in. Exits.* **Maureen** *enters, clocks in, goes and sits down at a knitting machine. Looks at her watch, goes to* **Kate**'s *phone, dials.*

Maureen Hello, is that you, Mr McAuley? It's Maureen Reilly. Our Johnnie's not well, he won't be into school the day . . . what? . . . he's got . . . a cold . . . and a sore throat . . . he'll be in the morra . . . no he's not mitchin', he's not well, so he's not.

Kate *comes in, overhears part of the conversation.*

Maureen Sorry Kate, I would've asked, but ye weren't about.

Kate It's all right.

Maureen I'll see ye later.

Kate Maureen?

Maureen What?

Kate Sit down a minute.

Maureen I've a lot on the day.

[1] 'Clocks' are Belfast cockroaches.

Kate What's the matter with Johnnie?

Maureen He's not well.

Kate What way not well? (*Pause.*) Has he been on the glue again?

Maureen No . . . I don't know . . . he was in bed when I got home last night. About six o'clock this mornin' I heard him vomitin'. He was as sick as a dog.

Kate Where is he now?

Maureen In the house. He's all right, just a bit green aroun' the gills. He'll sleep it off. He got fish an' chips in Larry's last night. I'm always tellin' him not to eat anything out of that dirty hole. The health man shoulda closed that dive down years ago. I don't know how that oul Larry gets away with it.

Kate When does Johnnie see his probation officer again?

Maureen Friday.

Kate I think you should give her a call today.

Maureen No.

Kate Maureen, Claudia's job is to help Johnnie and you. She's on your side.

Maureen She works for them, and they wanta put Johnnie away.

Kate Her job is to prevent that happening.

Maureen You shoulda seen the oul magistrate, old as the hills kep' sayin' to me 'Speak up, girl, I can't hear you.' As if it was my fault he was half deaf. He told our Johnnie if he got caught doin' anything again he'd put him away an' no more chances.

Kate He would have been put in a home if Claudia hadn't convinced the magistrate that you were capable and reliable and fit to look after him. She made promises on your behalf, Maureen. Don't let her down. You have got to let her know if Johnnie's on the glue again.

Maureen He's not. It was Larry's oul re-heated fish.

Kate If he's sniffing again, he'll be out joyriding before the week's out.

Maureen I told you. He's not sniffin' nuthin'. That Larry has a lot to answer for.

Kate Claudia will have a lot to answer for if Johnnie gets himself injured, or injures somebody else.

Maureen You're not worried about our Johnnie nor me. You're just afraid yer chum Claudia'll get intil trouble for not doin' her job right.

Kate I'm afraid that Johnnie might get shot.

Maureen Don't say that.

Kate Not saying it doesn't mean it's not happening.

Maureen The ones what got shot were big lads. Our Johnnie's only twelve.

Tommy *has come in and overheard part of the conversation.*

Tommy I never heard of the security forces checkin' anybody's age, name and address before they opened fire.

Maureen *walks out. She passes* **Arthur** *who is clocking in.*

Arthur Mornin' sweetheart.

Maureen Away an' jump.

Arthur What did I say?

He puts on a white coat and a chef's hat. Gets things ready for the morning tea break. Sets out cups, fills the tea urn with water, etc.

Kate Okay, Tommy. Where's the paint?

Tommy What paint?

Kate Two litres of white gloss, two litres of varnish, and a plastic container of white spirit.

Tommy I'm only in. Ask themens in the joinery section.

Kate I was here very early, long before any of you got in. Stocktaking. The stuff was already gone.

Tommy Some bugger broke in durin' the night?

Kate Stop acting the innocent. It went missing yesterday when you were in charge of the sixteen-year-olds who were painting the lockers.

Tommy The wee buggers. Wait'll I get the houl of them.

Kate Has it already been sold?

Tommy How would I know?

Kate Is this one for yourself or are you doing another wee homer? Redecorating some poor old pensioner's flat?

Tommy It would take more than a licka paint to make any of them flats fit to live in.

Kate I want it back, Tommy, and I want it back today.

Tommy What's a couple of friggin' tins of paint till the government?

Kate When you nick paint from here, you're not stealing from the government, you're stealing from your own people.

Tommy You can't steal from people who own nuthin'.

Kate Yes you can Tommy. You can steal away the only chance they have.

Tommy Of what! Of workin' fer slave wages? . . . Why are we not allowed to make a profit on what we do here?

Kate We must not come into competition with local industry.

Tommy What local industry! What you mean is, it would be really embarrassing if this underfunded project made a profit. People might start askin' if we can do it, why couldn't John de Lorean.

Kate Tommy, this project is not about profit . . .

Tommy No, it's about keepin' the unemployment figures down and keepin' the likes of us off the streets.

Kate It also keeps you out of borstal.

Tommy An' that's the only reason I'm here. Me an' all the other ones on probation or suspended sentence. Like they said, ye can go on the scheme or get locked up.

Kate So why don't you help to make it work?

Tommy I never promised to enjoy it.

Kate Tommy, there are a lot of people who would be delighted if this place closed, who never wanted it opened in the first place. They think teenagers like you should be horsewhipped and dropped into a bottomless pit, not trained to do something with all that energy . . .

Tommy Trained! Fer what! At the end of the fuckin' year, we'll be back on the fuckin' street with no fuckin' jobs.

Kate If I fiddle the books any more, I'll have no job either. I have a year to prove that we can employ young offenders here for a tenth of what it costs to lock them away in approved institutions. If, at the end of the year, we are running at a loss and it can be proved that any of that loss was due to thieving, we've had it. The opposition will rub their sweaty hands with glee and say 'We told you so' and this place will close. (*Pause.*) Do you want to be responsible for proving that all their prejudices are right? (*Pause.*) I want that paint back, Tommy.

Tommy I'll have a word. See what I can do . . .

Kate You want to do something. Try putting your Robin Hood ideas to good use in here. Stop fighting me . . . please . . . I need all the help I can get.

Tommy I won't hinder ye . . . but I won't help ye neither.

Kate Well, will you at least help the younger kids who do want to be here?

Tommy Nobody wants to be here.

Kate That's not true. Not everyone on this project came through the courts. Twenty per cent chose to come.

Tommy Only because they get eight quid more here than they would on the dole.

Kate It's not just that. There's a real enthusiasm among a lot of them, even the ones who did come through the courts. They want to make a go of it. They want it to work. For the first time in their lives they have teachers who are genuinely interested in them and what happens to them . . .

Tommy For what we are about to receive may the government make us truly thankful.

Kate I don't want your gratitude. I want you to stop wrecking this scheme until there's something better to take its place.

Arthur *comes in.*

Arthur Hey Kate, there's no tea nor coffee in the kitchen.

Tommy Not now Arthur.

Kate There had better be tea, coffee, sugar and a lot more besides in that kitchen or none of you are going to eat or drink all week. I am not buying as much as an extra pint of milk! Is that clear!

She walks out.

Arthur What did I say? What's the matter with everybody the day? I thought it was goin' to be a good day, you know? I woke up this mornin' and the oul leg wasn't as bad as it sometimes is. I was able til get outa bed myself without havin' to get my ma to do her big Goliath crane act. I think the oul leg's gettin' better. My da says if I stop limpin' before the court case, he'll friggin' kill me.

Tommy The tea an' coffee's in one of the lockers in the joinery section. Ask wee Oliver, he'll show you where it is.

Arthur Listen you, you wanna thieve, you do it in your own section. I take a pride in my kitchen so I do.

Tommy What's on the menu the day?

Arthur Ragout. (*He pronounces the 'T'.*)

Tommy What?

Arthur French for stew.

Tommy For Jesus sake, Arthur, nobody here wants anything that doesn't have chips with it.

Arthur I'm doin' chips as well. And pommes-de-terres. (*He pronounces both 'S's.*)

Tommy What time's yer break?

Arthur Two to three. Why?

Tommy What are you doin' then?

Arthur Eatin' the leftovers.

Tommy What else are ye doin'?

Arthur Chattin' up big Sandra.

Tommy Will you give me a hand to do somethin'?

Arthur What?

Tommy I need some money quick. Is that oul deaf guy still operatin' the petrol pump at the garage?

Arthur Ferget it. My case is comin' up. I'm not blowin' that fer a couple of quid out of a cash register.

Tommy What'll ye do if ye get the money?

Arthur Make big Sandra an offer she can't refuse.

Tommy Don't you have no ambitions?

Arthur Aye, to die of old age.

Tommy I mean like helpin' other people.

Arthur What for? Nobody ever helped me.

Tommy Come on, I'll get ye the tea an' coffee.

As they exit they bump into **Sandra** *as she rushes in.*

Arthur Mornin' darlin'.

Sandra Piss off.

Arthur (*to* **Tommy**) It must be the time of the month or somethin'.

Tommy *and* **Arthur** *exit.*

Sandra *punches her card. Looks at it.*

Sandra Shite!

She goes to **Maureen** *in the knitting machine section.*

Sandra One minute past. That's another fifteen-p off my wages.

Maureen It's ten past.

Sandra I'll hafta nick a new watch, this one's hopeless. What's up with you?

Maureen Nuthin'.

Sandra You still mopin' about that stupid play?

Maureen It wasn't stupid.

Sandra What does it matter why people get shot? If you get shot you get shot and that's all there is to it. (**Maureen** *looks away*.) Is your ma worse, is that what's the matter?

Maureen It's our Johnnie. I think he's on the glue again.

Sandra He was never off it.

Maureen He was.

Sandra He's a no-hoper. He always has been.

Maureen I won't let them take him away.

Sandra You'd be better off without him.

Maureen He's all I've got.

Sandra He's your brother. The way you talk you'd think he was your son.

Maureen He's nobody's son. My da's God knows where, and my mother . . . She might as well be dead for all she knows.

Sandra Are ye goin' up to see her the night?

Maureen I might.

Sandra I'll come with ye if ye like.

Maureen What for?

Sandra I've nuthin' better to do.

Maureen There's not much to do there. She just sits, starin', sayin' nuthin'.

Sandra Does she never speak?

Maureen Every nigh an' again she opens her mouth as if she's gonna say somethin' an then she screams. It's awful. They give her an injection an' she sleeps an' when she wakes up she just stares again.

Sandra Fuckin' Brits.

Maureen It's not as if she got hurt bad, not like some of them . . . Have you ever seen a plastic bullet?

Sandra Loads of them. Every time there's a riot our kid collects them. He's small and he's fast. Dives in an' out between the legs of the Brits and the rioters. He's fuckin' magic to watch.

Maureen What for?

Sandra He sells them.

Maureen Who to?

Sandra Tourists. Americans mostly, and some of them people what come here and write about us. A pound a bullet he gets. It's better than a paper round. He'll go far our kid. He'll have his own business when the rest of us is still on the dole.

Maureen It's better here than bein' on the dole.

Sandra What's better about it, except that you get more money?

Maureen You've got somewhere to go. Somethin' to do.

Sandra Like knittin' stupid sweaters that nobody wants.

Maureen I have orders for five more.

Sandra Only because they're dirt cheap. I told Kate we'd get more down the market for them than selling them roun' here.

Maureen We're not allowed. Kate has to keep to the rules. If she doesn't, they'll close the place down.

Sandra I don't know why they opened it in the first place. It's a friggin' waste of time.

Maureen It's better than hangin' roun' the house all day.

Sandra My granny worked in here. It used to be a linen mill ye know.

Maureen I know. My granny worked here too.

Sandra Did she ever tell ye about what it was like?

Maureen She died young. I don't remember.

Sandra My granny was one of the lucky ones. Lived long enough to draw the pension. Most of her mates coughed their lungs up or died of lead poisonin' before they were forty. An' they got paid even less than we do.

Maureen It's not that bad nowadays.

Sandra No, now ye get to die of cancer or boredom, if the Army or the police don't get ye first.

She takes a screwdriver out of her pocket, unscrews part of the knitting machine.

Maureen What are ye doin'?

Sandra I'm not doin' this no more. If the machine's broke they'll hafta put me on the cars. Friggin' Lady Summerville.

Maureen Who?

Sandra Lady Summerville. She donated the machines. Were you not here the day she come on the visit? The week before Christmas it was.

Maureen I had the flu.

Sandra She brought us a turkey. Arthur stuffed it with chestnuts. Friggin' chestnuts! It was diabolical. Anyway, the Lady Summerville give us a wee pep talk about how wonderful we all were, and how she give us the machines because when she was young there was a sewing room in her big house an' the girls from the village come in and made garments for the poor. Life's a geg isn' it?

Maureen Maybe if we asked her, she'd give us a machine when our year's up here. We could go into business on our own.

Sandra Maureen, grow up. Nobody is never gonna give us nuthin'.

> *Song*
>
> What will it be when we leave school
> Will it be ace schemes or YTP
> Will it be useful, will it be paid
> We'll have to wait and see.
>
> Hope it's work, real work
> We hope it's work, real work
> We hope it's work, real work
> And not the dole.

Scene Three

Kate *sorting out papers on her desk. She lifts a small dictaphone, speaks into it.*

Kate Molly, I have a meeting this morning with the fund-raising committee, so will you go ahead and type out the progress reports and I'll sign them when I get back. Also, will you type a reply to this letter from Councillor Margaret Anderson. As you will see, she is requesting, among other things, a breakdown on the Catholic/Protestant ratio of teenagers in each of the sections here. Now what is that bigoted old bat up to now I wonder . . . Give her all the necessary detail . . . we started out with sixty participants and are now down to fifty . . . three have been arrested and the other seven, all Protestants, have been transferred to other schemes at their own request. Make sure she understands there was no intimidation here . . . maybe that's what she's angling for . . . they all left because they

were understandably nervous about working in this area . . .
oh, and do point out (politely of course) I did warn the
powers that be, this would be a problem when we were
offered these premises, not a stone's throw away from IRA
territory . . . However, there are still six cheeky, cheerful,
undaunted Protestants in the car maintenance section, and
I'm confident they'll stay and complete the course, because
they're very keen to participate in the stock-car races we're
planning to organize in the summer . . . God and the fund-
raising committee willing . . . maybe her husband would like
to sponsor us . . . maybe he'd like to offer all the kids here
jobs in his factory . . . Tell our beloved councillor there are
fifty kids here and we'll be lucky if we can find jobs for five of
them at the end of the year, regardless of what religion they
are . . . they fuckin' know it, we fuckin' know it, and she
fuckin' knows it . . .

She stops as **Arthur** *comes in with a cup of tea, is embarrassed that he
has heard her swearing.*

Arthur (*grinning*) Cuppa tea, Kate?

Kate Tea turned up, did it?

Arthur And the coffee. Some dope-head shifted it intil
another cupboard . . . by mistake.

Kate Arthur?

Arthur What?

Kate The old woman who lives next door with all those
stray cats. When you give her a free dinner, make sure you
get the plates back. We're running low.

Arthur You don't miss much do ye Kate?

Kate I assume it's leftovers, that you're not making her
special meals or giving her free cartons of milk. We can't
afford that.

Arthur Here's yer tea.

Kate Thanks . . . Arthur, if you get this compensation
money, will you leave here?

Arthur I'll be eighteen soon. I'll hafta leave then anyway.

Kate No, you can stay on until the end of the year. (*Pause.*)
You're a good cook, a natural.

Arthur It's dead easy. You know them big restaurants must
make a fortune. It's as cheap, cheaper even to make that sort
of food fresh than buy it freezed or in a tin, but they get away
with chargin' double for it.

Kate If I could arrange it, would you be interested in
coming back next year to teach the new intake about
cooking, catering, all that?

Arthur I don't have no exams nor nuthin'.

Kate Would you be interested?

Arthur I dunno. Would I get paid?

Kate Yes. Not a lot, but more than twenty-seven pounds
and thirty pence.

Arthur Money fer oul jam. They'd never wear it.

Kate They might.

Arthur Why do ye bother, Kate?

Kate Because I'm an incurable optimist. I still have a
romantic belief that if an idea is good and right, then it's
possible. You're a bit of an optimist yourself, Arthur.

Arthur I'm not awful sure what an optimist is . . .

Kate It's someone who believes that . . . things will turn out
all right in the end . . . or at least that it's possible to make
things turn out all right.

Arthur Like, if ye wanta be a cook, ye can be a cook?

Kate Yes.

Arthur They make fun of me round here, ye know. Men
don't cook in West Belfast. I don't care. What's so great
about bein' a casual labourer on a buildin' site? Ye get
soaked to the skin an' wore out before yer time. But you see
kitchens? They're magic. Bein' the youngest, I was always

home from school first. Mondays in the winter was the best. My ma always did two things on a Monday, she did the weekend washin' an' she made a big pot of vegetable broth. The kitchen walls would be streamin' with the steam from the washin' and the soup, an' I'd come in freezin' an' my ma would light the gas oven an' I'd take off the wet shoes an' socks an' put my feet in the oven an' sit drinkin' a cup of the soup . . . soapsuds an' vegetables . . . it sounds revoltin' but it was great . . .

(*He becomes self-conscious about what he is saying.*)

You don't know what I'm bletherin' on about, do ye?

Kate Smells.

Arthur What?

Kate Smells . . . my mother smells of lavender water and silk. Expensive but discreet, and in terribly good taste . . . Did your mother really let you warm your feet in the oven?

Arthur We don't have no central heatin'.

Kate (*laughing wryly at herself*) I will get you a job here, Arthur, if only to stop me getting romantic notions about things which are purely practical . . . and now you don't know what I'm blethering on about, do you?

Arthur I know yer sorta puttin' yerself down. Yer always doin' that. You shouldn't. Yer too good fer in here.

Kate What's a nice girl like me doing in a place like this?

Arthur What?

Kate It's a saying . . . from the Hollywood movies . . . you've never heard it.

Arthur No.

Kate I keep forgetting you're all a generation beyond me.

Arthur Yer not that much older than us.

Kate I'm thirty-four, Arthur.

Arthur Ye don't look it.

Kate I feel it, and more.

Arthur Why'd you never get married, Kate? Are all the fellas roun' your way deaf, dumb and blind or what? . . . Sorry, I'm speakin' outa turn . . .

Kate It's not that I've never been asked, Arthur, it's just that . . . I'm not sure what I want . . . or who I want . . .

Arthur My sister Mary's like you, over thirty an' not married an' in no hurry neither. My da goes spare about it. 'There's niver been no oul maids in our family' he keeps tellin' her, as if she's stayin' single just to annoy him, like . . . sorry . . . I don't mean I think you're an oul maid, Kate . . . it's just the way my da talks . . . my da's stupid . . . our Mary says if she can't have Clint Eastwood she doesn't want nobody . . . If you could have anybody ye wanted, who would it be?

Kate Donald Sutherland.

Arthur Who?

Kate Donald Sutherland. He's a very famous actor. One of my favourite films is the one he made with Julie Christie. *Don't Look Now* it was called.

Arthur Never seen it.

Kate I've seen it three times. Once in the cinema. Twice on television.

Arthur What's it about?

Kate Love . . . and death . . . there's a scene in it where they make love in an apartment in Venice . . . it's unbelievably beautiful . . . tender . . . erotic . . . perfect . . . everything we all want.

Arthur Hung like a horse is he?

Kate What?

Arthur Dead good-lookin' is he?

Kate I think so . . . (*Then realizing that* **Arthur** *is obliquely referring to his scarred appearance.*) But a lot of people don't find him attractive at all . . . beauty is in the eye of the beholder . . .

Arthur So my ma keeps tellin' me . . . See ye later . . .

He exits.

Kate My mother keeps telling me I'm not getting any younger, and if I don't make a decision soon about Roger Elliott MD he's going to find himself someone else . . . someone younger who will devote herself to providing the home and family he says he wants . . . she never asks what I want. She just hopes that this job is some sort of aberration I'll grow out of before my child-bearing years are over . . . (*She lifts the dictaphone.*) Dear mother, I know I'm running out of time . . . nobody knows that more than me . . . more and more, I find myself looking at babies in prams, knowing I don't want to waken up some day to the realization that I've left it too late. Men can have babies till the day they die, but not women. It's not fair . . . I want a baby and I don't want to get married and I don't have the courage to have a child alone. (*She sets the machine down.*) There's never been no oul maids in my family, Arthur . . . nor no unmarried mothers either . . . and the only man who ever touched me the way Donald Sutherland touched Julie Christie was committed to violence, and I sent him away.

She lifts the tape again, wipes her words away.

In the hairdressing section, **Sandra** *is cutting* **Tommy**'s *hair.*

Sandra You know somethin' Tommy, your hair's a brilliant colour. Sorta blue-black like Superman's.

Tommy (*pleased*) Do you think so?

Sandra Aye . . . pity ye haven't got the body to go along with the hair.

Tommy All-American white . . .

Sandra I was talkin' about muscles, not colour. You're too touchy you, do ye know that? What's wrong with your da bein' an Indian? My da's a cowboy, an' it doesn't bother me.

Tommy He wasn't an Indian.

Sandra Well what was he then?

Tommy I dunno . . . my mother doesn't talk about it . . . she doesn't need to, everybody round here does enough talkin' for her.

Sandra Tommy, people round here don't talk about you because you *might* be a half-caste, they talk about you because you're *definitely* an eejit. Ye go on all the time as if ye'd swallowed a dictionary or somethin'.

Tommy A prophet without honour . . .

Sandra What?

Tommy Karl Marx had to leave the country of his birth.

Sandra Was he your da?

Tommy You take nuthin' serious.

Sandra I take a lotta things serious, but you're not one of them.

Tommy You're as bad as the rest of them round here. You make jokes when somebody tries to tell you the history of your own country.

Sandra I got enough of that at school.

Tommy I don't mean the great religious political con. I mean the true history of the division of the workin' classes by the owners, the capitalists.

Sandra Listen you. Every mornin' I get outa bed an' I look outa the window an' the soldiers is still there. That's all the history I need to know.

Tommy You need to know why they're there.

Sandra I don't, Tommy. I just want them to go away.

Tommy My mother says it's all God's will an' it'll pass. She believes everything's God's will, includin' me. It's how she copes.

Sandra Maybe yer da was an angel, Tommy. Maybe you were one of them virgin births . . . there's about one a year on this road . . . God knows how many there are in the whole of Ireland.

Tommy Angels are fair-skinned and blue-eyed.

Sandra Says who?

Tommy Have you ever seen a small brown angel with blue-black hair in a stained-glass window?

Sandra You don't believe in all that Tommy. You're a communist. It shouldn't bother ye.

Tommy It doesn't bother me.

Sandra *makes a disbelieving face behind* **Tommy***'s head.* **Arthur** *comes in.*

Sandra Hey, Arthur, you want yer head shaved?

Arthur You off the knitting machines?

Sandra Mine's broke. I'm fillin' in the time till they let me work on the cars.

Arthur You should stick to the hairdressin' Sandra, yer dead good at it.

Sandra Friggin' waste of time. They can't teach me nuthin' here I don't know already. I've always done everybody's hair in our house.

Arthur When my hair grows will ye streak it for me?

Sandra Your hair's never gonna grow. Hair doesn't sprout through a steel plate.

Tommy It'll grow roun' it. Like one of them climbin' plants. You can put a wee trellis on yer head Arthur an' train it, like an ivy.

Arthur The surgeon says it'll take a year or two. I don't want it to grow yet anyway. I hafta go intil the court scarred limpin' an' bald to get the big compensation.

Sandra It'll never grow.

Arthur I'm a skinhead, I don't care.

Sandra You're a chancer. Skinheads shave their hair off on purpose. Yours got shot off by the army.

Tommy Did you know that the white men were the first to take scalps off the Indians? The Indians only copied what they done first. I read it in a magazine.

Sandra It's knowin' things like that gets ye a job.

Tommy I'm only sayin'.

Sandra Will ye sit still or *ye'll* end up scalped.

Arthur I don't remember gettin' hit. I was walkin' down the street an' all of a sudden there was all this gunfire. A wee lad about that high run past me, an' I thought, you wee bugger you nearly got me shot. An' then I looked down an' there was all this blood, an' I thought, Christ, some poor bugger *has* got shot. An' I looked aroun' an' there was nobody there but me. An' then I fainted. There was no pain nor nuthin'. That come after.

Tommy If that had happened anywhere else in the British Isles you woulda died. Lucky fer you it happened here.

Sandra Will you sit still.

Tommy There are surgeons here what are the best in the world at puttin' broken bodies together. I read it in a magazine.

Sandra They get a lotta practice here, thanks til the terrorists.

Tommy An' the Army an' the police. (*As if he's quoting from a text book.*) Terrorists only exist because of corrupt governments.

Sandra Listen dick-head, if somebody gets blowed to bits, what does it matter who done it, or why they done it?

Arthur It matters if yer lookin' compensation.

Tommy If ye never ask why, yer never gonna change nuthin'.

Sandra I'm forever askin' why I'm stuck in this hole. Askin' changes nuthin'.

Arthur When I get my compensation I could change yer life for yer Sandra.

Sandra Don't hold yer breath.

She walks off.

Arthur She really fancies me, you know. It's only a matter of time.

Tommy Wee Oliver says you fancy Kate.

Arthur Wee Oliver's head is fulla white mice.

Tommy You've no chance there, Arthur. Kate's doin' a line with a rich doctor up in the City Hospital, drives a big flash Volvo, so he does.

Arthur How would you know?

Tommy Friend of mine, works there.

Arthur Oh aye, brain surgeon is he?

Tommy No, he's one of the real workers. Cleans up the blood and guts after Kate's fancyman has finished cuttin' up the dead bodies.

Arthur (*grabbing hold of* **Tommy**) Take that back!

Tommy It's true. He does the post mortems.

Arthur He's not her fancyman. She's no tart.

Tommy They've been knockin' round together fer years, and he's doin' a line on the quiet with one of the nurses as well.

Arthur You're a lyin' hound.

Tommy They're puttin' bets on in the hospital about how long he can keep the two of them goin' without Kate findin' out . . . maybe we should do her a favour an' tell her . . .

Arthur I'm warnin' you. You say one word of that shite gossip to Kate an' *you'll* end up on a slab in the City Hospital.

Tommy All right! All right! Keep yer hair on.

Arthur Ye made it all up, didn't ye? Didn't ye?

Tommy I'm away to get some fegs . . . (*He moves off.*) Are ye comin'?

Arthur Some of us have work to do.

Tommy *exits.* **Arthur** *goes to* **Kate**'*s desk where she is sitting writing. As he approaches, she sets down the pen and sighs.*

Arthur You all right, Kate?

Kate I'm bored, Arthur. Bored out of my mind writing reports, filling in forms and trying to make sense of official letters. I seem to spend more and more time sitting in here, and less and less out there with you lot.

Arthur You spend a lot of time with us.

Kate Not enough.

Arthur My sister was on a trainin' scheme for over six months an' she says she only clapped eyes on the man what run it once. An' even then somebody had to tell her he was the boss.

Kate The boss . . . is that how you all see me?

Arthur Well . . . that's what ye are.

Kate What do they really think of me, Arthur? The kids out there? Sorry, I shouldn't ask you a question like that.

Arthur They think yer dead-on.

Kate But they're never completely at ease with me, are they? They don't chat to me the way they do with their section heads, the people who actually teach them how to repair cars and make things.

Arthur Ach, that's because they know all themens. They're from roun' here, same as us.

Kate And I'm not the same as you, am I? I don't speak the same language.

Arthur You speak dead nice. You wouldn't wanta be like one of them pain-in-the-arse social workers what put the Belfast accent on, would ye? Ye can spot them a mile off. All training shoes an' black leather jackets. They think rollin' their own fegs and wearin' dirty jeans makes them one of the people. They're a joke. Nobody takes them serious. You're all right Kate. You don't try to be what yer not.

Kate You know what I am, Arthur? I'm a bored middle-class female who got excited by the civil rights movement in the sixties, and was so terrified by the violence that erupted around us when we marched from Belfast to Derry in the name of equal opportunities for all, that I stopped marching, stopped protesting, and kidded myself that by getting a degree in social studies I could change the system from within. And here I am, fifteen years later, one of the bosses.

Arthur We could do with more bosses like you.

Kate When I was your age, Arthur, I believed there shouldn't be any bosses.

Arthur That's oul commie talk. That's fer people like Tommy. Not fer people like you, Kate.

Kate You know what I am, Arthur? A shadow of a socialist. The only difference between me and Donal Davoren is that I'm bluffing nobody but myself.

Offstage the teenagers chant.
Arthur *goes off to join them.*

First Voice
  No job, nothing to do
  No money, on the Bru
            Repeat

Second Voice
  No job after school
  No future that's the rule
            Repeat

All Unemployment. Unemployment.

Third Voice
'O' Levels. 'A' Levels. 'X' 'Y' 'Z' Levels.
'O' Levels. 'A' Levels. 'X' 'Y' 'Z' Levels.

All Unemployment. Unemployment.

(*Then a mixture of all the chants simultaneously rising in volume.*)
Kate *puts her hands over her ears. Shouts 'Stop!'*

Scene Four

Mid-March. **Sandra** *and* **Maureen** *enter, followed by* **Tommy**.

Sandra You told Johnnie's probation officer? Are ye out of yer friggin' mind?

She begins to do **Maureen**'s *hair.* **Tommy** *sits watching and reading a magazine.*

Maureen I didn't know what else to do. I don't want him put away. I can't watch him all the time. When I'm here I never know if he's at school or roamin' the streets. She's nice, Claudia. She cares what happens til us.

Sandra She cares about keepin' her job. They all do.

Maureen No, she's different, like Kate.

Sandra A do-gooder.

Kate *comes in, listens. They don't see her.*

Tommy Doin' her bit fer the poor. It's her job.

Maureen She does a whole lot more for us she doesn't get paid fer doin'.

Tommy An' then goes back til her posh house up the Malone Road. If she's so liberated, why does she still live there with her ma instead of roun' here like us.

Kate Because I'm lazy, that's why. My mother runs the house, and that leaves me free to run this place. It suits both of us.

Maureen There's nuthin' wrong with livin' in a nice house. You mind yer own business, Tommy.

Sandra How many lives in your house, Kate?

Kate Just the two of us. My father's dead. My two brothers are married.

Sandra I wish some of our ones would go off an' get married. There's ten of us an' three bedrooms. Ye can call nuthin' yer own.

Tommy If Arthur wins ask him to buy ye a big house in the country.

Maureen I wonder how he's gettin' on?

Tommy It'll be all over by now. Sorry son, if the Army says you were joyridin' that's good enough for us. No compensation.

Kate He has a good case, you know. That solicitor wouldn't have taken him on if he hadn't thought he might win.

Tommy Sure, they get paid anyway, win or lose or draw. They'll take anybody on.

Arthur *comes in. He is wearing a suit.* **Sandra** *and* **Tommy** *fall about laughing.*

Sandra Frig, get him. Man from C an' A.

Tommy Where did ye get that outfit?

Sandra His ma's been shoplifting again.

Kate Leave him alone you lot. You look very nice Arthur.

Sandra He looks like a tailor's dummy.

Tommy He looks like yer man, Yorkie.

Kate Who's Yorkie?

Sandra The Secretary of State. Big, rich an' thick. Well, you're big an' yer thick, Arthur, but are ye rich?

Arthur *says nothing. Slowly takes off his tie.*

Tommy I knew ye wouldn't get nuthin'.

Sandra He's smirkin'. He got somethin'.

Tommy Did ye?

Sandra Look at his face.

Arthur You are now lookin' at the most illegible bachelor in West Belfast.

Tommy How much did ye get?

Arthur *takes twenty Benson & Hedges from his pocket. (Normally the teenagers have tens of cheap cigarettes.) He slowly counts out five cigarettes onto a table.*

Maureen Five . . . five hundred pounds?

Tommy You got yer costs.

Arthur *shakes his head. Places another two cigarettes on the table.*

Sandra Jeesus, he got seven thousand. (**Arthur** *grins.*) Ye did, didn't ye?

Arthur *shakes his head.*

Sandra Well, what then?

Arthur I got seventy. (*There is a stunned silence.*) Seventy friggin' thousand pounds!

Tommy I don't believe ye.

Sandra Yer a lyin' hound.

Arthur Hand on my heart an' hope to die.

Maureen It's a fortune.

Kate Well done, Arthur.

Arthur I done nuthin'. It was the solicitor. He was brilliant, like the fella in the big picture. I mean it was all dead borin' at first, statements from witnesses an' hospital reports fulla big words. I couldn't make out the half of it, an' then the oul solicitor gets up and tells the court about the oul steel plate an' the hair not growin' an' the headaches, an' how my social life's ruined with the scars an' the limp . . . I never let on you were mad about me anyway, Sandra . . . I tell ye, he was that good he nearly had me in tears, I was that sorry fer myself.

Maureen Seventy thousand pounds.

Arthur I always hoped I'd get somethin', a couple of thousand maybe, an' then the day when I heard him talkin' I thought, they're gonna give me more, maybe ten, an' then the judge said seventy . . . I thought I was friggin' hearin' things.

Kate You deserve it, Arthur, every penny and more. It sounds like a lot of money, but it has to do you for a lifetime.

Sandra Where is it? The money? Are Securicar waitin' at the front door?

Arthur They don't give ye the loot in a suitcase, Sandra. You're as bad as my da. He thought he was gonna walk out of the court like Al Capone. Seventy G's in used notes.

Tommy Do they give ye a cheque or what?

Arthur They give me nuthin'. It goes intil a trust till my eighteenth birthday.

Sandra There's always a catch.

Arthur That's what my da said. You shoulda seen his face when he heard he wasn't gettin' his hands on it. When we come outa the court he puts his arm roun' my shoulders an' he says, 'Arthur son, you'll see me an' your mother right, won't ye? All them sleepless nights we sat up in the hospital prayin' for ye.' My ma sat up in the hospital, he did his prayin' in the pub. I never remember my da puttin' his arm roun' me before the day.

Tommy It's a wonder he let ye out of his sight.

Sandra Did they not give ye nuthin' in advance?

Arthur No.

Sandra Frig. I never thought ye'd get it, but I thought if ye did we'd all get a drink outa it anyway.

Kate I knew he'd win.

She produces a bottle of champagne from her bag.

Arthur Is that real?

Kate The real McCoy.

Sandra Where'd ye nick it?

Kate The Forum Hotel. I won it, at a supper dance.

Maureen In a raffle like?

Kate Tombola. I think you should open it, Arthur.

Arthur I've always wanted to open a bottle of champagne.

Kate You just turn this until the cork comes up . . .

Sandra Here, it pops out, doesn't it? Quick, Maureen, cups. Arthur, wait a minute it'll spill all over the place.

Maureen *and* **Sandra** *run to the kitchen, get cups, the cork pops. They catch the champagne.*

Kate To Arthur.

Teenagers Arthur!

They taste it.

Tommy So that's what it's like.

Maureen It's different from what I thought . . .

Sandra It's diabolical.

Arthur I like it.

Sandra They seen ye comin' Kate. It's like fizzy dishwater.

Tommy Somebody gettin' rid of their oul cheap muck in a raffle.

Arthur I like it.

Kate Actually it is one of the best champagnes.

Maureen Like the pop stars drink?

Kate Yes.

Arthur I like it.

Tommy What does it cost, if ye were buyin' it?

Kate Around twenty pounds a bottle.

Sandra Yer friggin' jokin'.

Arthur I knew it was good. It's like the difference between saute potatoes an' chips.

Sandra Saute potatoes *is* chips, undercooked.

Arthur No it's not.

Sandra Yes it is, unless you're doin' it wrong. An' somebody puttin' a fancy name on it doesn't make it better, just different an' more dear.

Tommy (*admiringly*) Sandra, I wish you would join the Party.

Sandra What for? To end up typin' letters fer wankers like you?

Maureen It gets nicer, the more ye drink.

Arthur Could anybody lend us a fiver till pay day? Only I would like to buy yiz all a drop of what ye fancy.

Sandra Seventy thousand friggin' quid, and he's lookin' a sub fer a six pack.

Maureen What are ye gonna do with all that money, Arthur?

Arthur I have plans, baby, I have plans.

Kate Have you any plans for tonight?

Sandra It's Wednesday, nobody roun' here has any readies on a Wednesday.

Tommy Arthur's credit'll be good in the pub. His da'll be drinkin' on the slate already on the strength of what's to come.

Kate Do you fancy coming up to my house, the four of you? I'll supply the drinks and Arthur can cook the supper.

Sandra Your house?

Kate Yes. (*There is an awkward pause.*) It was just a thought.

Maureen I'd like to go.

Tommy Your ma wouldn't want the likes of us in your house.

Kate My mother's staying with her sister for a few days.

Maureen You all on yer own like, Kate?

Kate Look, you don't have to . . . I just said it on the spur of the moment . . .

Arthur You got a big posh kitchen, Kate?

Kate Yes.

Arthur An' ye'd let me cook in it?

Kate I'd love you to cook in it, I hate cooking.

Arthur Yer on. Can I cook anything I want?

Kate Within reason.

Tommy What had ye in mind?

Arthur It'll be a surprise.

Sandra Your food's always a friggin' surprise.

Arthur Ye don' have to come if ye don't want to.

Sandra Might as well. I've nuthin' better to do.

Kate Tommy? You want to see how the other half live?

Tommy I know how the other half live.

Sandra He read it in a magazine.

Tommy Have you got a library?

Kate I've got a lot of books.

Tommy Can I look at them?

Sandra He wants to colour in the pictures.

Kate Of course you can look at them.

Sandra Don't lend him none, he'll flog them.

Maureen What time'll we come, only I'll hafta make our Johnnie his tea first.

Sandra Why can't the wee bugger make his own tea?

Kate Whatever time you like. Oh, and Arthur, you'll need money to buy in the ingredients for the surprise meal. Do you mind? I'll be here until after six. I won't have time to go shopping. (*She hands him some money.*) You'd better go now before the supermarket closes.

Sandra I'm goin' with him, he'll go mad an' buy a lot of oul daft rubbish.

Arthur Hey Sandra, I've always wanted to push a trolley roun' the supermarket with you.

Sandra Well, enjoy it the day. It'll be the first an' last time.

They exit.

Tommy Do you want me to get you some booze Kate? Only I know a place where you can get it cheap.

Kate Eh, no thanks Tommy, I have some at home.

Tommy Next time yer stockin' up, give us a shout.

He exits.

Maureen Do you know what must be the best thing about having money? Never havin' to go to the Social Security. I hate that place. Do you think I'll get a job when my time's up here?

Kate You're hard working, conscientious, no police record. You have a high chance.

Maureen You've no chance when the Job Centre finds out yer from Divis Flats.

Kate I'm hoping to organise a typing course. Would you like to do it?

Maureen Me work in an office?

Kate Why not?

Maureen The only office work I'm likely to get is washin' floors.

Kate You can do better than that.

Maureen It wouldn't bother me. I just want a job. Any sort of a job. I don't care what it is. I wanta earn my own money, never stand in no more queues pleadin' poverty. Never have to fill in no more forms. 'Where's your father? – I don't know. Where's your mother? – In the looney bin.' I'll spend a year here and at the end of it I'll be back where I started off. No job, no money. Arthur spends a year in the hospital, an' at the end of it he gets seventy thousand pounds . . . I wonder would the Army like to shoot me?

Pause.

Offstage, the song 'Children of Divis Flats'.

Blackout.

Act Two

Scene One

Kate's *house after the meal.* **Arthur** *sings 'Oh I was out walking'.*

Arthur (*sings straight*)
Oh I was out walking outside Divis Flats
Where the happiest tenants are surely the rats
Where we all breathe asbestos and no one is well
I walked down the steps and I tripped and I fell
And I never knew when I had my fall
The Executive owned the steps, and the DOE owned the
    wall

I was took to the doctor all aching and sore
My ankle is swollen, can't walk any more
He gave me some tablets and we had a talk
They made me feel dizzy, I still cannot walk.

All
And he never knew, when he had his fall
The Executive owned the steps, and the DOE owned the
    wall.

Arthur (*parodying the worst type of Irish nasal country and western singer*)
My mother was raging, she went for a claim
She looked up a number and solicitor's name
She told him my story and he was all ears
But he shook his head sadly 'This claim will take years'

All
Pity he didn't know when he had his fall
The Executive owned the steps, and the DOE the wall.

Arthur

It's now five years later, and the claim's still not paid
There's wrangles and tangles, no settlement made
There's 'phone calls and letters, they argue and talk
I'm stuck in the flat now; I still cannot walk.

All

And nobody cares about you at all
When the Executive owns the steps, and the DOE owns
   the wall.

And nobody cares about you at all
When the Executive owns the steps, and the DOE owns
   the wall.

They all cheer, applaud. **Kate** *and* **Arthur** *go off to the kitchen.*

Maureen It was lovely, wasn't it. Arthur's awful good at the cookin'.

Sandra Do ye want more wine?

Maureen Leave some fer Kate an' Arthur.

Tommy Plenty more where that come from. I wonder what the poor people are doin' these days?

Sandra I thought the party didn't approve of this sorta livin'.

Tommy We want everybody to live like this, not just the privileged few.

Sandra Oh aye? An' who's gonna do the dirty work while everybody's livin' like this?

Tommy Machines.

Sandra You been readin' them star-wars comics again?

Tommy Some of the ornaments in this house would feed a family fer a fortnight. (*He picks up a photo in a silver frame.*) Here, look at this . . . to Kate, all my love, Roger. Must be her fella.

Sandra Give us a dekko . . . here, he's not bad lookin' . . . for a Roger.

Maureen He's lovely lookin'.

Sandra A wee screw.

Maureen You make everything cheap so ye do.

Tommy Nuthin' cheap about this place.

Maureen Can the two of yiz not just enjoy yourselves. It's lovely here.

Sandra She'll be day dreamin' all day the morra.

Maureen There's nuthin' wrong with day dreamin'.

Sandra There is if you believe in it. None of us is never gonna live nowhere but them stinkin' flats . . . unless we emigrate . . .

Tommy Nobody'd have us.

Maureen If you could live anywhere in the world, where would ye go?

Sandra Dunno, but I'll tell ye where I wouldn't go, friggin' America. Once was enough.

Maureen You don't know what side yer bread's buttered on. You got a free holiday, an' all ye ever done was complain about it. Half the school wanted to go, an' you were the one got picked.

Sandra I never had no luck.

Maureen Vera Cosgrove went one year an' she thought it was brilliant.

Sandra Vera Cosgrove's a lick.

Maureen I'm tryin' to get our Johnnie on one of them trips.

Sandra With his record? Are ye jokin'?

Maureen They haven't said no yet.

Tommy They will. They only take the well-behaved deservin' poor.

Maureen They must be considerin' him. They give me a whole lotta stuff to read.

She rummages in her bag, produces some leaflets.

Tommy Let me see . . . (*He reads.*) The Tennessee Summer Holiday Program for Irish Children . . . was that where you went, Sandra?

Sandra I was in North Carolina. Must be the most borin' place on God's earth. They never stop prayin'.

Kate *and* **Arthur** *come in carrying liqueurs.*

Arthur I told Kate she'd get done fer aidin' an' abettin' under-age drinkin', but she says this is a special occasion.

Kate And I'm running you all home afterwards to make sure you don't get picked up.

Maureen It's lovely roun' here. No army nor police nor nuthin'.

Tommy No need. They don't make petrol bombs roun' here, just money.

Sandra (*sniffing the liqueur*) What's this?

Kate It's a coffee liqueur.

Sandra *swallows a large mouthful coughs, splutters.*

Sandra Jeesus!

Arthur Yer supposed to sip it slow, ye ignoramous.

Maureen (*sipping hers*) It's lovely.

Sandra It beats glue.

Kate Do you sniff glue, Sandra?

Sandra Nigh an' again.

Kate Why?

Sandra Why do flies eat shite?

Tommy Because they can't afford gin and tonic.

Kate Do you all do it?

Arthur I usta. After the accident I never bothered no more.

Sandra He's afraid it'll rust the oul steel plate.

Maureen I never done it. It's the road to nowhere.

Sandra You never do nuthin'. That's why yer so miserable all the time.

Tommy *is reading the leaflets about America.*

Tommy You'd think we were refugees. Have you read these, Maureen?

Maureen Only some of them. I only got them the day.

Tommy Listen to this . . . 'You will love America. You will be coming to a peaceful place, a happy place, a safe place. No rioting, no shooting, no bombs, no soldiers.'

Sandra No hope . . .

Tommy 'Things you should know about the American people . . .'

Sandra When they're not talkin' they're eatin'.

Tommy 'Americans bathe or shower regularly, at least several times a week, or even every day. Your hosts will expect you to do this too. You will find American showers a lot of fun.'

Sandra See what I mean? They think we're still washin' under the pump in the yard.

Tommy (*reading from the leaflet*) An' they think we might not of heard of foods like baked potatoes, mustard, cucumber an' spaghetti . . .

Kate Let me see that. What is it?

Sandra Free holidays fer the poor an' needy.

Kate (*reading*) 'In America we call baps, dinner rolls . . .' Is this a joke?

Sandra It's a friggin' insult.

Kate (*reading*) Many Americans are of Irish descent, so you will find some familiar foods such as spam and Campbells Scotch Broth.'

Sandra *pretends to be sick.*

Arthur My ma says they usta send food parcels over here durin' the war. Now they're taking the kids over there to eat their leftovers.

Kate We'll have to send you over, Arthur. Teach them how to cook.

Sandra When I was in America, the Bible-thumper I stopped with says one day . . . little girl, we are going to give you a special treat. We're taking you to a real Chinese restaurant. Won't that be exciting? She got all huffed when I told her that we've more friggin' Chinese restaurants than chip shops in Belfast. An' anyway, I hate Chinese food.

Arthur I didn't see you turnin' up yer nose at my sweet an' sour pork the night.

Sandra I knew what was in it. I was with ye when ye bought the stuff. See in them restaurants? They cook dogs an' cats an' dead pigeons, so they do.

Maureen They do not.

Sandra They do, it's a well-known fact.

Tommy I'll tell ye sumthin' that's not a well-known fact . . .

Sandra The Pope's doin' a line with Maggie Thatcher.

Arthur What's the fastest thing on two wheels?

Sandra The Pope ridin' up the Shankill on a bicycle. What's the fastest thing on two legs?

Arthur Ian Paisley runnin' after him.

Tommy What language is spoken by most of the people in Ireland?

Sandra Are you talkin' or chewin' a brick or what Tommy?

Arthur I dunno that one.

Tommy It's not a stupid joke. It's a question. What do most people speak here?

Arthur English.

Tommy An' what's the next language what most people speak here?

Sandra Jail Irish.

Tommy No, not even school Irish.

Arthur What then?

Tommy Chinese.

Arthur Yer head's cut.

Tommy It's true.

Arthur How do ye know?

Sandra Picked his nose an' it fell out. -

Tommy I read it in a magazine. There are so many Chinese restaurants here that Chinese is the second language of Ireland. Do ye not think that's an' amazin' fact?

Sandra No.

Tommy I don't understand you, Sandra.

Sandra You don't understand me?

Tommy Yer bright an' yer stupid all at the same time.

Sandra An' you were definitely a forceps delivery.

Tommy An' you were born up an entry.

Sandra At least I know who my da is.

Maureen (*screams*) Stop it. Tell them to stop it, Kate!

They all stare at her.

Kate Maureen?

Maureen They're spoilin' it. They always spoil it . . . everything nice . . . makin' a joke of it . . . makin' it rotten . . . I don't like dirty talk . . . yiz spoil everything so ye do . . .

She runs out. **Kate** *goes after her. There is silence for a moment.*

Tommy What's up with her these days? Every time you look roun' she's cryin' about somethin'.

Sandra It's that head-the-ball Johnnie. If he was my brother I'd kick his friggin' head in.

Arthur People keep kickin' his head in. It makes no difference.

Tommy He's addicted til it. He wasn't even ten the first time he went joyridin'. Him an' another wee lad. They were that small, one of them had til turn the steerin' wheel, while the other one worked the foot pedals. An oul green van it was. They drove it intil a brick wall an' scarpered. The wall an' the car was wrecked, an' they got out without a mark on them.

Sandra Jammy wee buggers.

Arthur There'll be more than a mark on him if the Provos get the houl of him. They gave Frankie Devlin a terrible hammerin'.

Tommy They wouldn't do that to Johnnie. He's only twelve.

Sandra It's freelance thieves they're beatin' up these days. You'd better start stealin' for them instead of for yerself Tommy, or ye'll be gettin' yer knees broke with the hurley bat.

Kate *comes back with* **Maureen**.

Maureen I'm sorry. I dunno what got intil me. I musta drunk that liqueur too quick.

There is an awkward silence.

Kate Shall I make some coffee?

Maureen I'll hafta go soon. The woman next door said she'd keep an eye on Johnnie, but she goes to bed early so she does. I don't wanta spoil yer night out. I'll go home on the bus.

Kate You'll do nothing of the sort. It's time we were all going.

Arthur Aye, I need my beauty sleep.

Sandra You need a body transplant.

Maureen We never done the dishes or nuthin' Kate.

Kate There's no need. We have a dishwasher.

Arthur We have a dishwasher in our house too. My granny.

Sandra Ha friggin' ha.

Kate Come on, let's go.

Maureen It was lovely Kate, thanks very much.

Kate, **Maureen** and **Tommy** exit. **Sandra** goes to follow them, stops, drains a couple of glasses.

Arthur Sandra?

Sandra What?

Arthur Put it back.

Sandra What?

Arthur Put it back.

Sandra Ye want me to spit it intil the bottle?

Arthur The bottle in yer bag. Put it back.

Sandra What bottle?

Arthur I seen ye, earlier on.

Sandra They put eyes in the back of yer head up in the hospital?

Arthur Put it back.

Sandra They'll never miss it.

Arthur You don't steal from yer own.

Sandra She's not one of us.

Arthur She's as near as makes no difference.

Sandra She's a pain.

Arthur She's a lady.

Sandra An' you're plannin' to be a gentleman now yer rich?

Arthur Put it back.

Sandra You know the only reason you got the compensation? 'Cause you've got no record. An' that's only because you never got caught. You're no better than me.

Arthur I never said I was.

Sandra You fancy her. You do, don't ye?

Arthur Put the bottle back.

Sandra *takes the bottle from her bag. Puts it on the table.*

Sandra Put it back yerself.

Arthur *replaces the bottle.*

Sandra Honest Arthur the boss's friend. You'll be gettin' religion next.

Arthur You'll be gettin' jail next time yer caught.

Sandra What's that to you?

Arthur Nuthin'.

Sandra If I do you can always bail me out with all that money yer gettin'.

Arthur *grabs her. Kisses her, clumsily. She pushes him away.*

Sandra Get off, scarface.

She walks out. **Arthur** *stands, looking slightly forlorn for a moment, then shrugs.*

Arthur Cheeky get.

He looks around the room.

Arthur Won't be long til I can afford a place like this.

> *Song*
> Damp, damp, damp, damp, damp, damp, damp, damp.
> Mushrooms on my ceiling, drips on the wall
> Steaming soaking bedclothes, blackened flaky halls
> Spiders on the woodwork, mould on the clothes
> Children lying in the beds, they're nearly froze.

I went to the Housing Executive, to explain my situation
I said 'I've got terrible damp'
They said 'It's only condensation.'

No, it's damp, damp, damp, damp,
damp, damp, damp, damp.

Toilets overflowing, carpets all wet
If you think that's bad, take a look at that.

It's rats, rats, rats, rats, rats, rats, rats, rats.

Rats will bite your nose off, then just slink away
They're living in our bedrooms, they are here to stay.
Rats are full of poison, carry germs and fleas
You don't know what you could catch – some horrible
    disease.
Old Mother Hubbard went to the cupboard to get a piece
    of bread
She put her hand in the breadbin, and found something
    else instead
AUGH!
She found rats, rats, rats, rats, rats, rats, rats, rats.
They bring their families with them for breakfast, lunch
    and tea
I am paying heat and rent, but they are living free.

Every little tiny rat is out to get your child and cat!

Damp, damp, damp, damp, damp, damp, damp, damp.

Scene Two

The Lagan Mill. End of March.

Kate, *sitting reading an official letter. She phones* **Claudia**.

Kate Hello Claudia? It's Kate, look I'm sorry, but I can't
meet you for lunch today, I've a meeting with the hierarchy
later this morning, and I've been asked to partake of a civil
service lunch afterwards. Cold cuts and cheap white wine to
cushion the bribe . . . I'm being manipulated into having an

open day. You know the sort of thing – important official comes in, swans around making patronizing comments about the kids' work, pats them all on their dear little well-scrubbed heads, and hopefully goes off feeling righteous enough to recommend funding for another year . . . no, of course I know it's not ultimately up to me . . . it's just that I would like to have the courage to say 'Stuff your open day and your pompous VIP. I will not have the kids here paraded out like a chimps' tea party. Give them the bloody money as a right not a privilege for good behaviour.' But I won't. I'll make the nominal protest, which will be noted in the minutes (black mark, Kate) and then I'll be grown up and reasonable and will organise the event to perfection (gold star, Kate) . . . Claudia, you don't have to justify my reasons for agreeing. I've become very adept at doing that for myself. I'm just saying out loud what I want to do, before I agree to what I have to do . . . God, isn't it a long time since we sang 'We Shall Overcome' and believed it . . . Listen, do you fancy going to the Opera House this evening? I've got complimentary tickets, and Roger's working late. Oh . . . no, no, it's all right, I'll take mother . . . have a good time. I'll give you a call next week . . . Thanks, bye.

She replaces the receiver. **Sandra** *comes in.* **Kate** *looks at her watch.*

Kate I don't believe it. Were you up all night?

Sandra We were all up all night. They got Tommy. Four o'clock this mornin'.

Kate Who got Tommy?

Sandra The great lads he's always bummin' he's so friendly with.

Kate What happened?

Sandra They broke both his hands. Stupid bugger. I warned him, we all did. You don't steal round here. You do it in the big shops in the town. They don't mind that.

Kate They broke his hands?

Sandra They'da done worse, only his ma run intil the street, squealin'. Next thing the Army was in. They used it as an excuse to take the flats apart. You wanna see the state of the place. Glass everywhere.

Kate There was nothing about it on the news this morning.

Sandra Our windows is always gettin' broke. It's not news. Who cares about the Army smashin' up the windows and the doors in Divis Flats. The bloody place is fallin' to bits anyway. Walls streamin' with water, toilets overflowin', rubbish chutes that don't work. If the rats an' the bugs don't get ye, the asbestos will . . . or the police, or the Army, or the IRA . . . who cares?

Kate Did you see Tommy?

Sandra No. But I heard him. Pigs! An' they're supposed to be on our side.

Kate Sandra, you're worn out. Go back home and get some sleep.

Sandra And get my pay docked? Are you jokin'? I'm down the best part of a pound already this week.

Maureen *comes in.*

Maureen Did she tell you?

Kate Yes. Did you see Tommy?

Maureen Johnnie an' me hid under the bed till it was all over.

Sandra Did they not come in til your place?

Maureen Somebody hammered on the door, but we never let on ourselves an' they went away.

Sandra Couldn'ta been the Brits. They'da broke the door down.

Maureen Is Arthur not in yet? I'm dyin' fer a cuppa tea. They've cut off the water as well as the electric, Kate.

Kate Who?

Maureen It happens all the time.

Sandra Arthur got picked up.

Maureen What for?

Sandra He came out onto the balcony to see what was goin' on, an' they had him in the back of the landrover before his feet had time to touch the ground.

Kate He wasn't doing anything?

Sandra Jeesus, Kate, you might as well live on the moon fer all ye know. You don't have to be doin't nuthin'. Ye just hafta be there. He's a stupid get, Arthur. He's got picked up like that before. One look at that face of his an' they haul him in fer questioning.

Maureen It's not right.

Sandra His solicitor'll have him out before lunchtime. He's used to it. Can I make some tea Kate?

Kate Yes, of course you can. I'll go and see who's in.

Maureen There'll not be many in the day. They'll all be sleepin' or standin' aroun' talking about it . . .

Kate Did anybody else from in here get picked up?

Sandra That wee lad Oliver from the joinery section. He was lobbin' milk bottles at the Brits. He got three of them before they grabbed him. He's dead good. He plays darts.

Kate Anybody else?

Sandra Not from in here. The rest they lifted was on the dole. Can I make a bitta toast as well, Kate? Only I'm starvin'.

Kate Yes.

She exits.

Sandra She takes it all dead serious, doesn't she? Do ye want toast, Maureen?

Maureen No, just a cuppa tea.

Sandra How did ye keep your Johnnie in? He loves all that. Did ye nail his feet til the floor?

Maureen I give him a pound.

Sandra Yer mad. He'll be out buyin' glue with it.

Maureen He doesn't do that no more.

Sandra Like he doesn't joyride no more? Wise up, Maureen. He's wired to the friggin' moon that wee lad.

Maureen You usta go in the back of the cars.

Sandra I grew out of it.

Maureen Our Johnnie's grew out of it too. (**Sandra** *gives her a long look.*) . . . I asked him why he keeps doin' it. He says it's a laugh.

Sandra It usta be a laugh. It stopped bein' funny the day the Brits stopped shoutin' halt an' opened fire. Do ye know Geordie Quinn? They got him right there. (*She points to below her navel.*) He showed me his stitches. Another two inches an' he'd a got the DSO. Why do ye not want any toast?

Maureen I'm not hungry.

Sandra You ate nuthin' these days. What's up with ye?

Maureen What do ye mean?

Sandra Suit yerself. Aw frig, there's no milk.

Maureen The crate's at the front door. I'll get it.

Sandra It's heavy. I'll get it.

There is a pause.

Maureen What am I gonna do, Sandra?

Sandra What are ye askin' me for?

Maureen You asked me. How did ye know?

Sandra I've two older sisters. I've seen that look. Candles to the virgin an' promises never to do it again. How far gone are ye?

Maureen Four week an' three days.

Sandra You could still be all right.

Maureen I went to Boots. I'm not all right.

Sandra Have ye told him?

Maureen He's away home for a month. He's a student.

Sandra Away home where?

Maureen I met him in the Botanic Gardens.

Sandra Where?

Maureen The Botanic Gardens. It's behind the university.

Sandra I only know roun' here. What were ye doin' away over there?

Maureen It's not far from the hospital. I go an' look at the plants sometimes. There's a palm house and a tropical ravine and the Ulster Museum. It's lovely. Ye should go sometime.

Sandra Is that where ye done it?

Maureen He lives in a flat, roun' the corner. Not like our flats. In an old house with a garden. It's lovely.

Sandra Jeesus, you musta been at the back of the queue when they were handin' out the brains.

Maureen What am I gonna do, Sandra?

Sandra How would I know?

Maureen What would you do?

Sandra I don't do it. Nobody's never gonna catch me like that.

Maureen I thought . . .

Sandra Ye thought what?

Maureen Nuthin'.

Sandra You see fellas? They talk about ye if ye do it, an' they make it up if ye don't.

Maureen They'll all talk about me.

Sandra This road's hivin' with kids. One more won't make no difference.

Maureen It'll look different.

Sandra What way different?

Maureen He's not from roun' here.

Sandra Tommy's da wasn't from roun' here. My ma says he was a half-caste what come roun' the doors sellin' floor polish. She says that's why Tommy has a bit of a tan all the year roun'.

Maureen They'll take Johnnie away when they find out.

Sandra They're gonna take Johnnie away anyway . . . Has he any money, Cairo Fred or whoever he is? You can make him pay. It's the law.

Maureen We only done it twice.

Sandra Once is enough. God but you're thick. I suppose he told you he loved you?

Maureen He was lovely. He talks awful nice. Not like the ones round here. (**Sandra** *rolls her eyes in disbelief*.) I'll get the milk.

Sandra I'll get the friggin' milk. You rest yer swelled ankles.

Maureen His father's a prince or somethin'.

Sandra Aye, an' Tommy's da was Omar Sharif.

She exits. **Maureen** *looks down.*

Maureen There's nuthin' the matter with my ankles . . . (*She begins to work the knitting machine, stops, looks down.*) Don't heed her baby . . . he loves me . . . I know he does . . . he said he did . . . and he's a gentleman . . . (*She operates the knitting machine again, stops.*) We're gonna live in an old house behind the university . . . and every day I'll put you in your pram and wheel you round the Botanic Gardens . . . a proper pram . . . Silver Cross with big high wheels . . . and everybody'll look at you, you'll be that beautiful . . . your father's dark eyes an' your grannie's blonde hair . . . (*She stops at the thought of her mother.* **Sandra** *comes in, sets the milk down, watches and listens to* **Maureen** *who doesn't see her.*) Your granny was like the sun . . . all golden . . . she lit up everything she touched . . . she come from the country and got cooped up in the flats like a battery hen . . . the day your granda went to England to look for work, we were that miserable she took me an' Johnnie to the pictures . . . *The Wizard of Oz* . . . it was lovely . . . an' the next day she bought seven pot plants . . . seven . . . an' she put them in a row on the kitchen window sill an' she said . . . 'They'll all flower except for the fourth one. That one has to stay green.' And she wouldn't tell us why. 'Wait and see' she said . . . 'Wait and see.' We watched an' we waited for a while an' nuthin' happened, an' we lost interest. Didn't even notice them anymore. And then one day I come in from school an' all the pot plants had flowers except the fourth one, just like she said. (*She smiles and counts on her fingers.*) Red, orange, yellow, green, blue, indigo, violet . . . 'See,' she said, 'we have a rainbow on our window sill.' (*She look round, sees* **Sandra**.) You come in that day . . . do you remember?

Sandra You an' your Johnnie were dancin' round the kitchen singin' 'Somewhere over the rainbow' an' your mother was laughin' an' she said 'We're all mad in this family, Sandra. Some day the men in the white coats are gonna come in and take us all away.'

Maureen Our Johnnie doesn't remember it. I asked him the other day.

Sandra It was a long time ago.

Maureen He's the spittin' image of her. Blond curly hair, blue eyes. Like one of them cherubs in the stained-glass windows. How can he look so like her and be so different? She only had to smile at you and you felt warm . . . Johnnie's light doesn't warm . . . it burns . . . it burns . . . and I can't get anywhere near him . . . (*She is incoherent, sobbing.*) And I don't know what to do . . .

Sandra Maureen, don't, you'll make yourself sick . . .

Maureen You mean mad . . . like her . . .

Sandra No I don't. Come on Maureen . . . into the loo . . . wash your face an' I'll make ye a cuppa tea . . . come on . . . you don't want anybody to see you like this . . . you know the way they talk . . . come on . . .

She looks as if she wants to touch **Maureen**, *but can't.* **Maureen** *walks, dazed, towards the exit, turns back to* **Sandra**.

Maureen Sure you won't tell nobody . . .

Sandra Cross my heart and hope to die.

She walks off. **Sandra** *follows her.*

Scene Three

Open day at the Lagan Mill. Mid-April.

Tommy *(his hands in plaster) is sitting watching* **Sandra** *who is writing on a large sheet of paper with a felt-tip pen. A radio is playing, very loudly, 'Alternative Ulster' by the Belfast punk group Stiff Little Fingers.* **Kate** *is rushing about. She turns the radio down. Exits.* **Arthur** *comes in carrying prepared food. He grins at* **Tommy**.

Arthur Hiya, Tommy. Clap your hands. How're ye doin'?

Tommy Okay.

Sandra It's one way of stoppin' smokin', eh Tommy? Here ye are Arthur.

She pins up a sign. 'Get Your Non-Sectarian Nosh Here.' Sits down and begins writing again.

Tommy They'll make ye take that down. (**Sandra** *shrugs.*) What time are the big nobs comin' in?

Arthur They're comin' for lunch an' then they're havin' a look roun' the sections.

Tommy An' then they'll pat yiz all on the head an' tell ye what good children yiz all are.

Arthur There's some real big nob comin' in. He's a Royal or somethin'.

Tommy He's not a Royal. He's from the Home Office. They're interested in this scheme. Yous should be boycottin' his visit, not feedin' his face.

Arthur Sandra, you're supposed to be helpin' me.

Sandra In a minute. Houl yer horses.

Arthur What are ye doin'?

Sandra Makin' an Irish welcome for the English civil servant.

Kate *comes in. Turns the radio off.*

Kate Does anybody know where Maureen is? Sandra?

Sandra Haven't seen her.

Kate It's not like her. She's never late.

Sandra What do ye think, Kate?

She holds up another sign. It says 'Never Mind What The Papers Say. We All Love Ye, Conn.'

Kate Who's Conn?

Sandra The man from the Home Office

Kate His name is Jeremy Saunders. Who's Conn?

They all grin.

Kate Okay. I'm a thick middle-class moron. Would somebody like to explain it to me?

Maureen *rushes in. She is carrying a Marks & Spencer carrier bag.*

Maureen Sorry I'm late Kate.

Kate That's all right. Are you all right?

Maureen I had a message to do this mornin'. Forgot to tell ye.

Kate Are you sure you're all right?

Maureen Why shouldn't I be all right?

Kate Do you know who Conn is?

Maureen Conn who?

Arthur It's a name for any English civil servant.

Tommy It's short for constipation, the shite you can't get rid of.

Kate Are you planning to pin that up?

Sandra They'll never know what it means, an' they'll be too polite to ask.

Kate It would be really embarrassing if this scheme didn't get a second year's funding because an English civil servant was brighter than you lot thought.

Tommy I'm away. See yiz all later.

Kate Are you not staying to heckle?

Tommy We're stagin' a demonstration.

Kate Outside.

Tommy We're protestin' about Mr Jeremy Saunders bein' here. Do you know his da owns the half of Cornwall or somewhere?

Kate God give me strength.

Tommy You shoulda said no, Kate.

Kate I didn't want this open day. I was told it had to take place. Will you tell the Party that I don't care if Jeremy Saunders' father owns all of Cornwall. All I care about is getting enough money to keep this place going for at least another year. While you lot are trying to change the face of the world, I am just trying to get the kids here through another rotten day.

Tommy Yer wrong, Kate.

Kate I know I'm wrong. But it's the best I can think of till the revolution comes.

Sandra Yer both wrong. When we're all drawin' the pension there'll still be head-the-balls like him an' there'll still be well-meanin' people like you, an' nuthin' will be no different. Do ye know what this scheme is? It's a friggin' Government joyride. A good laugh for a year, an' then ye grow up.

Kate Put your poster up, Sandra. If Mr Jeremy Saunders is intelligent enough to know what it means, he'll be too sophisticated to care.

She walks out. **Tommy** *follows her.*

Arthur Do ye know what they're talkin' about Maureen?

Sandra Maureen doesn't know what time of day it is. What's in the bag?

Maureen None of your business. What's all the glasses for?

Arthur Wine.

Sandra We get lectures about the demon drink, an' they can't manage a meal without a bottle of wine.

Maureen Where's the wine?

Arthur Kate has it hid away. She's no dozer.

Sandra *looks in the Marks & Spencer's bag.*

Maureen Put that down!

Sandra I was only lookin'.

Maureen Well don't. Yer hands is all felt tip.

Sandra Well you show me then.

Maureen Not now.

Sandra Arthur!

Arthur What?

Sandra On yer bike!

Arthur What?

Sandra Maureen wants to try on her new frock.

Maureen I don't!

Arthur I won't look.

Sandra Bugger off when yer told.

Arthur I've a lot to do. Yiz have ten minutes.

Sandra Don't come back in till yer called.

Arthur *exits*.

Sandra Well, come on then. Let us see.

Maureen *takes an expensive matching outfit out of the bag. Jacket, skirt, trousers, top, shoes.*

Sandra You rob the meter or what?

Maureen I've been savin' up since Christmas. I've always wanted this outfit. It was reduced in the sale. You can wear the skirt or the trousers with the jacket, swap them roun'.

Sandra Try it on.

Maureen Kate might come in.

Sandra Kate hasn't got nuthin' we haven't got.

Maureen *takes off her skirt and shoes. Puts on the new jacket, skirt and shoes.*

Maureen No mirror. Is it nice?

Sandra The jacket's awful big.

Maureen It's the fashion. It's supposed to be big.

Sandra It would fit two. It'll come in handy later on . . . ach, fer God's sake, Maureen, I was only jokin'. Stop lookin' like a wet week all the time.

Maureen I'm not sure about the colour. They had it in pink as well.

Sandra Ye can always get it changed.

Maureen I want to wear it the day.

Sandra What for? Are ye hopin' Mr Saunders'll fall for ye an' offer ye a job in Stormont Castle?

Kate *comes in*.

Kate Oh, that's nice Maureen. Is it new?

Maureen Why shouldn't it be new?

Kate No reason . . . I . . .

Maureen I've as much right to new clothes as the next one, so I have.

Kate You look lovely.

Maureen I look a sight. It's too big.

She takes the outfit off. Stuffs it back into the bag.

Kate Careful. Don't crease it or they won't give you your money back.

Kate *takes the clothes out, folds them, puts them back into the carrier bag.* **Arthur** *comes in.*

Arthur Hey Kate, the Law's back. They want to see you.

Kate They've already checked the building twice. What do they want now?

Arthur They never said. I suppose when Jeremy Saunders comes in the place'll be crawlin' with them.

Kate Mr Saunders will have his own heavies in tow. Would you two give Arthur a hand with the food? I won't be long.

Arthur What about the wine?

Kate They won't be here for a while. We'll open it later.

Arthur The red should be opened in advance.

Kate There's plenty of time.

She exits.

Sandra Good try, Arthur.

Arthur Do ye think they'll let us drink the leftovers?

Sandra Yer ever hopeful.

Arthur Are ye not wearin' your new frock for them, Maureen?

Maureen No.

Sandra *puts her finger into one of the bowls, tastes the contents.*

Sandra Jeesus, Arthur, what's this?

Arthur Cheese dip.

Sandra It's revoltin'.

Arthur Try this one.

Sandra What is it?

Arthur Celery, date an' walnut salad.

Sandra I hate dates.

Arthur Do ye like cooked ham?

Sandra It's all right.

Arthur Well do ye think ye could stop complainin' an' roll the ham up, put a cocktail stick through it an' sprinkle it with chopped parsley?

Sandra What for?

Arthur Because it looks nicer that way, than lyin' flat on a plate.

Sandra They're gonna ate it, not take pictures of it.

Arthur Maureen, will you do the ham? (*To* **Sandra**.) You do the lettuce, it's all yer fit for.

Sandra Up yer nose Arthur.

Kate *comes in.*

Sandra Hey Kate, do the Law know there's a suspect device in Arthur's potato salad?

Kate Would the two of you go outside for a moment. I want to talk to Maureen.

Sandra What's up?

Kate Just do as you're told!

Arthur Is there somethin' wrong, Kate?

Kate Just go.

Sandra Do as yer told and ye'll live long enough, Arthur.

Sandra *and* **Arthur** *leave.*

Kate Is it true Maureen?

Maureen Is what true?

Kate I said I wanted to talk to you first. They gave me five minutes.

Maureen How did they know it was me?

Kate Oh Maureen, what got into you?

Maureen How did they know?

Kate When you ran out of the shop, there was a policeman across the street. He recognized you. He was in court the day Johnnie was put on probation. They went to your home, and Johnnie told them you were here.

Maureen What's Johnnie doin' in the house? He should be at school.

Kate Never mind that now. Why did you do it? What on earth possessed you?

Maureen My fella's back in Belfast, he's been away for a month. I was goin' to see him the night. I wanted to look nice.

Kate Why didn't you ask me? I could have lent you something to wear.

Maureen I wanted somethin' new. My own. I'm fed up wearin' other people's cast-offs . . . I didn't go in to do nuthin' . . . I only went in to look . . . I've been eyin' that suit fer months . . . I heard they was all reduced . . . I only went in to see . . . I was standin' there, tryin' to make up my mind . . . the jacket was still too dear, but I had enough saved for the skirt or the trousers . . . I thought maybe the skirt . . . he said I had nice legs . . . an' then this woman an' her daughter come up, an' the girl tried on one of the jackets . . . an' it was lovely on her so it was . . . an' she said . . . she said, 'Do ye think I should get the trousers or the skirt an' the woman said, 'Get both, it's not every day you're seventeen . . .' I followed them roun' the shop . . . they bought matchin' shoes an' a top . . . the shoes were real leather, reduced til twelve pounds . . . everything she was wearin' was brand new. What did she need with more clothes? Her mother bought her the lot . . . wrote a cheque . . . I just walked behind them . . . watchin' . . . an' then they stopped at the blouses . . . they set the bag on the floor while they were lookin' . . . an' I just lifted it . . . an' I run . . . it's not even my size . . .

Kate Oh Maureen, Maureen . . .

Maureen They'll lock me up an' put Johnnie away, an it'll all be my fault . . .

Kate I'll phone a solicitor, ask him to go to the station . . .

Maureen I'm sorry . . . I don't know why I done it . . . it was wrong . . .

Kate It's all wrong, and none of it is your fault, so stop apologizing.

Maureen I've let ye down, I'm sorry . . .

Kate No, I've let you down . . . you know what my reaction was when the police told me. How could Maureen do this to me . . . my star pupil . . . I'm becoming more and more like them . . . expecting you to be grateful for nothing. Sandra's right. I might as well live on the moon for all I know. Everything I have taken for granted all my life, you have had to fight for. Ordinary things like a warm dry house, nice clothes, education, opportunity, choice. You have no choice. None of you have. Poverty on the dole, or poverty on a Youth Opportunities Programme. And if you're very good and aspire to be like us, we might even find you a job.

Maureen I've no chance of gettin' a job in an office now, have I? Not with a police record.

Kate Maureen, you are going to have to learn how to fight, or they'll destroy you . . . I'll phone for a solicitor.

Kate *goes to the phone. As she dials there are noises, shouts from the street outside.* **Tommy** *rushes in.*

Tommy Maureen! It's your Johnnie! He's nicked the fuckin' police car. He's coked to the gills, ridin' it round and round the block. The Army's in the next street. Somebody'd better stop him before they do . . .

Maureen No!

She runs out. **Kate** *runs after her.* **Arthur** *comes in. He is nervous, agitated.*

Tommy It's Johnnie.

Arthur I know. I seen him.

They look out of the window.

Tommy (*admiringly*) Jeesus, look at him. He's like the friggin' 'A' Team . . . go on ye wee bugger. You show them . . .

There is a rattle of gunfire, screams, shouts.

Tommy Jeesus Christ!

Arthur *turns away from the window, puts his hands on his head, walks abruptly to the kitchen. He lifts a lettuce, pulls it apart. He is shaking.*

Tommy What are ye doin'?

Arthur Shreddin' lettuce . . . you shouldn't cut it ye know . . . it destroys the vitamin C content if ye use a knife.

He is very agitated. His head hurts as he tries to block the memory of being shot and the subsequent slow, painful recovery.

Tommy Arthur?

Arthur There is no pain ye know . . . not when yer hurt that bad . . . the brain shuts down . . . it's what saves ye . . . the oul brain knows when you've had enough . . . when it's more than a body can take . . . an' it shuts down . . . that way ye don't die of shock . . . you know what the worst bit is? . . . when ye sort of come to . . . an' ye can hear, but ye can't see an' ye can't speak . . . I remember I was shit scared they might think I was dead an' bury me alive . . . I thought I'd go mad . . . I thought maybe I *was* dead . . . but I wasn't . . . I wasn't. You can be shot to bits an' not be dead . . .

Tommy Arthur . . . Arthur!

Arthur What's happenin' out there?

Tommy *looks out of the window again.*

Tommy The street's fulla kids, dozens of them. They're all over the place, screamin' shoutin' throwin' stones at the Army and the police . . . the kids won't let them near the car . . . an' yer man Saunders has arrived, an' the Brits are tryin' to protect him, get his big Mercedes outa the street . . . it's like bedlam out there . . . I can't see . . .

Sandra *comes in. She is carrying* **Maureen**. **Maureen** *is a horrific, bloody mess.*

Sandra (*quietly, without expression*) Lock the door.

Tommy *locks the door.* **Sandra** *sets* **Maureen** *on the chair below the hairdryer.* **Maureen** *sprawls grotesquely, half on the chair, half on the floor.*

Sandra (*expressionlessly*) She run between the car an' the army.

Arthur I know. We seen her.

There is a brief moment when he might offer **Sandra** *comfort, when she might accept. Then* **Sandra** *turns away, grabs hold of* **Maureen** *shakes her, screams.*

Sandra Ye stupid bitch, ye daft stupid bitch! Ye haven't the sense ye were born with!

Arthur Sandra . . .

Sandra What are you lookin' at, face-ache!

Arthur She's dead, Sandra.

Sandra I know she's friggin' dead. Her guts is everywhere. That's what dying's like. (*She shakes* **Maureen**.) This is what it's like. Do you hear me? It's not lovely, an' it's not romantic like in stupid friggin' plays!

Arthur Don't, Sandra.

Sandra Nobody's every gonna write poetry about you! Nobody!

Arthur Don't. It's not right.

There is a loud hammering on the door.

Sandra Fuck off! If you let the Brits touch her, so help me, Arthur, I'll stove in yer steel plate . . .

Kate (*offstage*) Arthur, Sandra, Tommy, please . . . open the door . . .

Sandra Give them a signed statement. Tell them she done it for love.

Kate Please let me in.

Arthur Ye just can't keep her here, Sandra.

Sandra Why not? Nobody else wants her.

Arthur Let Kate in, Tommy.

Kate Please, open the door.

Tommy Are ye on yer own, Kate?

Sounds of argument outside.

Kate Yes.

Tommy Swear.

Kate I swear. Please, let me in.

Tommy *opens the door.* **Kate** *comes in.* **Tommy** *locks the door again.* **Kate** *looks at* **Maureen**. *Looks away.*

Kate Move her out of that chair.

Sandra Put her back on the knittin' machine.

Arthur *pushes the food and the glasses off the table on to the floor. Lifts* **Maureen**. *Lays her gently on the table.*

Kate Cover her with something.

Sandra Look at her. Everybody should look at her.

Tommy Did they get Johnnie as well?

Kate He got a few cuts from the windscreen, that's all.

Tommy Jammy wee bugger. He always did have the luck of the devil.

Hammering on the door.

Sandra Do you know what it'll say in the papers the morra? 'Shoplifter gets shot.'

Blackout.

In the darkness **Sandra** *sings quietly 'Wouldn't it be good to be in your shoes Even if it was for just one day'.* **Maureen** *is carried offstage by* **Arthur**. **Tommy** *chants 'No job nothing to do, no money, on the Bru'.* **Sandra** *sings quietly 'We are the Divis girls we wear our hair in curls'.*

Kate *sings 'Damp, damp, damp, damp, damp, damp, damp, damp'.* **Arthur** *returns singing 'Oh I was out walking outside Divis Flats, Where the happiest tenants are surely the rats'.*

In semi-darkness, **Kate**, **Arthur**, **Sandra** *and* **Tommy** *clear the stage, singing excerpts of the songs from the play, which merge into a distorted medley.*

Rats, rats, rats, rats, rats, rats, rats, rats.
What will it be when we leave school?
Will it be ace schemes or YTP?
No job after school. No future that's the rule.

Unemployment. Unemployment.

Hope it's work real work
We hope it's work real work
We hope it's work real work
And not the dole.

Old Mother Hubbard went to the cupboard
To get a piece of bread
She put her hand in the breadbin
And found something else instead
AUGH!

Sandra *sings loudly, defiantly*

> We are the Divis girls we wear our hair in curls
> We wear our skinners to our knees
> We do not smoke or drink
> *That's what our parents think*
> We are the Divis girls
> We are the Divis Street crowd of rowdies
> We are a nuisance to the public I agree
> I agree!
> See us stand and talk to each other
> We are mates, we are great, we agree

Kate, **Arthur** *and* **Tommy** *exit.* **Sandra** *sits down on a chair, lights a cigarette.*

OR *alternatively:*

After Sandra's line '. . . Shoplifter gets shot'

Blackout.

Maureen *is carried offstage and there is no singing, only the sound of broken glass being swept up. (This is the sound that usually follows violence in Belfast.)*

Scene Four

Early May. The Belfast Arts Council Gallery. **Sandra** *sitting smoking a cigarette.* **Arthur** *comes in. He is wearing the 'Compensation Day' suit casually (sleeves rolled back and an expensive T-shirt.) Already he looks more prosperous, more middle-class.*

Arthur What's the use of comin' til an art exhibition if ye don't look at the pictures.

Sandra I have looked at the pictures. They're a load of crap.

Arthur The man what done them is downstairs. He's from Russia.

Sandra If he was from roun' here, nobody'd give them a second look. I've seen better at the primary school open day.

Arthur Kate says people are payin' hundreds for them.

Sandra Why don't ye put in an offer fer one. You'll be gettin' yer money any day now, won't ye?

Arthur I have it all earmarked.

Sandra You treatin' yerself till a brain transplant?

Arthur I'm takin' over Larry's.

Sandra Yer what?

Arthur I've made him an offer he can't refuse. I'm gonna do it all up. Serve good food.

Sandra Did they pack yer head with green cheese in the hospital? Ye'll go broke in a year.

Arthur I'm gonna have candles on the tables an' a man playin' the accordion.

Sandra I'll take you home again, Kathleen.

Arthur Real French stuff. Ye hafta get them in the mood.

Sandra They'll set fire til the tablecloths with the candles.

Arthur Not if you were there.

Sandra Me?

Arthur The family's gonna help me out, part time, till I get goin . . . but I need somebody full time . . . a supervisor . . . to keep an eye on the place while I'm doin' the cookin' . . . make sure my da keeps his hands outa the till.

Sandra What makes ye think I would keep my hands outa yer till?

Arthur No point in robbin' a business if yer a partner . . .

Sandra A what?

Arthur I mean proper . . . one of the family.

There is an awkward, embarrassed pause.

Sandra Arthur . . . will you just go away an' leave me alone. Yer wearin' me out.

Arthur Suit yerself.

He walks away. **Sandra** *sits for a moment.*

Sandra The one an' only time I ever wore a white lace frock Arthur, was for my first communion . . . an' my mother parades me down the road to get my photo tuk, an' she says to the photographer, 'Isn't our Sandra a picture? Won't she make a beautiful bride?' an' I told her I was never gonna get married, an' she got all dewy-eyed because she thought I wanted to be a nun . . . A bride of Christ, or forty years' hard labour . . . my mother thinks anything in between is a mortal sin . . . She married a big child like you, Arthur, an' what did it get her . . . eight kids an' twenty years' cookin' cleanin' an' survivin' on grants an' handouts . . . You're too like my da fer comfort. Fulla big plans that'll come to nuthin' because yer too soft an' yer too easy-goin' an' havin' all that money won't make ye any different. Whatever your da an' the rest of your ones don't steal from ye, the world will. They'll ate ye alive . . . You know what the big trick in this life is? It's knowin' what ye don't want, an' I don't want to be a back-seat joyrider, content to sit and giggle behind the fellas who do the stealin' an' the drivin' . . . I stole a car once . . . all by myself . . . I never told nobody, doin' it was enough . . . I just drove it roun' them posh streets in South Belfast until it ran outa petrol, an' then I walked home. Didn't need to boast about it the way the fellas do . . . just doin' it was enough . . . When the careers' officer come til our school, he asked me what I wanted to do, an' I says, 'I wanna drive roun' in a big car like yer woman outa Bonnie an' Clyde, an' rob banks,' an, he thought I was takin' a hand out him, so I says, 'All right then, I'll settle fer bein' a racin' driver.' An' he says, 'I'd advise you to settle for something less fantastic Sandra.' . . . They're all the same. They ask ye what ye wanta be, an' then they tell ye what yer allowed to be . . . Me wantin' to be a racin' driver is not more fantastical than Maureen believin' the fairy stories . . . dilly day-dream, just like her mother before her . . . somewhere over the rainbow, bluebirds die . . .

Kate *comes in.*

Kate You know the best thing about this exhibition?

Sandra What?

Kate The free wine.

Sandra Somebody's payin' for it. Nuthin's free.

Kate Tommy's right. You should join the Party.

Sandra I went to visit Tommy on the way here.

Kate How is he?

Sandra His left hand's okay. The right hand . . . they're gonna hafta break it an' reset some of the bones.

Kate Oh God.

Sandra Lucky he's left-handed . . . born klute as well as half-caste. God gave him a good start in life, didn't he . . . Did you get to read the report the hospital done on Maureen?

Kate Yes.

Sandra What did it say?

Kate It said that she died of gunshot wounds.

Sandra Did it say anything else about her?

Kate *pauses. They look at each other for a moment.*

Kate Why didn't she tell me . . . Why didn't you tell me?

Sandra I thought maybe she imagined it. She was forever day-dreamin' . . . Have you ever been to the Botanic Gardens, Kate?

Kate Yes. It's really lovely. As well as the park, there's a palm house and a tropical ravine, and the Ulster Museum . . . Would you like to go sometime?

Sandra No.

The lights dim to sound of Nik Kershaw recording of 'Wouldn't it be Good to be in Your Shoes.'

The Belle of the Belfast City

For Susan Hogg

The Belle of the Belfast City was first produced by The Lyric Players Theatre Belfast in May 1989, with the following cast:

Dolly Dunbar Horner	Sheila McGibbon
Vi, *Dolly's daughter*	Stella McCuskar
Rose, *Dolly's daughter*	Fay Howard
Belle, *Dolly's granddaughter*	Suzette Llewellyn
Janet, *Dolly's niece*	Lindy Whiteford
Jack, *Dolly's nephew*	John Hewitt
Davy Watson	
Tom Bailey	
Issac Standaloft	Richard Howard
Customs Man	
Peter	

Directed by Tim Luscombe
Designed by James Helps
Lighting Designer Patrick Dalgety
Production Manager Rose Morris

The Ballad of William Bloat was written by Raymond Calvert and *Ballad to a Traditional Refrain* ('May the lord in His Mercy be kind to Belfast') by Maurice James Craig. My thanks to both authors and also to Irene Calvert, Agnes Bernelle, the Blackstaff Press, The Linen Hall Library, Belfast Leisure Kids, The Kingham Mission for The Deaf and The Council for the Advancement of Communication Skills with Deaf People, Belfast And a very special 'Thank you' to John and Agnes Carberry for teaching and translating their language of signing during rehearsals.

Act One

Scene One

Belfast, November 1986

Dolly *(aged 77) sits looking at a photo album. She wears a dressing gown. Her walking stick is propped against a dressing-up box alongside her chair. The room has many framed photographs, old and new. The largest and most dominant image is of the young* **Dolly** *on a concert poster circa 1925 when she topped the bill in the halls as 'The Belle of the Belfast City'.*

Dolly *(sings)*
    I'll tell me ma when I go home
    The boys won't leave the girls alone
    They pulled my hair they stole my comb
    Well that's all right till I go home
    She is handsome she is pretty
    She is the Belle of the Belfast City
    She is courtin' One Two Three
    Please won't you tell me who is she

Davy *taps out the rhythm of the song on the spoons,* **Dolly** *listens, and in the distance, as if she is conjuring it, we hear her family singing. It is 1958.* **Dolly**'s *daughters* **Vi** *(aged 29) and* **Rose** *(8), and her niece* **Janet** *(8) come running to her from the past. They dress up with clothes from the box and perform the song.* **Dolly**'s *nephew (* **Janet**'s *brother* **Jack**, *aged 12) beats out a drum rhythm with his hands.* **Jack** *does not dress up nor join in the love and laughter that envelops the girls. During the singing and dancing,* **Dolly** *joins in and becomes an agile woman of 49. Her 18-year-old granddaughter* **Belle** *watches with delight.* **Belle** *is in the present time and watches as if seeing an often-heard story re-created.*

Vi, **Rose** *and* **Janet** *sing.* **Dolly** *joins in.*

Joe Horner says he loves her
All the boys are fightin' for her
They knock at the door and they ring the bell
Saying 'Oh my true love are you well'
Out she comes as white as snow
Rings on her fingers bells on her toes
Oul Dolly Dunbar says she'll die
If she doesn't get the fella with the rovin' eye

I'll tell me ma when I go home
The boys won't leave the girls alone
They pulled my hair they stole my comb
Well that's all right till I go home
She is handsome she is pretty
She is the Belle of the Belfast City
She is courtin' One Two Three
Please won't you tell me who is she

Back to the present time. **Jack** *and* **Janet** *exit.* **Dolly** *looks at the photo album.* **Vi** *is in the family shop with* **Davy**. **Belle** *and* **Rose** *are in Aldergrove Airport, Belfast, waiting for transport to the family home.*

Belle   She is my grandmother. Dolly Dunbar. Child star of the twenties. Songs, recitations and tap dancing. She won a talent competition when she was ten and was top of the bill before she was thirteen. I'm called after her. Not Dolly, but Belle. That was her stage name and my grandfather Joe never called her anything else.

Rose   My mother, the Belle of the Belfast City, happened to be performing in an Orange Hall in Belfast one night when my father Joe Horner was at a Lodge meeting in an upstairs room. They say he heard her singing and walked out of the meeting and into the concert like a man under a spell. And that was it. They eloped a fortnight later, and from then on she gave up the stage and did all her dressing-up and singing and dancing just for him.

Vi   Our Rose is nuthin' if not romantic. The truth is that my mother's family were still dressin' her up as if she was thirteen instead of goin' on nineteen, an' trailin' her round draughty oul halls to sing to audiences of twenty or thirty. My father took her away from all that, and waited on her hand and foot for the rest of his life. Still, as they say, it's a poor family can't afford to support one lady.

Dolly An' a poor story that doesn't improve with the tellin'.

Rose When I was very small I used to lie in bed with my big sister Vi and listen to our parents gossiping and giggling like a couple of kids in the room next door. When the bed-springs started to creak, our Vi used to stuff cotton wool in my ears.

Vi Forty-one mother was when she had our Rose, and me already over the age of consent. It was the talk of the neighbourhood.

Rose Bad enough to be still doing it at their age, but even worse to be enjoying it so much that she was careless enough to get caught. Our Vi was that mortified she wouldn't go out of the house. My mother and father were over the moon.

Dolly (*looking at the album or pointing to one of the framed photos*) He was as proud as a peacock. My Joe. The cock of the North.

Vi Mother! That'll do!

Dolly She always calls me mother when she's bein' prim an' proper. She must of got that from your side of the family, Joe. But you see our Rose? She's like *my* ones. Fulla life an' rarin' to go. She's travelled the world you know, takin' pictures. Imagine that!

Rose *walks to* **Belle**.

Rose No sign of the airport bus yet?

Belle It's been delayed indefinitely. There was a demonstration earlier today near Belfast city centre and some of the roads are still blocked.

Rose What sort of a demonstration?

Belle A loyalist protest against the Anglo-Irish Agreement. The speakers were the Reverend Ian Paisley and your cousin Jack.

Rose Welcome to the land of your forefathers, Belle. Come on, let's see if we can get a taxi.

Dolly (*sings*)
>Let the wind and the rain and the hail blow high
>And the snow come tumblin' from the sky
>She's as nice as apple pie
>And she'll get her own man by and by
>When she gets a man of her own
>She won't tell her ma when she comes home
>Let them all come as they will
>For it's Joe Horner she loves still

Scene Two

Dolly *sits in the room off the family shop. The shop is small and sells crisps, sweets, cigarettes, newspapers, magazines and a few groceries and carry-out snacks (sandwiches, pies etc). There is a small table and chairs for the occasional customer to eat on the premises.*

Vi *is setting out the local magazines which have been delivered by* **Davy** *who is deaf and mute.* **Vi** *and* **Davy** *communicate through lip-reading and/or hand signals. If* **Vi** *has her back to* **Davy***, he attracts her attention by clapping his hands.*

The shop is in East Belfast in a side street that the Army has closed to traffic.

Jack *walks into the street. He is very neatly and expensively dressed and wears slightly tinted glasses. He moves silently. All* **Jack**'s *movements are very careful and controlled.*

Vi *takes two bars of chocolate from a shelf.*

Vi Thanks for bringin' the magazines round, Davy. Here, that's for you and one for your mother. Don't you be eatin' both of them, mind.

Davy *shakes his head and signals thanks.* **Jack** *has come into the shop quietly without* **Vi** *and* **Davy** *being aware of him. He deliberately moves one of the chairs to make a noise.*

Vi God, Jack, you made me jump!

Jack They say that's the sign of a bad conscience Vi.

Vi A bad conscience? Me? Huh! Chance would be a fine thing!

Dolly (*sings*) There was an oul woman down Donegall Street, who went to the doctor 'cause she couldn't . . .

Vi Mother!

Jack Aunt Dolly sounds in fine form the day.

Vi Did you ever know a day when she wasn't?

Davy *becomes aware of* **Jack** *and talks rapidly in sign language to* **Vi**. *He is very excited that* **Jack** *is there.*

Vi He says, can he get you anything, Mr Horner? A cup of tea, a sandwich, a hot pie . . .

Jack Tell him no . . . thanks. I have to go to a meeting. (**Vi** *signals to* **Davy** *who looks crestfallen.*) I just called to ask you if you're still thinking of selling the shop.

Vi (*glancing nervously towards the room where* **Dolly** *sits*) It's not something I've thought out, Jack, nor mentioned to nobody else . . . why do you ask?

Jack I have a friend who's looking for a shop and dwelling around here.

Vi What friend?

Jack Nobody you know. A business acquaintance. An Englishman. He's in Belfast for a few days, looking at property. I mentioned this place to him and he's very interested. It's the right size and in the right area. He's got the money to make you a good offer.

Davy *signals to* **Vi** *again.*

Vi Have a quick cup. Just to please him, Jack. The kettle's already boiled, it won't take a minute, and you can have a wee word with Dolly.

*She signals to **Davy** that **Jack** will have a cup of tea. **Davy** is delighted and almost runs behind the counter. **Vi** moves quickly towards the other room, anxious that **Jack** won't pursue the subject of selling the shop. **Jack** follows her.*

Vi Here's Jack to see you, mother.

Dolly Jack who?

Vi Our Jack.

Dolly The one with the haircut that's never off the television?

Vi You know right well who he is, now stop actin' the eejit.

Dolly *points out a photo to **Jack**.*

Dolly That's you, with a face like a Lurgan spade as usual. An' that's me, and Rose and Vi and your wee sister Janet, God love her. My Joe took that photo the week after we brought the two of you here to live with us. (*Pause.*) Janet's stoppin' here again, ye know. Left her man. Don't know what's goin' on there at all. (*At **Vi**.*) Nobody never tells me nuthin' these days.

Jack *looks sharply at **Vi**. **Vi** looks away. **Dolly** reaches out as if to take off **Jack**'s glasses. **Jack** recoils.*

Dolly I only wanted to have a look at your sore eye.

Jack (*off-guard*) I haven't got a sore . . . (*He stops, realizing that **Dolly** is making fun of him.*)

Vi Mother! Behave yourself!

Jack *walks angrily back to the shop. **Vi** gives **Dolly** an exasperated look. **Dolly** smiles innocently. **Vi** follows **Jack**. **Davy** rushes forward eagerly with a cup of tea for **Jack** and sets it on the table. **Davy** signals to **Vi**.*

Vi He says, God bless you, John Horner, and God bless Ian Paisley. He says you're the boys'll see Ulster right.

Jack What's all this about Janet?

Vi She's left Peter. She's been here about a week.

Jack Why wasn't I told?

Vi She didn't want . . .

Jack You should have phoned me immediately.

Vi It wasn't my place.

Jack What's happened?

Vi I don't know. She won't say.

Jack She'll say to me. Where is she?

Vi She's out.

Jack You tell her I'll be back and I want to see her. Has *he* been here?

Vi Just the once. Peter hasn't a lot of free time. The RUC are on full standby, what with one thing and another . . .

Jack I knew no good would come of that marriage. Sneaking off to a registry office instead of standing up and declaring themselves without shame in the eyes of the Lord. I suppose he's got himself another woman. Catholic licentiousness. It never leaves them.

Vi Peter's a good man.

Jack A Catholic policeman! It's the like of him who've infiltrated the Royal Ulster Constabulary. Corrupted the force into fighting against us instead of standing alongside us as they've always done.

Dolly (*recites loudly*)
    Holy Mary Mother of God
    Pray for me and Tommy Todd
    For he's a Fenian and I'm a Prod
    Holy Mary Mother of God.

Jack That old woman should be in a home!

Vi If that old woman hadn't taken you and Janet in when your mother died, that's where you'd have ended up, in a home! And don't you ever forget that, Jack!

Jack I'm sorry if I offended you, Vi. I . . .

Vi You offended *her*. This family never badmouths its own.

Jack I apologize. I said it without thinking. Not like me. One of the first things you learn in politics. Never speak without knowing exactly what you're going to say . . . I was angry with Janet. That marriage has always been a thorn in my side. (*He becomes aware of* **Davy** *watching them.*) Does he understand what we've been talking about?

Vi No. He needs to be close up and facing you to lip-read.

Jack I don't want family business gossiped about.

Vi I don't think you need worry about Davy doin' much gossipin', Jack. (*She signals and talks to* **Davy**.) Away in and sit with Dolly for a while and look at the photos. Here. (*Putting some sweets in a bag.*) Share these with her.

Davy *goes to* **Dolly**. *Holds out the bag of sweets.* **Dolly** *takes one. Turns up her nose and calls to* **Vi**.

Dolly Brandy Balls! Are they not makin' it in bottles any more? (*She turns the pages in the photo album.* **Davy** *gets excited and points when he sees* **Jack** *as a boy.*) Aye, that's Jack when he was a wee lad, wearin' the National Health specs. Suited him better than them Miami Vice jobs he wears these days.

In the shop, **Jack** *stands hesitantly as* **Vi**, *still angry at what he has said, tidies up the magazines.*

Jack You wouldn't fall out with me, would you, Vi? We've always been friends, haven't we?

Vi Yes, of course we have.

Jack I've always appreciated what your parents did for me and Janet. I'm not ungrateful. But I . . .

Vi It's all right, Jack.

Jack I just want you to know that I've not forgotten how *you* looked after *me* . . . Dolly always sided with Janet and Rose . . . you're the only person in the world I've ever enjoyed singing with . . . do you know that? (*They are both awkward about this declaration.*) Do you still sing?

Vi There's no children here to sing for any more, and she does enough singin' for both of us.

Jack You had a good voice.

Vi You weren' so bad yourself.

Dolly (*sings*)

In the county Tyrone near the town of Dungannon,
Where many's the ruction myself had a hand in
Bob Williamson lived there, a weaver by trade
And all of us thought him a stout Orange blade

On the Twelfth of July as it yearly did come,
Bob played on the flute to the sound of the drum
You may talk of your harp, your piano or lute
But nothing could sound like the oul Orange flute.

Vi (*to* **Jack**) We used to sing it better than that. When you were a wee lad.

(*Sings.*)

But Bob the deceiver, he took us all in
And married a Papish called Brigid McGinn
Turned Papish himself and forsook the oul cause
That gave us our freedom, religion and laws

Jack (*sings*)

Now the boys in the townland made comment upon it
And Bob had to flee to the province of Connaught
He flew with his wife and his fixin's to boot
And along with the latter the oul Orange flute

Vi

At the chapel on Sundays to atone for past deeds
Bob said Paters and Aves and counted his beads
Till after some time at the priest's own desire
Bob went with his oul flute to play in the choir

Jack

And all he could whistle and finger and blow
To play Papish music he found it no go.
'Kick the Pope' and 'Boyne Water' and such like it would
     sound.
But one Papish squeak in it couldn't be found

Vi
> At the council of priests that was held the next day
> They decided to banish the oul flute away
> For they couldn't knock heresy out of its head
> And they bought Bob another to play in its stead

Jack
> So the oul flute was doomed and its fate was pathetic
> It was fastened and burned at the stake as heretic
> As the flames licked around it they heard a strange noise
> 'Twas the oul flute still playin' 'The Protestant Boys'!

Dolly *points to the album and cackles with laughter.* **Jack**'s *rare moment of pleasure is broken.*

Jack And then Rose came sneaking in and took a photo of us.

Vi She meant no harm. I never could understand why you were in such a state about it.

Jack I don't like being caught off-guard like that. Rose always was a sly one. (*Hurriedly, in case* **Vi** *objects to him slighting one of the family.*) When's she arriving?

Vi Now how did you know about that?

Jack You must have told me.

Vi I haven't seen you since Rose phoned to tell me that her and Belle were coming.

Jack She's bringing her daughter here?

Vi She is indeed. And about time too. That child's over eighteen and been all over the world with our Rose and never in her own home town. It's a disgrace, so it is. I told Rose, now that Dolly's not able to travel to London no more you'll have to bring Belle here to see us. She must have took it to heart, for the pair of them are arrivin' the day . . . and would you look at the state of this place. (*She fusses about, tidying the shop.*) Don't mind me gettin' on, Jack, I don't want Belle thinkin' we run this shop like a midden. I want her to think well of Belfast and have a holiday she'll never forget.

Jack Oh, Rose is on holiday, is she?

Vi (*slightly puzzled at his tone of voice*) Aye, and Belle's on half term from her college.

Jack What's she like, this daughter of Rose's?

Vi Like you. Clever. She's studying Drama and Irish History at University. I suppose she gets the drama from Dolly. And she's beautiful lookin' too. Mind you, it's over a year since I've seen her, but Rose keeps us up to date with photos. Great they are, but then they would be, wouldn't they, it's Rose's job. Janet brought some lovely photos back from London. Would you like to see . . .

Jack Nobody told me that Janet had been in London.

Vi You're not around much these days to be told anything, Jack.

Davy *comes back into the shop. He takes a crumpled newspaper cutting out of his pocket. Signals to* **Vi**.

Vi He says, would you autograph this for him. It's you and Ian Paisley the day of the last strike on the platform at the City Hall.

Jack (*to* **Davy**) A great day. Were you there?

Vi Yes, he was there, Jack, and that's something I want to talk to you about. Davy's mother asked me if I would ask you to tell him that he's not to go to the big demonstration next Saturday.

Jack I can't do that.

Vi He's deaf. His sight's poor. He shouldn't be in a crowd like that. It's dangerous. His mother is worried sick about him. He won't heed her, but he'll do anything you say. He worships the ground you walk on.

Jack He has faith in me because of what I believe in. I can't weaken that loyalty by telling him not to go to the rally. Every good Protestant must go.

Vi Look at him, Jack. In God's name, do you need the like of him on the streets of Belfast in order to win? He has a mental age of ten.

Jack Saturday is the first anniversary of the signing of the accursed Anglo-Irish Agreement. Every loyal man woman and child must take to the streets to show the British government they will never defeat us. Never! Never! Never!

Vi He can't hear the grand speeches, Jack. He goes because the flags and the banners and the crowds excite him. The violence excites him.

Jack There will be no violence. It will be a peaceful protest.

Vi You said that last time, and look what happened.

Jack It was not our doing. The police created the violence.

Vi There was a riot, Jack. I was there. I saw it.

Jack The Catholics riot. We do not. We are a respectable people.

Davy *points proudly to the newspaper cutting. Signals.*

Vi He says that's him there, in the crowd directly in front of the platform.

Jack He must have been there early to get so near the front. You know it's said that simple people like him are truly the Children of God?

Vi Try tellin' that to his mother.

Jack God works in mysterious ways. Ours not to reason why. Don't you consider it miraculous that he can neither hear nor speak, but he knows instinctively what we're fighting for.

Vi He knows because he lip-reads the television and reads the papers. He had partial hearing until he was about ten, and before it left him entirely, his mother taught him to read. That's the miracle her love and faith worked when all them clever doctors said it was impossible. He's all she has, Jack. Please tell him not to go.

Jack God will look after him.

Dolly (*sings*)
  I don't care if it rains or freezes
  I am safe in the arms of Jesus.
  I am Jesus' little lamb.
  Yes by Jesus Christ I am

Jack *takes the newspaper cutting from* **Davy** *and signs it.* **Rose** *and* **Belle** *come into the shop.*

Rose Shop!

Vi Oh Rose, you're here! And Belle – look at you, all grown up! You're not a child any more. You're a young woman. Not too big to give your oul aunt a hug, are you?

A lot of hugging and kissing between the women. **Rose** *becomes aware of* **Jack**.

Rose Hello, Jack.

Jack Hello, Rose. How are you?

Rose I'm very well. And you?

Jack I'm well too, thanks be to God.

Rose This is my daughter Belle. Belle, this is my cousin John Horner. Jack to the family.

Belle Hello, Jack.

She half moves to shake his hand but doesn't as he just nods his head slightly to acknowledge the introduction.

Vi And this is Davy Watson, lives round the corner, gives me a hand in the shop nigh an' again.

Belle Hello, Davy.

She holds out her hand to **Davy** *who has been staring at her since she came in. He hesitantly touches her hand then shyly almost touches her face. Stops and signals to* **Vi**.

Vi (*laughs*) He's all of a dither because he's never seen nobody with dark skin before, except on the television.

Belle Is this a joke?

Rose There aren't many like you in Belfast, Belle. And those that are, are well-to-do. Restaurant owners, doctors, university lecturers, overseas students. They don't live round here.

Belle No working-class black ghettos?

Rose None.

Belle (*looking directly at* **Jack**) No prejudice?

Davy *signals to* **Vi** *again.* **Vi** *shakes her head at him and looks sideways at* **Belle***, who grins, and surprises* **Vi** *by signalling to* **Davy** *as she talks.*

Belle No Davy, I'm not from Africa. I'm from England. And my mother is from Belfast and my father is from America. I think that makes me an Anglo/Irish Yank.

Vi Now, where did you learn to do that?

Belle I have a friend who's deaf.

Vi Isn't that great? Now Davy'll have three people to talk to. You, me an' his mother. It was *her* taught *me*. (*She looks at* **Jack**.) She's a nice wee woman.

Davy *signals self-consciously to* **Belle**.

Belle Thank you, Davy. I may take you up on that.

He signals goodbye to everyone, then shakes **Belle***'s hand and leaves very quickly. He passes* **Janet** *in the street and signals to her excitedly and runs off.* **Janet** *stands for a moment outside.*

Rose What did he say?

Belle He offered to be my escort if I want to see Belfast.

Vi Hey girl, I think you've clicked there.

Jack I must go.

Rose Affairs of state Jack?

Jack Think over what I mentioned, Vi. And don't forget to tell Janet I want to talk to her. (**Rose** *and* **Vi** *exchange looks.*) I see *you* know about it.

Rose I know she's here. She phoned me.

Jack She tells everybody but not her own brother.

Rose Some things are easier discussed between women.

Jack Women! That's always been the trouble with this house. Women having secrets, whispering, gossiping.

Vi I told you, Jack, I don't know anything to gossip about.

Jack But *you* do. Don't you, Rose?

Janet *comes in. There is a strained silence.*

I'm late for a meeting. I'll talk to you later, madam.

He walks out.

Belle God, he's a bundle of laughs, isn't he?

Vi He's under a lot of strain at the moment. He's all right when you get to know him. (**Rose** *and* **Janet** *exchange looks.*) And we'll have less of the looks between you two if you don't mind. It's a long time since this family were all together under one roof, and I want it to be happy. Like the old days. No troubles.

Janet I'm sorry. This is all my fault.

Rose (*sharply*) No it's not, Janet! (*More gently.*) You have got to stop always blaming yourself when it's Jack who's at fault.

Dolly (*sings*)
In and out go the dusty bluebells
In and out go the dusty bluebells
In and out go the dusty bluebells
I'll be your master.
Tapper-rapper-rapper on her left-hand shoulder
Tapper-rapper-rapper on her left-hand shoulder
Tapper-rapper-rapper on her left-hand shoulder
I'll be your master

Scene Three

Dolly *and* **Belle** *sit turning the pages in the photo album.*

Belle Not so fast. I want you to tell me about every one of them. What age everybody is. Where you were at the time. What you were doing. I want to know all about my family. I want to know all about Ireland.

Dolly Well, I can tell you all about the family. But as for Ireland, I've lived here all my life and I still can't make head nor tail of it. Better leave that to them clever professors at your university.

Belle So many photographs.

Dolly Aye, my Joe was a dab hand with a camera. That was one of the last photos he ever took, God rest him. That's me and your mammy and Janet and Vi settin' off one August mornin' for the Dublin train. I give your mammy Joe's oul camera after he died, an' she took to it like a duck to water. Then me an' Vi bought her a good camera when she was older an' she's never looked back since.

Belle You all look so happy.

Dolly We had good times. Outin's an' parties an' sing-songs an' dressin' up, you don't know the half of it.

Belle It must be lovely being part of a big family.

Dolly You *are* part of a big family.

Belle I mean, having a big family around you all the time. A granny who lives nearby. I miss you not coming to London.

Dolly I've missed you too. You'll have to come here now and see me. I'm sure Rose misses you now you're at the university.

Belle She's all right. She has lots of friends.

Dolly Friends are not the same as family. Does she have a man?

Belle Sort of.

Dolly Oh aye. Does that mean he's married?

Belle No. It means that *he* has *his* flat and *she* has *hers*. She's an independent woman, my mother.

Dolly She always was. She takes that after me.

Belle But you ran off and got married before you were nineteen.

Dolly But I was never a housewife. My Joe never wanted that. He was a rare bird. An Ulsterman who could cook.

Pause.

Belle Did you ever meet *my* father?

Dolly Not at all. We knew nothin' about any of it till you were born an' he was back in America by then.

Belle I met him last Christmas, when mum and I were in New York. I told her I wanted to see him and she got in touch with him through some mutual friends. He arranged to meet us in a very expensive restaurant. Bought us lunch. Kept looking over his shoulder in case someone he knew might see us. He's a very respectable married man now. A pillar of a Baptist Church. He made a great point of telling me that he hadn't left my mother. I already knew all that. Rose has never lied to me about anything. I told him that now that I'd met him I could understand why she'd thrown him out. He's a sanctimonious American bible-belt prig. I bet he votes for Ronald Reagan. I asked him what he told his God about me, and he got up and walked away.

Dolly I'm sorry, child.

Belle I'm not. Now that I know what he's like, I can get on with my life knowing I haven't missed much. I didn't like him. I don't like your nephew Jack either. Does he always talk to Janet like that?

Dolly Has that skittery ghost been gettin' at Janet again? I should never have told him that she was here. I only said it to annoy him. To let him know that when Janet was in trouble it was us she come to an' not him.

Belle Why is she afraid of him?

Dolly I thought I'd put a stop to all that years ago. But maybe it was too deep ingrained by the time me and Joe got them. God knows what went on before that. Their father was a Presbyterian Minister, you know. Joe's only brother, Martin. Martin died young an' the mother took the two childer back to Scotland where she come from. An oul targe of a schoolteacher she was. You know the sort. Goes to church on Sunday, an' prays to God to give her strength to beat the kids on Monday.

Belle She beat them?

Dolly Into the ground. Not with a big stick. With words. Words like sin, the world and the devil. And the worst sins were the sinful lusts of the flesh. Jack's job as the man of the house was to protect his sister from temptation. I used to wonder how his mother and Martin ever had kids. I mean, it's not as if they were Catholic an' he could dip it in the Holy Water first. May God forgive her an' Jack for the way they scared that wee girl, for I know I never will. Do you know, the day me an' Joe arrived in Scotland to get them, I picked Janet up an' she stiffened like a ramrod. An' then she sort of crumpled up an' she cried, an' she fell asleep in my arms. Eight years old an' nobody had ever cuddled her. That's what I call a sin.

Belle And what about Jack?

Dolly Jack doesn't like bein' touched. Did ye not notice? I suppose that's why he never married.

Belle I thought perhaps it was just me he didn't want to touch.

Dolly Do ye come in for much of that? I mean, is it a bother to ye, bein' neither one thing nor the other?

Belle Only when it bothers other people.

Dolly Well, you needn't worry about round here, love. All they're interested in is what religion ye are.

Belle Do you believe in God, gran?

Dolly I believe I'll be with my Joe someday, an' I hope it'll be soon.

Belle Oh no, gran!

Dolly Ach, I don't mean right this minute, love. I'm all right for the time bein'. But I don't want to outlive my time. End up bein' kep' goin' by machines in a hospital. I have a horror of that. I can cope with not bein' able to dance with my feet no more. But I couldn't cope with not bein' able to dance in my head. I want to go under my own steam when my time comes. If you're around, will you see to that?

Very slight pause.

Belle Yes, I will.

Dolly I knew you'd say that, without a moral debate. You think straight. You see clear. Like me. Vi's too responsible, an' Rose is too romantic, an' Janet . . . Janet's fallin' to bits an' I think I know why, but I can't say till I know for sure. The rest of them think I'm a daft oul woman who can't be told certain things. But I know more about life than they'll ever know. It's got nuthin' to do with age. I was born knowin'. Like you. (*Pause.*) Will you tell me what happened to Janet in London?

Belle Yes, I will.

*She takes **Dolly**'s hands and talks quietly to her about **Janet**. In the shop **Rose** is helping **Vi** to clean and tidy.*

Vi Man, that's great. It's weeks since I had the time to give the place a proper reddin' out.

Rose Do you do much business, Vi?

Vi Not the way we used to. Since the Army closed the street to traffic, we don't get the passin' trade. An' apart from that we can't compete with the prices in the new supermarket. I've cut out most of the groceries. But we get by on the snacks, an' people comin' in for the cigarettes an' the papers an' the magazines.

Rose *has been looking at some of the magazines as she tidies the rack.*

Rose Why do you sell this stuff, Vi?

Vi It's what all the shops round here sell. It's a good local paper for local people.

Rose (*holding out a copy of* Ulster) And what about this load of racist propaganda?

Vi What are ye talkin' about? The UDA aren't against the blacks.

Rose Racism is not necessarily to do with colour, Vi.

Vi Don't you be startin' on one of your grand political speeches, Rose. You're only back five minutes. Give your tongue a rest. An' put that magazine back in its place. An' don't be creasin' them, or they won't sell, an' I'll have to pay for them.

Rose What else do you have to pay them for, Vi?

Vi What do you mean?

Rose I mean the man in the black leather jacket, who came in late last night for a sandwich. Does everybody who buys a sandwich here get a sealed envelope with it?

Vi We've always given to the Loyalist Prisoners Fund.

Rose That was no voluntary contribution in a collecting tin. That was notes by prior arrangement. How much do they make you pay, Vi?

Vi They protect the shop.

Rose From what?

Vi From vandals.

Rose You give them money and in return, they tell their vandals not to break your windows. Is that it? Or are you afraid they'll publish your name in their 'Did you know' column? (*She reads from the* Ulster Magazine.) Did you know that Paul Reilly & Sons, building contractors in Newry, employ workmen from the Irish Republic. Are these IRA spies working in your area? . . . Did you know that the new canteen manageress in the Protestant-owned firm of Spencer Brothers is a Catholic and has a brother with known terrorist links in the town? Staff and customers who have any links with the security forces – Beware!' Do you never worry, Vi, that you might sell this distorted information to a customer who'll go out of this shop and shoot an innocent canteen manageress?

Vi Don't you lecture me, Rose! It's all very fine and easy livin' in London and makin' noble decisions about what's right and what's wrong about how we live here. I'm the one who has to live here. You've been on your travels since you were seventeen. You don't even talk like us any more. Talk's cheap. And it's easy to be brave when you've somewhere safe to run.

Rose So you admit that you pay them because you're afraid.

Vi I admit nuthin'! (*Slight pause.*) I talked to the police about it. They said there was nuthin' they could do. Advised me to pay. The sergeant said 'Think of it as doin' your bit to keep the peace, Miss Horner. It's cheap at the price.'

Rose What's the going rate for intimidation? Do they give you a discount because John Horner was raised in this house?

Vi Jack has no connection with them. He's a politician.

Rose Jack's a gangster. He's well connected with the Protestant paramilitaries here, and other right-wing organizations in the United Kingdom.

Pause.

Vi Why are you here, Rose? It's not just a holiday, is it? Jack knew you were comin' before I told him.

Rose Did he now? That's interesting. But not surprising. Jack's English allies are very well informed.

Vi About what?

Short pause. **Janet** *comes into the shop from the street.*

Janet Look what I've got. Dulse and yellowman for Belle. (*Pause.*) What's the matter?

Rose Nothing that dulse and yellowman won't cure. Come on. Let's introduce my daughter to the gastronomic delights of her homeland. (*They go to* **Dolly** *and* **Belle***.*) Hey Belle, Janet's bought you a present.

Belle (*peering into the two small paper bags*) What is it?

Janet The sticky stuff is called yellowman. It's a sort of toffee.

Belle And the black stuff?

Janet It's called dulse. You'll love it. Try a bit.

Belle *eats some dulse. Splutters and coughs.*

Belle What is it?

Janet Dried seaweed.

Belle Dried seaweed!

Rose It's very good for you.

Vi Puts hairs on your chest.

Belle It's revolting!

Dolly It's an acquired taste, love. You have to start on it young. This lot were weaned on it.

Vi Have a bit of the yellowman. It'll take the taste of the salt out of your mouth.

Dolly Remember that wee shop in Dublin sold the great yellowman? We always bought some for the train journey home. Look, there's a photo of us all in the station. Laden with pruck.

Belle Pruck?

Vi Pruck. Pickin's. Smuggled goods. Did your mother never tell you that you come from a long line of customs dodgers?

Sound of a train. A British customs officer walks on. **Belle** *watches as* **Dolly**, **Vi**, **Rose** *and* **Janet** *dress up from the box. They assume position as if on a train. They eat the dulse and yellowman. The year is 1959. (***Dolly** is 50; **Vi** 30; **Rose** 9; **Janet** 9.*)

Dolly (*sings*)
    At the Oul Lammas Fair boys
    Were you ever there
    Were you ever at the fair at Ballycastleo
    Did you treat your Mary Ann
    To some dulse and yellowman
    At the oul Lammas Fair at Ballycastleo

Customs Man Anything to declare, ladies?

Dolly Ach no, son. Sure me and the wee childer have just been visitin' a sick oul aunt in Dublin. All I've got's the wee drop of whiskey she give me for my man an' a few sweets for the wains. We're allowed that without payin' the duty, aren't we?

Customs Man (*to* **Rose** *and* **Janet**) And did your poor old aunt put the sweets in those pretty little handbags?

They open the bags which contain only sweets.

Dolly (*aside to* **Vi**) The oul get. Searchin' innocent childer. (*She smiles sweetly at the* **Customs Man** *as he turns to her and* **Vi**.)

Customs Man And now you two.

They hold out their bags. He looks inside. Removes a half bottle of whiskey from **Dolly**'s *bag.*

Dolly Like I said, son. Just the half bottle.

Customs Man What about your pockets? (*They turn out their pocket linings. They are empty.*) Are you telling me that you've been to the south and haven't bought anything?

Dolly No money, son. It was as much as we could do to scrape up the spondulics for the train fares. The oul aunt wanted to see the wains before God took her.

The **Customs Man** *looks totally unconvinced.*

Rose (*quickly, to distract him*) Janet bought an ornament for our bedroom. Show him, Janet.

Janet *takes the 'ornament' out of her pocket. It is a religious statue of the Virgin Mary.*

Vi Mother of God!

Dolly (*aside to* **Vi**) She didn't know what it was, an' I hadn't the heart to tell her she couldn't have it, she was that taken by it.

Vi Jack'll go mad.

Dolly Ach, he'll never see it in the girls' bedroom.

Janet It's a pretty lady. Isn't she lovely?

The **Customs Man** *is completely distracted from his suspicions by* **Janet**'s *sweet, innocent face. He smiles at her.*

Customs Man It's very nice, dear. Have a pleasant journey.

He exists. **Dolly** *laughs delightedly.*

Dolly God. You're great, Rose, distractin' him like that. For a minute I thought he was considerin' takin' us off the train for a body search. They took my cousin Annie off the train one time. Made her take all her clothes off. Every stitch. Mortified she was. Particularly when they found the two bottles of whiskey an' the hundred John Players she'd hid in her knickers.

Vi Mother!

Janet *and* **Rose** *go to get up.*

Dolly Sit down, the pair of ye! Yer not to move one inch til we're well clear of the border. Sometimes the oul buggers start the train an' stop it again just to catch ye on.

(*The train noise starts up again. They all sit very still for a minute.*) Right! All clear!

Janet *and* **Rose** *jump to their feet and hand* **Vi** *the smuggled goods they've been sitting on.*

Rose Two bags of sugar, and a carton of cigarettes for daddy.

Janet Two bags of tea and a bottle of gin for Auntie Dolly.

Vi *gets up.*

Vi Pair of shoes for me an' two bottles of whiskey for my father.

Dolly Never mind all that. Will yous get this curtain material off me before I suffocate!

She gets to her feet and removes her dressing gown. There are layers and layers of lace curtain material wrapped round her body. **Rose** *and* **Janet** *unwind the material by dancing round* **Dolly** *as if she's a Maypole.* **Dolly** *dances and sings.*

Dolly
> Our Queen can birl her leg
> Birl her leg, birl her leg
> Our Queen can birl her leg
> Birl her leg leg leg.

All (*sing*)
> Our Queen can ate a hard bap
> Ate a hard bap, ate a hard bap
> Our Queen can ate a hard bap
> Ate a hard bap bap bap

Dolly *puts her dressing gown on again and falls exhausted back into her seat.*

Dolly Now I know how a swaddled child feels. I thought I was gonna expire with the heat. Oh dear God, I forgot about the sausages. They must be half-cooked in the perspiration.

She removes a package from her brassière.

Rose What's that, mammy?

Dolly Two poun' of Haffners sausages. Best sausages in Ireland. They're for Jack's Church Brigade Supper the marra night.

Rose Jack won't eat anything that was made in the South of Ireland.

Dolly Jack won't know where they come from. Nor how they were smuggled over the border. With any luck, they'll choke the Church Lad's Brigade.

Rose Can we tell Jack after they've eaten them, mammy?

Dolly I don't see why not, darlin'.

Vi You're a wicked woman, mother, an' stop encouragin' them wee ones to be the same.

Dolly Our Rose doesn't need any encouragin', do ye love?

The group freezes with the exception of **Janet** *who lifts the statue and dances into the shop. She sings quietly.*

Janet
    Our Queen can birl her leg
    Birl her leg birl her leg
    Our Queen . . .

She stops singing as **Jack** *as a boy of thirteen walks towards her.*

Jack What's that you've got?

Janet She's my pretty lady. I bought her in Dublin.

Jack *grabs the statue. Shouts at* **Janet**.

Jack That's no pretty lady. It's a blasphemous Popish statue. A heathen image of Christ's mother. Thou shalt not make unto thee any graven image, or any likeness of any thing that is in heaven above, or that is in the earth beneath, or that is in the water under the earth. Thou shalt not bow down thyself to them, nor serve them; for I the Lord thy God am a jealous God, visiting the iniquity of the fathers upon the children unto the third and fourth generation of them that hate me. You have sinned, Janet. You have broken the fourth commandment. You must be punished.

Janet Leave me alone. I'll tell aunt Dolly.

Jack No you won't, or God will punish you. You must repent, you must atone. You have broken His commandment. Now you must break this.

He holds out the statue.

Janet No!

Jack Then I must break it for you. I am the guardian of your faith.

He raises the statue above his head.

Janet If you hurt her I'll tell the Church Brigade about the sausages!

Jack What!

Janet Nothing.

Jack What did you say! What about the sausages?

Janet Nothing.

Jack *grabs her. Twists her arm.*

Jack Tell me! Tell me!

Janet They were from Dublin. Dolly bought them. It wasn't me! It wasn't me!

Jack Women! Women! Temptation! Deception! You're the instruments of the devil! The root of all evil!

He smashes the statue on the shop counter and scatters the pieces. Turns furiously towards **Janet**.

Janet Leave me alone! Leave me alone!

Jack *exits.* **Janet** *continues shouting. The frozen group look up. It is 1986 again.*

Dolly In the name of God, what was that! Where's Janet?

Rose I'll go.

Vi *moves to follow* **Rose** *into the shop.*

Dolly No Vi. Sit down. I want to talk to you about Janet. (*To* **Belle**.) She has to be told, Belle. This family always looks after its own, no matter what. And maybe it's Vi's common sense that's needed here as much as anything else.

Rose *finds* **Janet** *kneeling on the floor in the shop, sobbing and picking up little pieces of the broken statue.*

Janet Shattered . . . Shattered . . . Not just seven . . . twenty-seven . . . twenty-seven years' bad luck . . . the luck of the Irish . . . the luck of the devil . . .

Rose Janet.

Janet Too many little pieces. It can never be put right.

Rose *picks up a piece of broken china.*

Rose It's only a plate. One of the cheap ones Vi uses in the shop.

Janet Cheap . . . damaged goods . . . like me . . .

Rose No.

Janet Every morning I waken filled with the knowledge of him. And I think maybe I dreamt it. Maybe I made it up. But I didn't. And I don't know what to do. Tell me what to do, Rose.

Rose I don't know what you want.

Janet I want it never to have happened.

Rose Why?

Janet Sin.

Rose No. Sex.

Janet And shame.

Rose What are you ashamed of?

Janet I don't feel guilty, and I should feel guilty. I need to feel guilty.

Rose Why?

Janet There is no forgiveness without repentance. And I'm not sorry.

Rose Good.

Janet Good? I go to a party in London. I spend all that night and most of the next day in bed with a . . . a boy . . .

Rose Martin should be so flattered. He's twenty-six if he's a day.

Janet And I am thirty-six and married.

Rose To Peter Pan. You can't be worried about *him* forgiving you. He forgives everybody.

Janet I never give Peter a thought. All I think about is Martin. His face, his hair, his hands, his smell. Maybe I'm possessed. Maybe Martin is the devil my mother said was always there. Waiting at your shoulder. Fornication. Adultery. Adultery. Adultery . . .

Rose Stop it! Stop it! That's Jack talking. Not you.

Janet Ashes to ashes. Dust to dust.
If the Lord don't get you, the devil must.
Jack won't rest till he knows.

Rose There's no need for Jack to know.

Janet He'll make me tell him.

Rose You don't have to tell Jack anything. It's none of his business. He's only your brother. Not your keeper. Not your God. You don't need Jack's permission to do anything. You're a grown woman.

Janet I've been avoiding Vi. Can't look her straight in the face. What am I going to tell her?

Rose Whatever you want to tell her.

Janet I want to tell her the truth. She'll despise me.

Rose Don't be daft. She'll be a bit shocked, and then she'll get over it, and then she'll be on your side regardless of what she thinks, because you're family and the family always comes first with Vi. You know that. Remember when Belle was born? Vi was on the next plane to London. I didn't ask her to do that. She just came. Before they brought Belle in from the nursery, I said to her, 'Vi, so that it doesn't come as a bit of a shock, I think you should know that although the father's Protestant, he's not exactly what you'd call a white Anglo-Saxon.' And Vi just gave me one of her long looks and she said, 'See you, Rose? If there's an awkward way of doin' a thing, you'll find it.'

The telling of this story has relaxed **Janet**. *She manages a smile.*

Janet Does Martin care about me at all?

Rose (*carefully*) Martin, like Peter, fell in love with your innocence.

Janet And now that's gone. And so has Martin.

Rose He's married.

Janet I know. He told me. Before we went to bed. So I can't even claim I was tricked. Or seduced. I don't even feel guilty about that. It wasn't true when I said I wish it had never happened. It was everything I ever dreamt it might be. Did you love Belle's father like that?

Rose I suppose I did. At first. Don't remember it clearly any more. It's a romantic notion that first love is always an unforgettable, special, never-to-be-equalled experience. I've had better love since. What I remember most clearly about Belle's father is how inadequate and dependent he made me feel. How outraged he was when I turned down his noble offer to make an honest women of me. Admitting that it was a fucking shambles made an honest woman of me.

Janet Peter wants me to come home. I had a letter from him this morning.

Rose What do you want?

Janet Remember the little girl in the Just William stories who wanted to scream and scream and scream? (*She walks away from* **Rose**. *Talks to herself as if in a dream.*) I want what I can't have. I want it to be like it was. Like the old days in the photo album. I want Dolly to put her arms around me and sing me to sleep. And when I waken, I want Jack to have gone away for ever. And Peter too. I'm tired being the sister of a devil and the wife of a saint.

Jack *walks on stage.* **Peter** *in RUC uniform walks on from the other side.* **Janet** *is situated centre stage between them. She looks from one to the other.*

Peter (*sings*)

Green gravel, Green gravel
Your grass is so green
You're the fairest young damsel
That ever I've seen
Green gravel, Green gravel
Your true lover's dead.
So I've sent you a letter
To turn round your head
I washed her and I dressed her
And I robed her in silk
And I wrote down her name
With a glass pen and ink.
Green Gravel, Green Gravel
Your grass is so green
You're the fairest young damsel
That ever I've seen.

Jack (*quoting from St Paul*) It is good for a man not to marry. But since there is so much immorality each man should have his own wife and each woman her own husband. The husband should fulfil his marital duty to his wife, and likewise the wife to her husband. The wife's body does not belong to her alone, but also to the husband. In the same way, the husband's body does not belong to him alone but also to his wife. Do not deprive each other except by mutual consent. Then come together again so that Satan will not tempt you because of your lack of self-control. I say this as a concession, not as a command. I wish that all men were as I am.

Peter I love you. Come back to me.

Jack I love you. Come back to me.

Janet Out of the frying pan into the fire. A devil and a saint are the same thing. Afraid of women. Afraid we'll tempt you. Afraid we won't. They say there are no women in Ireland.

Only mothers and sisters and wives. I'm a sister and a wife. But I'll never be a mother. Will I, Peter? Why did you marry me? Why did I marry you? (*To* **Jack**.) Because he was everything you were not. Quiet. Gentle. Kind. After the ceremony we went to Dublin for a week. It was the one city I could be sure you wouldn't be in. But you were with me, all the way there on the train. (*To* **Peter**.) It was very late when we got to the hotel. I wanted you to take me . . . to teach me . . . I wanted to exorcize him . . . to find out that it wasn't an act of sin and shame and pain and guilt. But as soon as you touched me I turned away. And then I turned back to you and you said, 'It's been a long day. Let's go to sleep.' The next day we hired a car and drove around Dublin. When we got back to the hotel we were both very tired. You told me that there was nothing to worry about. You said lots of newly married couples didn't . . . for a while. You said there was no hurry. I felt grateful because you were so patient, so kind. It was years before I realized that you were relieved, that you didn't want . . . had never wanted . . . that you were content with things that way. (*To* **Jack**.) And I suppose I was content too. Knowing that I would never have to contend with you and Peter's mother fighting over the religion of the children of this unholy union. Peter's very fond of children. He's a community policeman. Does a lot of work with teenagers. One of them asked him once, 'Why does an Irish Catholic join a sectarian force like the Royal Ulster Constabulary?' And Peter said, 'It will always be a sectarian force if Catholics never join.' He was such a good little boy that his mother expected him to become a priest, but Peter sees his mission in life as doing something more positive towards peace and reconciliation. (*To* **Peter**.) Was marrying me part of that mission?

Peter I love you.

Janet I am not your mother! I am not your sister!

Jack I love you.

Janet I am not your virgin mother, nor your virgin wife!

Peter I love you. Come back to me.

Jack I love you. Come back to me.

Janet *throws back her head and screams.* **Rose** *runs to her. The two men exit.* **Janet** *runs past* **Rose** *to* **Dolly**. **Vi** *storms into the shop and shouts at* **Rose**.

Vi What have you and your loose-livin' English friends done to that child? Look at the state of her!

Rose She's not a child!

Vi (*indicating to where* **Dolly** *and* **Belle** *are comforting* **Janet**) You call that bein' grown-up?

Rose It's a damn sight more grown-up than living in Never Never Land!

Vi By God, you have a lot to answer for.

Rose When in doubt, always find a woman to blame. If it's answers you want, ask Peter, ask Jack!

Vi And what about this Martin? This so-called friend of yours! I suppose he has nuthin' to answer for either! A married man in no position to stand by her. The road to nowhere. And you set her on it. May God forgive you.

Dolly *sits cradling* **Janet**'s *head in her lap. She strokes* **Janet**'s *hair and sings.*

Dolly
  I know where I'm goin'
  And I know who's goin' with me
  I know who I love
  But the dear knows who I'll marry.

  I'll wear gowns of silk
  And shoes of fine green leather
  Ribbons for my hair
  And a ring for every finger.

  I know who is sick
  And I know who is sorry
  I know who I've kissed
  But God knows who I'll marry.

Act Two

Scene One

Janet sits at **Dolly**'*s feet, looking through the photo album.* **Belle** *walks on and watches* **Dolly** *and* **Janet** *from the other side of the stage.* **Dolly** *recites.*

Dolly

In a mean abode on the Shankill Road
Lived a man called William Bloat
He had a wife, the curse of his life,
Who continually got his goat.
So one day at dawn, with her nightdress on,
He cut her bloody throat.

With a razor gash he settled her hash,
Oh never was crime so quick,
But the steady drip on the pillow slip
Of her lifeblood made him sick,
And the pool of gore on the bedroom floor
Grew clotted cold and thick.

And yet he was glad that he'd done what he had,
When she lay there stiff and still.
But a sudden awe of the angry law
Struck his soul with an icy chill.
So to finish the fun so well begun,
He resolved himself to kill.

Then he took the sheet off his wife's cold feet,
And twisted it into a rope.
And he hanged himself from the pantry shelf.
'Twas an easy end, let's hope.
In the face of death with his latest breath,
He solemnly cursed the Pope.

But the strangest turn to the whole concern
Is only just beginnin'.
He went to Hell but his wife got well,
And she's still alive and sinnin',
For the razor blade was German-made,
But the sheet was Irish linen.

Belle Before I came here, I had two images of Belfast. A magical one conjured by my grandmother's songs and stories and recitations, and a disturbing one of the marches and banners and bands on the six o'clock news . . . They are both true, but not the whole truth of this bizarre and beautiful city. Belfast is surrounded by soft green hills. All its inhabitants live within walking distance of the countryside, and like village people they are inquisitive, friendly, hospitable.

Belfast must be the best-kept social secret in the British Isles . . . There was a bomb scare in Marks & Spencer's today. A voice from a loudspeaker asked the customers to evacuate the building. Nobody panicked. Nobody ran. The general feeling was one of annoyance that the shopping had been interrupted. One woman was very cross because the girl at the checkout wouldn't finish ringing through her purchases. 'It'll be another one of them hoax calls,' she said. And it was.

I wasn't frightened by the bomb scare, but I was frightened by their complacency, by their irritated acceptance that it's a normal part of everyday life, like being searched before entering the shops. The situation has existed for so long now that the people have come to accept the abnormal as normal. Armed soldiers in suburban streets. Armed police in armoured cars. An acceptable level of violence. There's a new generation of citizens who've never known it to be any other way.

I accepted Davy's offer to show me around but discovered that he has only ever been round here and the city centre. That's not peculiar to him. Belfast is not so much a city as a group of villages forming an uneasy alliance. My Aunt Vi has lived here all her life and has never set foot in West

Belfast. Injun Country. The Badlands. Her images of the
Falls Road are conjured by Nationalist songs and stories and
recitations. And the news bulletins and the rhetoric of the
Reverend Ian Paisley confirm everything she fears to be true.
She votes for the Unionist Party to keep the Republican
Party out.

Dolly (*sings*)
Will you come to our wee party will you come?
Bring your own bread and butter and a bun
You can bring a cup of tea
You can come along with me
Will you come to our wee party will you come?

Will you come to Abyssinia will you come?
Bring your own ammunition and a gun
Mussolini will be there firing bullets in the air
Will you come to Abyssinia will you come?

Belle *walks into the shop where* **Vi** *and* **Rose** *are making sandwiches
and heating sausage rolls.*

Belle I've got party poppers and paper hats.

Vi What's a party popper when it's at home?

Belle It's a sort of friendly hand grenade.

She pulls one of the poppers and covers **Vi** *with streamers.*

Vi Sometimes I wonder if we're all mad or mental in this
family.

Belle Why?

Vi Havin' a party in the middle of all these terrible goin's on
with Janet.

Belle Janet's looking forward to it.

Rose Mum always has a party on dad's birthday.

Vi Dolly has had a party every day of her life.

Belle I think it's a wonderful idea. What good does it do
him or any of us making a mournful pilgrimage to a

graveside on a cold November day. Much better to be here, reminiscing and singing and celebrating his life.

Vi It's well seein' who you take after. I tell ye, Dolly'll never be dead as long as you're alive. Come the three minute warnin' an' no doubt the pair of ye'll be organizin' a wee sing-song to pass the time till the bomb goes off. I hope you have your party piece ready. Everybody has to do a turn, you know.

Rose Except Jack. Jack only ever did a party piece once because Dolly made him, and he refused ever to do one again.

Belle Jack's been invited?

Vi Of course he has. He's one of the family, whether your mother likes it or not.

Rose He'll only be calling briefly. He has a prior engagement.

Belle Does Janet know he's coming?

Vi She has to face him sooner or later. And I told her, better sooner while the family's all here gathered round her. And I've told Jack he's not to be gettin' at her. She has to work things out for herself.

Rose You didn't tell him about . . .

Vi I did not. And I don't intend to. Least said soonest mended. He'd never understand it. *I* don't understand it. I always thought her and Peter were the happiest couple in the land. Never a cross word between them, and neither of them lookin' a day older than the day they were wed. And as for this man in London . . .

Belle Sexy Martin? What a way to lose your virginity after fifteen years of celibate marriage. (*She grins at* **Vi**'s *outraged expression.*) Aren't you glad she enjoyed it? Wouldn't it have been awful if she hadn't, after waiting all that time?

Vi I have never heard such talk from a youngster in all my life. When I was your age . . .

Belle I'm the age now that my mother was when she had me.

Vi Maybe my trouble is, I never was that age. I never remember a time when I was really young, the way children are. As soon as I was tall enough to see over the counter, Dolly kept me off school to work in the shop. I tell you, Davy can read and write better than I can.

Dolly (*sings*)
  Our wee school's a good wee school
  It's made of bricks and mortar
  And all that's wrong with our wee school's
  The baldy headed master
  He doesn't care he pulls our hair
  He goes to church on Sunday
  And prays to God to give him strength
  To beat the kids on Monday.

Janet (*as a child*) Auntie Dolly?

Dolly What darlin'?

Janet Can I stay off school tomorrow and help in the shop?

Dolly Now you know what Vi's like about you wee ones missin' your schoolin' unless you're really sick. Not that she was ever all that keen on goin' to school when she was your age. Any excuse to get stayin' at home.

Janet *coughs exaggeratedly.*

Dolly An' there's no point in tryin' it on. It might work with me but it'll never fool Vi.

Vi and **Rose** *as a child come in with plates of sandwiches and sausage rolls.* **Jack** *as a boy stands sulking in the street.*

Dolly Where's the Prophet Isaiah?

Rose He's out in the street sulkin'.

Janet He says we should be thanking God for taking Uncle Joe to heaven and not having a sinful party.

Dolly Oh, does he indeed? I'll decide how we mourn my Joe. And Jack'll do as he's bid as long as he lives in Joe's house. Vi! Away an' tell him to come in this minute and join the party.

Vi Ach, leave him alone, mother.

Rose I'll tell him.

She runs gleefully to the street to fetch **Jack**.

Vi He doesn't like parties.

Dolly He'll sing for Joe along with the rest of the family.

Rose *returns, followed very reluctantly by* **Jack**.

Dolly Right. Now that we're all assembled, how's about 'Soldier, Soldier'? My Joe loved 'Soldier, Soldier'. You can play the man, Jack.

Jack I don't know the words.

Dolly 'Course you do. You've watched the girls often enough.

Jack I don't.

Rose I'll help you.

She smiles sweetly at him. **Jack** *gives her a murderous look.*

Dolly We'll all help you. Where's the dressin'-up box, Vi?

Vi It's here.

Dolly Right. Away ye go, Janet. You be the girl.

Belle *watches the performance of the song with the photo album on her knee.* **Janet** *sings the girl's part and fetches the clothes for the soldier from the box.* **Jack**, *assisted by* **Rose**, *sullenly sings the man's part.* **Dolly** *puts the clothes on him when he looks as if he is about to refuse.* **Dolly** *and* **Vi** *and* **Rose** *sing the chorus.* **Jack** *becomes increasingly angry and humiliated as the song progresses.*

Janet
Oh soldier, soldier, won't you marry me?
With your musket, fife and drum.

Jack

Oh no sweet maid I cannot marry you
For I have no coat to put on.

Chorus

So, off she went to her grandfather's tent
And got him a coat of the very very best
She got him a coat of the very very best
And the soldier put it on.

Janet

Oh soldier, soldier, won't you marry me?
With your musket, fife and drum.

Jack

Oh no sweet maid I cannot marry you
For I have no boots to put on.

Chorus

So, off she went to her grandfather's tent
And got him some boots of the very very best
She got him some boots of the very very best
And the soldier put them on.

Janet

Oh soldier, soldier won't you marry me
With your musket, fife and drum.

Jack

Oh no sweet maid I cannot marry you
For I have no hat to put on.

Chorus

So, off she went to her grandfather's tent
And got him a hat of the very very best
She got him a hat of the very very best
And the soldier put it on.

By this stage **Jack** *looks utterly ridiculous.* **Rose** *is making faces at him behind his back.* **Vi** *is trying hard not to laugh aloud.* **Dolly** *makes no attempt to conceal her mirth.*

Janet   Oh soldier, soldier won't you marry me . . .

She dissolves into laughter. **Jack** *is almost in tears with anger and humiliation. He grabs hold of* **Janet***, shakes her, shouts.*

Jack Oh no sweet maid I cannot marry you!
For I have a wife of my own!

He runs out.

Back to the present time. **Dolly**, **Rose**, **Janet** *and* **Belle** *are laughing at the memory.* **Vi** *looks uncomfortable.*

Belle Oh, I wish I could have seen that. Isn't there a photograph of Jack dressed up?

Dolly You must be jokin'. He run out of here like a scalded cat. Wouldn't speak to any of us for days after.

Vi It wasn't really funny.

Dolly Away on with ye. Ye were laughin' as much as the rest of us. Did him the world of good. He's always been full of his own importance.

Vi It wasn't easy for him, livin' in a household of women, with no man to . . .

Dolly My Joe was around for a year after he come here to live. I never noticed Jack makin' any effort to enjoy Joe's company. Jack likes to be the *only* man. The one in charge. Thought he'd be the man of the house when Joe died. I soon put him right on that score.

Vi It's gettin' dark. I'll put up the shutters on the shop.

Rose I'll give you a hand.

Dolly An' we'll open a bottle. With any luck Jack'll not turn up an' we can all get bluttered without him sittin' there like Moses makin' the tribe feel guilty.

Vi *and* **Rose** *go to put the steel mesh shutters over the shop windows for the night.*

Rose Why do you always defend him, Vi?

Vi Somebody has to defend him. Everybody needs a friend on their side.

Rose Even when they've done what he's done to Janet?

Vi Have you ever stopped to wonder what their mother and father done to Jack?

Rose They were Janet's parents too, but she's not cruel and vindictive.

Vi You're pretty good at bein' vindictive when it comes to Jack. You never give him a chance. You never liked him from the day and hour he come her.

Rose Do *you* really like him?

Vi He was that lost and lonely, I felt heart sorry for him. Nobody liked him . . . I didn't like him either and I felt bad havin' such feelin's about a child. It's a terrible thing not to like a child. Terrible. I always tried to make it up to him.

Rose By agreeing with his mad religious politics?

Vi I've never been strong on religion, I'm all for people worshippin' as they please. But I've never had to pretend to agree with Jack's politics. I'm with him all the way on that.

Rose No you're not, Vi.

Vi We need somebody strong to speak up for us. To tell the British government that we won't be handed over to a foreign country without a fight. That we won't be patted on the head and complimented on our loyalty and patriotism through two world wars, but now it's all over, thank you very much, and your loyalty and your patriotism are an embarrassment to us and our American and European allies. We are bein' sold down the river because England doesn't need us no more. An' what we need now is somebody to shout our cause an' our rights from the rooftops. We are as much a part of Great Britain as Liverpool or Manchester or Birmingham. How would they feel if they were suddenly told that the Dublin government was to have a say in the runnin' of their country?

Rose A third of the population of Northern Ireland were denied a say in how their country should be run.

Vi I've never been opposed to the Catholics havin' their say. Doin' their part. As long as they are prepared to do it with us and not against us. But they've made their position very clear. They don't want to share power. They want to take it.

Rose And the Unionists want to hold on to it. Absolutely. They have to. They will never agree to power-sharing because they can't. Northern Ireland was created as a Protestant State for a Protestant People, and if they agree to power sharing, they'll have agreed to do away with the very reason for the state's existence. Don't you see that?

Vi And isn't the South a Catholic State for a Catholic People! You only see what suits you, Rose. And don't try to tell me it would suit you to live in a country where priests make the laws and tell you how to vote from the altar. Where things like contraception and divorce are a legal and a mortal sin. It's written into their Catholic Constitution. You're a great one for women's rights. We wouldn't have many rights in a United Ireland!

Rose We won't have many rights here either, if Jack and his gang get the Independent Ulster they want. Their right-wing Protestant Church is in total agreement with the right-wing Catholic Church on issues like divorce and abortion, on a woman's right to be anything other than a mother or a daughter or a sister or a wife. Any woman outside that set of rules is the Great Whore of Babylon. One of the first things they'll do if they get their Independent State of Ulster is vote that into their Protestant Constitution.

Vi So, the choice is the devil or the deep blue sea, is that what you're sayin'? Well, in that case I'll stay with the devil I know . . . I don't see why we have to change anything. We were all gettin' on all right before the Civil Rights started the violence. We never had no quarrel with our Catholic neighbours.

Rose There was one Catholic family in this street, and they were intimidated out in 1972.

Vi By strangers. Fly-by-nights from God knows where. Not by the neighbours. Not by us. The Doherty's lived next door for twenty years an' we all got on great. I nursed two of them kids through the measles when their mother was in the hospital havin' her veins done. And she used to come in here regular on the twelfth of July and help my father put on his Orange sash for the parade.

Rose No! That's not true, Vi. Bridie Doherty came in here *once* on the twelfth of July. It was the morning that Granny Dunbar had the stroke, and instead of you and Dolly being here as usual to dress father up for the parade, the two of you were at the hospital. Bridie came in to enquire about Granny, and there father was blundering and bellowing like a bull because he couldn't find his sash.

Vi And Bridie found it behind the sofa and put it round his neck.

Rose She lifted it up and she held it out to him. And suddenly there was a terrible awkwardness between them. She hesitated, and then she placed the sash around his neck.

Vi Like I said.

Rose There was nothing neighbourly or affectionate about it. He was afraid that if he took it out of her hands it would look as if he didn't want a Catholic handling it. And she was afraid that if she set it down again it would look like an insult. That's why she put it round his neck. And then both of them were so uncomfortable and embarrassed that Bridie left without saying a word. That's the truth of what happened. I know, because I was there. I told you that story, Vi. And over the years, you and Dolly have romanticized it into something it wasn't.

Vi Better than demeanin' it the way you're now doin'.

Rose Oh, Vi. Belfast abounds with half-baked sentimental stories like that. About the good old days and how well we all got on with our Uncle Tom Catholic neighbours. Sure we did. As long as they stayed indoors on the twelfth of July and didn't kick up a fuss when the Kick-the-Pope bands marched past their houses, beating big drums to remind them of their place here. The stories are myths. Fables. Distortions of the truth. Bridie Doherty was the best neighbour we ever had. And what did this family do when the bully boys daubed red paint on her windows and stuffed petrol-soaked rags through her letter box?

Vi We put out the fire! We brought them in here! We . . .

Rose We helped them pack and move out.

Vi Now you're distortin' the truth. We didn't want them to go. We wanted them to stay. All the neighbours did. (**Rose** *raises her eyebrows.*) Well, all except that Sinclair clan up the street. But I soon give them a piece of my mind when they started mouthin' about the Dohertys bein' in the IRA. Molly Sinclair never said nuthin' like that within earshot of me again, I can tell ye.

Rose Yet you voted for Molly Sinclair's son in the council elections. Head-the-Ball-Harry. Don't be vague. Burn a Tague.

Vi I had no choice. He was the only Unionist Candidate.

Rose You could have voted for one of the more moderate parties.

Vi What! Split the vote and let the Sinn Feiners in? The mouthpiece of bombers and murderers. Sinn Fein. Ourselves Alone. Not much hint of power-sharin' in that! Maybe you'd like to see the IRA in control of Belfast City Council.

Rose I'd like to see the people here voting for, and not against, in every election. Sooner or later, Protestant or Catholic, we have all got to take that risk.

Vi We? That's easy to say, when you don't live in the middle of it. When there's no risk of losin' your nationality, your religion, everything you've lived your life by, and believed in.

Dolly (*sings*)
In and out the windows
In and out the windows

In and out the windows
As you have done before.

Stand and face your partner
Stand and face your partner
Stand and face your partner
As you have done before.

She pulls a party popper. **Belle** *hands her a drink.*

Dolly (*sings*) Vote vote vote for Maggie Thatcher
In comes Belle at the door, io
For Belle is the one that'll have a bit of fun
And we don't want Maggie any more, io.

As she sings, **Jack** *walks into the street with* **Tom Bailey**. **Bailey**
*is middle-aged, elegantly dressed, and has a soft, cultured British
accent. He has the calm self-assurance that comes from a life of wealth
and privilege. The two men stand for a moment looking at the street and
the shop before entering.*

Jack Vi, this is Tom Bailey, the English businessman I
mentioned to you last time I was here.

Tom How do you do, Miss Horner. It's a pleasure to meet
you.

Vi How do you do, Mr Bailey.

Jack We had hoped to have a quiet word with you . . .
alone.

Vi This is my sister Rose.

There is a pause as **Rose** *looks steadily at* **Tom Bailey**. *He smiles
and acknowledges the introduction with a slight nod of his head.*

Jack I just called to let you know that I can't come to
Dolly's party. I'm taking Tom to the airport after the
meeting.

Tom My apologies for this intrusion on a family occasion. I
had hoped for the opportunity of an informal private chat,
Miss Horner, but it's obviously inconvenient. Perhaps we
could arrange to meet later. I'll be back in Belfast in a couple
of days.

Rose In time for the Anglo/Irish Protest Rally?

Tom Of course.

Rose What business have you with my sister?

Jack Private business. None of your concern.

Vi Now you just hold on a minute, Jack. I don't know what's goin' on here, but anything to do with this house is not goin' to be a dark secret between you and me. It'll be discussed properly by the whole family before any decisions are made. You're rushin' me into somethin' and I don't like it. I never intended to consider this so soon.

Rose Consider what?

Vi I mentioned to Jack one time that I had a mind to move away from here. Take Dolly to end her days somewhere nice and quiet. By the sea, maybe. You know she always loved the seaside. Not right now, but maybe in a couple of years or so when I get the pension. I didn't intend so soon . . . so quick . . .

Jack We don't have to discuss this now, Vi. We'll call again next week.

Rose Oh no you won't. There is nothing to discuss. This house is not for sale to Tom Bailey as long as I have any say in the matter.

Vi You know this man, Rose?

Rose Let me introduce you properly, Vi, to the Reverend Thomas Bailey. Formerly of the Anglican Church, until his Bishop ordered him to sever his connections with the National Front. So Thomas took a leaf from the book of another reverend, Dr Ian Paisley, and formed his own Free Church where no one had the authority to tell him that all God's children are not necessarily blue-eyed, blonde-haired and white.

Jack This is outrageous. We don't have to listen to this.

Rose No. But Vi must.

Jack My apologies, Tom. I did warn you this would happen if she was here.

Rose (*to* **Tom**) He knew I would be here. Conceit. Arrogance. You couldn't resist letting me know personally.

Vi How do you know him, Rose?

Rose We met in court when he was prosecuted under the Race Relations Act.

Unlike **Jack**, **Tom Bailey** *has remained urbane and calm throughout* **Rose**'s *outburst.*

Tom Unsuccessfully prosecuted.

Rose His wife, the Lady Elizabeth Montgomery Bailey, Q.C., got him acquitted on a legal technicality. When Mrs Bailey isn't in court defending the British right to racism she advises the Ulster Unionists at Westminster on how to break the law within the law in order to keep Northern Ireland Protestant, Orange and White. I wonder, Vi, what a well-heeled, upper-crust couple like the Baileys would be wanting with a huxtery shop and dwelling in a small street in East Belfast? It's a far cry from their luxury flat in Westminster and their rolling acres in Surrey.

Tom A purely rhetorical question, Miss Horner. Your sister and her associates are well informed about my every move.

Rose Not as well as we thought, it would seem. I knew your associates were looking for premises. I didn't know it would be *you*. I didn't know it would be *my home*. Was that *your* idea? Does the notion of operating from my family home appeal to your bizarre sense of humour? Or is it just simple vindictive revenge?

Tom You flatter yourself, Ms Horner. You are not that important. You made a minor, misguided incursion into my life once. It scarcely caused a ripple.

Vi Would somebody mind tellin' me what's goin' on here? Jack?

Jack Tom, we must be going. We'll be late.

Tom There is no hurry. The meeting cannot begin without me. And I have nothing to hide from Miss Horner. Can her sister say the same?

Rose I have never tried to hide my part in bringing the activities of you and your family to the attention of the public. In fact I'm rather proud of those photographs. Some of the best I ever took, considering the circumstances.

Tom Blurred images from a concealed camera.

Rose Not so blurred that you and those other wealthy aristocratic Fascists in Nazi uniforms couldn't be identified.

Tom A man may dress as he pleases in the privacy of his own home.

Rose But not in the privacy of mine!

Vi What has all this to do with my shop?

Rose Mr Bailey doesn't parade publicly through the streets with the National Front. He's much too refined for that. But he does provide them with advice, legal assistance, money, meeting places. They're planning to open an HQ in Belfast. A twenty-four hour service for the faithful. A shop outlet for their propaganda. Back rooms for meetings. They've been here quietly for years. Observing. Participating. One of their leaders recently described Northern Ireland as the perfect springboard for their activities in the United Kingdom. They're now confident enough to crawl out of the woodwork, and go public.

Tom I have always had confidence in the loyalty of the Protestant people of Ulster.

Rose The type of loyalty you're talking about is of *some* of the Protestant people. Not *all* of the Protestant people. And not nearly as many as Paisley claims.

Tom You are mistaken, Ms Horner. You represent a very small minority. Without support. Without power.

Jack She is also, as ever, a deceiver. Even as a child you delighted in knowing and telling other people's secrets while being close about your own. Vi asked a question and you answer it with exaggerated gossip about why Tom Bailey is here, but carefully avoid mentioning why you are here.

Vi Rose?

Rose This week I am here for the pure pleasure of being with my family. Next week I won't be going back to England with Belle. I'll be moving into the Europa Hotel to work with two colleagues, journalists, who are here investigating the links between the National Front, the British Friends of Ulster, and the Democratic Unionist Party.

Vi You were plottin' to stay on in Belfast and not say?

Rose There was no plot, Vi. I happened to have a free week when Belle was on half-term holiday, and it was a perfect opportunity to come home with her. The fact that I have a job here next week is coincidental.

Vi Oh, I see. If you hadn't happened to be free this week, you would have sneaked into a Belfast hotel next week, without even lettin' the family know you were in the city?

Rose Yes. I would. Partly because it's business and it's confidential. But mainly, because it would be too risky to work from home. John Horner may be safe in the arms of Tom Bailey, but John Horner's cousins are not safe from abusive phone calls and threatening letters and other tactics of the violence Tom Bailey funds. I couldn't risk exposing you and Dolly to the possibility of that.

Tom I would commend your concern about your family, Ms Horner, if I didn't know how willingly you have already exposed them to possible risk in your determination to discredit your cousin John Horner. However, I suppose the betrayal of one's family is a minor consideration in one so ready to betray one's country.

Rose What country would that be, Mr Bailey?

Tom England. Ulster.

Rose You are as ill-informed as most of the English about this country. This is Northern Ireland, not Ulster. Not

Donegal, Cavan and Monaghan. The so-called Ulster Unionists gave those areas with a Catholic majority to the South in 1920 in order to create and maintain their own false majority.

Tom I see you've been reading your daughter's history books. I hear she's quite an intelligent student, despite her antecedents . . . and despite a rather dangerous tendency to support somewhat suspect left-wing causes . . .

Vi (*very quietly*) Get out of this house.

Jack Vi . . .

Vi Makin' threats about Belle . . .

Jack Tom didn't intend . . .

Vi I know a threat when I hear one. Even when it's made by a well-spoken gentleman. And nobody threatens our Belle, nobody! She's my sister's child with the same ancestors as me. She's my niece and your cousin. She's family, and by the looks of things, the only grandchild this family's likely to have.

Jack She's not family! She's . . .

Rose A black bastard?

Jack If the cap fits . . .

Rose She's a blood relation of yours whether you like it or not, Jack. Or maybe first cousins once removed don't count with your chums in the National Front?

Jack Why should I be considered responsible for your ungodly fornications?

He walks out.

Rose If you're going to join the war here, Thomas Bailey, never forget that loyalty to one's immediate family will always take precedence over loyalty to the Unionist family.

Tom I'll bear that in mind.

Rose You do that. Ireland has been the death of better Englishmen than you.

He smiles and leaves unhurriedly.

Pause. **Vi** *and* **Rose** *just look at each other.*

Rose Thanks, Vi.

Vi For what! For defendin' Belle? Or for havin' the fall-out with Jack that you've been engineerin' ever since you were a child! You never could leave well alone, could you? You were an indulged brat when you were wee and you haven't changed one whit. Still stirrin' it. Always gettin' away with it. A pretty face. A clever tongue. Father always said you could charm the birds off the trees. 'Look after Rose, Vi. She's our wee flower.' He never had a pet name for me. Good old Vi. Martha to your Mary. Vi'll make the dinner while Rose is makin' daydreams. No matter what I did for him he always took it for granted. No more than was his due. God, he had it made. A wife to play-act for him. A little daughter to pet and indulge. And a dutiful dependable grown-up daughter to cook his meals and starch his shirts.

Rose Don't Vi. Don't. You always loved him so. He loved you.

Vi Aye. Because I deserved it. But he adored you regardless. *He* adored you. *Dolly* adored you. *Everybody* adored you. (*Pause.* **Rose** *is very shaken that* **Vi** *might be about to say she hated her.* **Vi** *continues more quietly.*) *I* adored you. Silly oul maid. Pushing you round the park in that great Silver Cross pram they bought when you were born. 'Nothing's too good for our Rose.' Strangers used to stop and compliment me on my beautiful baby. And I let them assume you were mine. I expect they also assumed you got your good looks from my husband. Not from a plain lump like me. I used to get into these terrible panics in case one of them would happen to come into the shop and discover that you were really my sister, and tell Dolly about my foolishness. And then she would have told father and they would have laughed together in that close way of theirs as if they were the only two people in the world.

A long pause.

Rose I'm sorry, Vi. I don't know what else to say. Except that, if you and I had never been born, they would still have been totally happy, just the two of them.

Vi I know. (*Pause.*) Why have you never got married, Rose?

Rose Why haven't you? And don't say you were never asked, because I know you were.

Vi Nosy wee bitch. I knew you were listenin' at the door. He's an assistant manager in the Ulster Bank now. If I'd played my cards right, I could be livin' in a split-level bungalow in Holywood, Co. Down.

Rose And I could be singing hymns in a Baptist Church in America.

Vi Maybe it's just as well that growin' up with the real thing made us both too choosy, eh?

Belle *comes in.*

Belle Gran says if you two don't come in this minute, she's starting the party without you.

Vi Since when did Dolly ever need the go-ahead to start a party? You go in and monitor her drink allowance, Rose. Belle, you give me a hand with the shutters.

Belle *carries the shutters outside.*

Vi Don't let her go to the rally.

Rose Don't worry. I'll talk to her later. (*Pause.*) I love you, Vi.

Vi I love you too. Even if you are the most thrawn child this family has ever known.

Vi *goes outside.*

Rose *goes to* **Dolly** *and* **Janet**.

Dolly One down. Two to go.

Rose They're putting up the shutters. They won't be a minute.

Dolly You and Vi have had enough time to put shutters round the Great Wall of China. What's been goin' on out there?

Rose Jack's been and gone. He won't be back for the party.

Dolly That's the best bit of news there's been since the Relief of Derry.

Janet Do you want a drink, Rose?

Rose Yes, please.

Dolly Here, top mine up while you're at it.

Rose Take it easy. You know what the doctor said.

Dolly You're a long time dead. Here. (*Holding out the photo album.*) Remember this one? It was the time you an' Janet got saved down in the mission hall by that buck eejit Issac Standaloft and his sister Naomi.

Janet (*to* **Rose**) Remember? We only went down in the first place because we'd heard about Naomi crossing her hands when she played the piano.

Dolly God, the way that women murdered a good tune wasn't ordinary.

Dolly *sings (badly) and mimes* **Naomi Standaloft** *playing the piano with exaggerated gestures. Sound of a piano. As* **Dolly** *sings, she becomes* **Naomi**. **Janet** *and* **Rose** *join in as ten-year-olds. They are torn between giggling and fascination at* **Naomi**'s *elaborate playing.*

Dolly/Naomi (*sings*)
  Climb climb up Sunshine Mountain
  Singing as we go.
  Climb climb up Sunshine Mountain
  Faces all aglow.
  Turn turn your back on Satan
  Look up to the sky
  Climb climb up Sunshine Mountain
  You and I.

She shouts 'all together now!' and **Rose** *and* **Janet** *sing the song and march around the room. As they finish, the preacher* **Issac Standaloft** *walks on. He is a plump, perspiring man in an ill-fitting suit. He has a north of England accent.* **Naomi** *heralds his arrival with a fanfare on the piano.* **Issac** *stands for a moment, eyes shut, a tortured expression on his face.* **Dolly/Naomi** *goes to him and comforts him.*

Issac Behold a pearl among women. My dear devoted sister Naomi. But for her faith and goodness, I, Issac Standaloft, would still be sliding down the slippery slopes, towards the fires of Hell! I was a bad child, corrupted by the unholy passions of Satan's cinemas. I became a dissipated youth who forsook his Christian home for the drinking dens of the devil and the dreadful desires of women who dance! Be not like them. The devil's voluptuous temptresses with painted faces and lacquered nails and hair dyed red with sin. Beware of the devil who lurks in the dark dance halls and hostelries and picture palaces. He wants your youth. He wants your bodies. He wants your souls. Be as Naomi. Be unadorned. Be modest. Be chaste. Be not the foul instrument of the downfall of men. Your souls belong to God. Your bodies are his temple. Only your lawful wedded husband may worship and enter therein, not for pleasure, but purely for the procreation of God's children. But first, you must cleanse that temple of the original sin of your worldly birth. Ye must be saved. Ye must be born again. You must, or you will surely face the fiery furnace and burn forever. Come on to me. Come on to me, before it is too late.

Naomi, *who has been gazing at* **Issac** *with ecstatic passion brings the two children forward.* **Issac** *embraces* **Naomi**, **Janet** *and* **Rose**. *There are sexual overtones in how he touches them.*

Issac Sing, Naomi! Sing!

Dolly/Naomi (*sings*)
  There is one thing I will not do
  I will not stand in a cinema queue

Issac and **Dolly/Naomi**
> There is one thing I will not do
> I will not stand in a cinema queue
> I ain't a gonna grieve my Lord no more

Dolly/Naomi All together now!

All
> I ain't a gonna grieve my Lord
> I ain't a gonna grieve my Lord
> I ain't a gonna grieve my Lord no more.

Issac There are two things

Dolly/Naomi There are two things

Issac I do detest

Dolly/Naomi I do detest

Issac A painted face

Dolly/Naomi A painted face

Issac And a low-backed dress

Dolly/Naomi And a low-backed dress

All
> There are two things I do detest
> A painted face and a low-backed dress
> I ain't a gonna grieve my Lord no more
> I ain't a gonna grieve my Lord
> I ain't a gonna grieve my Lord
> I ain't a gonna grieve my Lord no more.

Issac There are three things

All There are three things

Issac I will not do

All I will not do

Issac I will not gamble, smoke nor chew

All
> There are three things I will not do
> I will not gamble, smoke nor chew

I ain't a gonna grieve my Lord no more
I ain't a gonna grieve my Lord
I ain't a gonna grieve my Lord
I ain't a gonna grieve my Lord no more.

During the singing of the last chorus, **Issac** *and* **Dolly/Naomi** *dance off.* **Rose** *and* **Janet** *sit down and look pious. They sing a few bars of 'Sunshine Mountain' without much enthusiasm.* **Dolly** *returns (as herself). She takes a photo of them. She shakes her head in exasperation.*

Dolly Tell me this an' tell me no more! How long are the pair of ye plannin' to keep up this daft carry-on? I mean, I can cope with a couple of ten-year-olds not boozin' nor gamblin' nor smokin' nor frequentin' the Plaza Ballroom. But I declare to God if I hear one more chorus about climbin' up that friggin' Sunshine Mountain, it's the friggin' Sunshine Home for Wayward Girls for you two before this day's over. Now away out to the street and play with the other kids an' give my head peace.

Janet There's nobody to play with. They're all away to the pictures.

Rose (*wistfully*) It's Lassie, so it is. An' Bugs Bunny.

Dolly What time does it start?

Janet Two o'clock.

Dolly I think I'll go an' see that. He's great crack, that oul Bugs Bunny. (**Janet** *and* **Rose** *watch with mounting anguish as* **Dolly** *prepares to go.*) If I rush I'll see the comin' attractions as well. I hear *A Hundred and One Dalmatians* is on next week. Now how much money do I have on me . . . (*She looks in her purse.*) Enough for three an' a bit over for choc ices . . . pity ye can't come with me. Still, yiz can say a wee prayer for me while I'm away sinnin'.

She moves towards the door. **Janet** *and* **Rose** *look at each other.*

Rose That oul Issac Standaloft's a smelly pervert, so he is.

She runs after **Dolly**.

Janet Wait for me! Wait for me!

She runs to **Dolly** *and* **Rose**. *Dolly links a child on each arm. They exit with* **Dolly** *singing 'Onward Christian Soldiers'.*

Scene Two

The morning of the protest rally.

Vi *carries the steel shutters from outside into the shop.*

Rose *comes in from the house.*

Rose What are you doing?

Vi What does it look like I'm doin'?

Rose You're opening the shop?

Vi No. I'm takin' up weight-liftin' in my old age. Here, prop that behind the counter instead of standin' there with both your arms the same length.

Rose I thought you were supporting the strike.

Vi Well, you thought wrong. I'm in support of the protest, but I'm gettin' out of the corner they've boxed us into. 'Close your shop, an' take to the streets if you don't support The Agreement.' I will never support that agreement, never. But neither will I be a part of what they've got us involved in. Civil disobedience aided and abetted by thugs. Them's IRA tactics, an' I'll have no part of it. I've paid my rates, despite their orders not to. I've never been in debt in my life, an' I won't start now.

Rose Vi, I never intended this . . .

Vi I'm not doin' it for you. I'm doin' it for me. And well dare anybody round here suggest I'm not as loyal as the next one. I'm British, an' that's what I'll fight to stay as long as there's breath in my body. But I'll do it respectably and with dignity. I won't be associated with the dictates of criminals.

Rose I should be at home today.

Vi No. Your place is with the rest of the media who've congregated here, hopin' there's goin' to be a riot this day.

Rose I don't hope that.

Vi Maybe not. But the rest of them surely do. A peaceful protest is no news.

Belle *comes in.*

Vi What are you doin' up at this hour of the mornin'?

Belle I want to get into town early. Get near the front. See the speakers.

Rose You are not going to the rally.

Belle I am going to the rally. It's a historical happening. When I get back to college, I can tell those dusty old history lecturers that while they've been reading about it, I've been there.

Vi You can watch it on the six o'clock news. You'll get a better view. And a safer one.

Belle I'll be all right. Davy has promised to hold my hand.

Vi The blind leadin' the blind. You said you would talk to her, Rose.

Rose I did talk to her. (*To* **Belle**.) Weren't you listening to a word I said!

Belle I listened. And I've thought about it. And I want to go to the rally. I'm not afraid of the National Front.

Rose Well, I am. And I'm telling you to stay indoors today.

Belle You can't tell me what to do. I'm eighteen. And I don't live at home any more. I can fight my own battles.

Rose I have worked day and night since you were born to make sure that you've never had to fight this battle. You've never known what it's like to be hated because you are black. I have kept you safe, well clear of poor, violent streets and schools, and . . .

Belle And now you want to live my life for me?

Rose I didn't give you a life to see it destroyed on the streets of Belfast. Now, stop being silly.

Belle And you stop being so melodramatic!

Vi Hey, hey, calm down the pair of you.

Rose It's always the same. I talk to her. I'm reasonable. She's not. She just goes off quietly and does whatever it was she decided to do in the first place.

Vi I wonder who she takes that after? (*To* **Belle**.) Listen, love. We're both worried. Nobody's tryin' to lead your life for you. We just don't want you to come to no harm.

Pause.

Belle The National Front are recent arrivals here. Like me. Why have I never been in Belfast before now?

Vi It was always easier for Dolly and me to visit you than for Rose to bring a baby across the water. Dolly loved them trips.

Belle I haven't been a baby for a long time.

Rose I couldn't afford the fare. You don't remember our early days in London. The rotten rooms we lived in before I began to earn decent money.

Belle You've had a well-paid job for as long as I *can* remember, and you've taken me all over the world with you. But never to Belfast. One hour away by plane. So if it wasn't the time and it wasn't the money, what was the reason?

Rose Belle, love, what is all this about?

Belle You haven't protected me from racism, you know. No amount of money can buy immunity from that. But I've always dealt with it in my own way. Quietly. Never told you because you're always too anxious to fight on my behalf.

Rose You're my daughter.

Belle You're not black. I am. You can decide not to be a Protestant. I can't decide not to be black. I have no problem about being black. Is it a problem to you?

Rose What are you saying?

Belle I don't know. (*Pause.*) I'm saying that I'm not as concerned about political issues like the National Front as I am by the thought that you . . . this family . . . might have been embarrassed by me. Maybe still are.

Rose How could you think such a thing?

Belle I don't know. Didn't realize it was in my head until I said it. Don't look at me like that. I feel bad enough already.

Rose And so you should.

Vi Better sayin' it than harbourin' it. And she has a right to know.

Rose There's nothing to know.

Vi Oh, come on, Rose. You know as well as I do, that although we never sat down and discussed it, we came to an unspoken agreement that it would be easier all round if me and Dolly visited you and Belle instead of you comin' here and copin' with the waggin' tongues. (*To* **Belle**.) Bein' an unmarried mother was scandal enough here all them years ago, but havin' a black child was unheard of. We may say we meant it for the best, but it's not to our credit that we took the easy way out at first, and then over the years just let it go on that way. If I'm ashamed of anything, it's us. Not you. The very idea! I couldn't love you more if you were my own.

Belle (*After a small pause. Smiles*) Me too. (*A longer pause, as* **Vi** *gestures/signals with her eyes that* **Belle** *is to make her peace with her mother.*) Sorry, mum.

Rose Me too.

But there is still a small awkwardness between **Belle** *and* **Rose**.

Vi (*deadpan*) Don't strain yourselves. (*To* **Rose**.) Away you to your warm work. (*To* **Belle**.) And you can give me a hand in the shop the day.

Belle Janet's here. I could go in with *you*, mum. Then you wouldn't need to worry about me.

Rose No. This is not an outing. This is work. And I'm late. But I'm not going in until I have your promise that you won't go in on your own.

Belle It's not fair!

Rose Please, Belle. This is one crowd I don't want you standing out in.

Belle (*reluctantly*) All right.

Rose Promise?

Belle I promise. Okay?

Rose Thank you. I'll get back as soon as I can. Take care, Vi.

Vi You too.

Rose *leaves*.

Belle Do you want me to make the sandwiches?

Vi No point. Nobody'll be in to buy them.

Belle Then why bother opening? We could go in to Belfast together. I only promised mum I wouldn't go in alone.

Vi Your mother did not say, don't go in alone. She said, don't go in on your own. Meanin' off your own bat. Under your own steam. With or without company.

Belle That's not how I understood it.

Vi Oh, is it not, clever clogs? Well, the answer is still no. I've made up my mind to open the day, an' I won't be deterred. Not even by the big brown eyes of the Belle of the Belfast City. Now you just content yourself and keep an eye on the shop while I get Dolly up and dressed. I'll send Janet down to keep you company and out of mischief.

Vi *moves towards the house*.

Belle Vi?

Vi What?

Belle Are you opening the shop, making a stand, just because of me? I mean . . . would you feel so strongly about the National Front being here if I were white?

Vi After the Second World War, your grandfather sent me and Dolly to the pictures to see the newsreels of what had been goin' on in them camps in Germany. He was there, when they were liberated, you see, an' he said everybody should see what he'd seen, an' never forget it, so that it could never happen again. He was a good man. A decent man. I wish you could have known him. He would have spoilt you rotten. He would never have condoned the followers of them butchers marchin' on the streets of Belfast. And neither will I.

She goes upstairs. There is the sound of bands in the road near the street.
Belle *goes out to look.* **Davy** *comes into the street. He is wearing even more red, white and blue badges and Loyalist slogans than usual. He has an 'Ulster Says No' poster taped to the back of his coat. He signals excitedly to* **Belle***, miming the bands and telling her to come with him.*

Belle I can't, Davy . . . I promised . . . (*She hesitates, then signals.*) Hold on a minute. I'll get my coat.

She puts on a coat. Scribbles a note to **Vi***. Leaves it on the counter. She holds out her hand to* **Davy***. He smiles shyly and takes it. The noise of the bands increases. As* **Belle** *and* **Davy** *leave the street,* **Janet** *comes in to the shop. She reads the note, grabs her coat and runs after them.*

Scene Three

Late afternoon the same day. A room in Unionist Party headquarters.
Jack *stands rehearsing a speech. At first he refers occasionally to his notes but by the end of the speech he is in a state of masturbatory ecstasy.*

Jack Today, the internal feuding within the Unionist family is ended. No longer divided, we shall not fall. Strong and reunited we stand. Unafraid in the face of our common enemy. We are at war with the British government, and our ranks will never be broken again. We will never submit to the conspiracy of the Anglo-Irish Agreement. Fight the Good

Fight. Rejoice in your strength. But beware of complacency. For therein lies weakness. And weakness may be seduced by that other great conspiracy – the corruption and perfidy of Rome.

Be constantly on your guard against the satanic smells and heathen incantations that pervade the Roman Catholic Church. The descendant Church of the Semitic God Baal. Baal the Sun God. Baal the Master. Baal the Possessor. Baal the Seducer.

Guard our women. Guard our children. Lest they succumb to the insidious evil that festers and grows in our land. The phallic worship of priests in scarlet and gold. The pagan rites of black nuns. Sisters of satan. Sisters of sin. Defilers of man's.

Guard your mothers. Guard your daughters. Guard your sisters and your wives.

And may God guard us lest we weaken and yield to Unholy Desire.

Janet *comes in. There is a long pause.*

Janet They said I would find you here.

Jack I gave instructions that I was not to be disturbed.

Janet I told them I was your sister. I have to talk to you.

Jack You'll have to wait. I'm about to address a meeting.

Janet This can't wait. I need your help.

Jack So. You've come to your senses at last.

Janet It's not for me. It's for Davy.

Jack Who?

Janet Davy Watson. You've met him in the shop. He's deaf and dumb.

Jack What about him?

Janet He's been arrested and I can't find out where they've taken him.

Jack Ask your policeman.

Janet Peter's on duty. I don't know where.

Jack I've more important things to do than wander round the police stations looking for a halfwit.

Janet I'll tell Vi I asked for your help and that's what you said.

Jack Wait. Tell me what happened.

Janet He went to the rally with Belle. She was told not to go, but she was determined to see it for herself. I went after them, but there was no stopping her.

Jack Every inch her mother's daughter. Disobedient and defiant.

Janet I couldn't talk her out of it, so I went with them. On the way home, we were stopped by a crowd of kids wearing National Front T-shirts. Five boys and two girls. The girls were wearing Union Jacks around their shoulders. Like cloaks. They couldn't have been more than fourteen years old.

Jack Will you get on with it? I haven't got all night.

Janet They made a circle round Belle. Started taunting her, pushing her about, pulling her hair. Davy went berserk. Dived on them like a madman. A police patrol came along and the kids ran away. All that was left was me and Belle trying to calm Davy down. The police assumed he was attacking us, and dragged him into the Land Rover. We tried to explain to them, but they weren't interested. One of them kept shouting about a colleague who'd been injured earlier on at the City Hall. I suppose they were determined to get somebody. Anybody. Then something came through on the radio and they drove off. Belle and me have been everywhere, Jack, and nobody will give us any information. So we came here.

Jack You've brought her here?

Janet She's outside. In a taxi.

Jack Go home! I'll make some phone calls.

Janet   Belle says she's not going home without him.

Jack   Tell her to clear off from here, or I'll leave him to rot!

Janet   Can you get him out?

Jack   We still have some friends in the RUC. Influential men. Not community do-gooders like your husband.

Janet   I no longer have a husband.

Pause.

Jack   You will always have a brother.

Janet   Goodbye, Jack.

She turns to leave.

Jack   You need me!

Janet   I never needed you. I was only ever afraid of your need of me. And now I'm not afraid any more.

Jack   What are you going to do? Live out your days with that mad old woman? She's already got one foot in the grave. She won't last for ever. And Vi's not getting any younger. What'll you do when they're both gone? You'll never manage alone. You never could. You've always needed somebody to take care of you.

Janet   It's time I took care of myself. I'm going to London.

Jack   You met a man there, didn't you? Didn't you!

Janet   Yes, I did. But I'm not running back to him. I want a life of my own. My own! Nobody else's! Not his, not Peter's. Not yours. Most of all not yours. I am walking away from this violence.

Jack   I am not a violent man. I abhor violence.

Janet   You love it, Jack. You need it. It excites you. Violence is the woman you never had.

Jack   I need no woman.

Janet   Then you don't need me.

She walks away.

Jack (*shouts after her*) I have never needed you! Harlot! Whore!

Dolly (*sings*)
> Let him go let him tarry
> Let him sink or let him swim.
> He doesn't care for me
> And I don't care for him.
> He can go and get another
> That I hope he will enjoy.
> For I'm goin' to marry a far nicer boy.

Janet *walks away into Scene Four.*

Scene Four

Evening. The same day.

Dolly, **Vi**, **Rose**, **Janet** and **Belle** *in the house.*

Vi There were two of them. A young lad of about fifteen and a middle-aged man. The boy was loud-mouthed, abusive, every other word a swear word. The man was quiet spoken. Quite reasonable I suppose. In his own way. He sent the boy outside and then he talked to me about the agreement and how we all had to oppose it. When I pointed out that the organizers had promised there would be no intimidation, he said there would be no damage done to the shop, but that it would be boycotted if I didn't close. After he left I put the shutters back on the windows. Just as well, as it turned out. They started comin' back from the rally in the late afternoon. A gang of them. Singin'. Shoutin'. I thought it was stones they were throwin'. It was golf balls.

Janet They smashed in the windows of a sports shop near the city hall. They used the golf balls to attack the police. The owner of that shop is a Protestant businessman. He'd closed his premises. But that didn't deter them.

Rose They wrecked and looted about a dozen shops. They were very selective in what they stole. Alcohol. Leather jackets. Ski anoraks. I got a great photograph of one young boy walking around with a bottle of champagne in each hand and a pair of ski boots round his neck.

Dolly Maybe the UDA are plannin' to open a ski resort in the Mourne Mountains.

Belle Was that a car?

Jack walks into the street with **Davy**. *He brings him into the house.* **Davy** *is in a distressed, confused state.*

Jack I don't know where he lives, and he couldn't tell me, so I brought him here.

Belle *and* **Vi** *try to comfort* **Davy**. *But he cowers and whimpers and won't let them touch him.*

Vi In the name of God, what have they done to him?

Belle It's all right Davy, it's all right. (**Davy** *signals that she is not to come near.*) I won't touch you. I won't come near. I promise. Just talk to me. Tell me.

After a pause, **Davy** *signals and* **Belle** *interprets.*

They put me in a room. No windows. Bright light. No toilet. They laughed. They made me take my clothes off. All of them. Cold. Cold. They gave me an old blanket. Pushing. Shouting. Shoving. Bright light. Stop. Don't. Cry-baby. Cry . . . I couldn't help it. It wouldn't stop. Dirty. All over the blanket. Don't laugh . . . don't laugh . . . Don't . . . They put the blanket over my head. (**Davy** *touches his hair, looks at his hands with disgust.*) Don't touch. Don't touch . . .

He rocks back and forward, weeping.

Vi Come on, son. Come with me. It doesn't matter. It'll wash off. I'll fill a bath for you. Come on now. You don't want to be going home to your mother in that state. Don't worry. It'll all wash away, and nobody need ever know. We won't tell it. Come on, now.

She leads **Davy** *off.* **Dolly** *and* **Janet** *have been watching and listening to the story with horror.* **Rose** *has been watching* **Jack**.

Rose But you'll tell it, won't you, Jack? What a godsend to distract attention from the violence of your gangsters today. I can just see the headline. 'Brutal RUC interrogation of innocent, retarded loyalist'. A heaven-sent piece of propaganda in your favour.

Jack You think they should be allowed to get away with it?

Rose No I don't. No more than I thought they should have been allowed to get away with it when they did that and worse during the interrogation of suspected IRA terrorists. But that never bothered the Unionists at all, did it? In fact you were all for it, as long as it was being done to the Catholics, innocent or guilty.

Jack They're all guilty. Potential traitors every one.

Belle Regardless of what your motives are, I'm grateful to you for getting Davy out of there.

Jack I did it for Vi, because she cares for him and I care about her. But as for the rest of this family, you can all go to hell!

Dolly I doubt there'll be much room left down there. It must be packed out with the clergy by now. (*She grins as* **Jack** *turns angrily to leave. She chants.*) Two little sausages frying in the pan. One went pop and the other went bang.

She starts to laugh and then falls forward out of the chair. **Belle** *runs to* **Dolly**, *cradles her in her arms.*

Rose Janet! Phone for an ambulance!

Dolly No ambulance . . . no hospital . . . my own time . . .

Jack *pushes* **Belle** *aside as* **Dolly** *stops breathing. He very expertly begins to resuscitate her.*

Belle Leave her alone! Leave her alone!

Rose Belle!

She restrains **Belle** *from pulling* **Jack** *away.*

Belle Make him stop! She doesn't want this! Let her go! Let her go!

Jack She's breathing again. Put a blanket over her, keep her warm.

Belle Who taught you to do that? The Church Lads Brigade? Why couldn't you leave her alone? I promised her! I promised her! People have the right to die when they want to. When their time has come.

Jack That is for the Lord God to decide.

Belle And you're the Lord God, are you?

Jack I am the instrument of His will.

Belle So were the thumbscrews and the rack.

Janet The ambulance is on its way.

Belle I'm sorry, gran . . . I'm sorry . . .

Scene Five

A few months later. A 'sold' sign on the shop.

Dolly *sits in the wheelchair. She looks very old. Vacant. Her mouth is slightly twisted. Some knitting lies in her lap.* **Vi** *is packing things in cardboard boxes.* **Belle** *sits on a suitcase at one side of the stage.* **Rose** *and* **Janet** *stand a little way off.* **Janet** *is looking at a newspaper.*

Vi We got a fair price for the shop. Better than I expected. I suppose I should have guessed. It sold so quick. She seemed a nice young woman. Paid cash. Transpired Tom Bailey put up the money, and as soon as it was all signed, sealed and delivered, she transferred the deeds into his name. Rose says he's buyin' up property all over the town. It's one of the ways he makes his money. Buyin' cheap an' waitin' an' sellin' dear. I suppose in the end that's what it all boils down to. Property. Land, who owns what. God, would you listen to me. Next thing, I'll be votin' for the Workers' Party.

She gives **Dolly** *a drink out of a child's plastic cup with a lid and spout.*

Vi You'll love the wee house in Donaghadee. You can see the sea and the Copeland Islands and the lighthouse. And the girls are comin' over from London to help us pack up and move. It'll be just like the old days, only better . . . and you'll get better. It'll take time . . . but you will . . . (*She picks up the knitting.*) Encourage her to knit, the doctor said. It'll help to get those hands working again. You never knit nor sewed nuthin' in your life, did you mother? I suppose it's a bit late in the day to expect you to learn new tricks. (*She puts the photo album on* **Dolly***'s lap.*) Here, look at the pictures. Turn the pages. That'll do your hands and your heart more good.

Dolly *stares at the album. Slowly turns the pages.* **Davy** *comes running in. He is wearing an expensive ski anorak and waving a local magazine. He signals to* **Vi** *to look, points to a photograph, points to himself.*

Vi Calm down. Calm down. I can see it's you. I'd know that ugly mug anywhere. (*She reads.*) British barrister to represent loyalist victim of RUC brutality. I hope the Lady Elizabeth has been forewarned to advise you not to appear in court in that jacket. Fell off the back of a protest lorry, did it? How much did they sting ye for it? (**Davy** *signals.*) A tenner? Was that with or without golf balls?

Janet *reads to* **Rose** *from the newspaper.*

Janet Mr David Watson has a mental age of ten. He is deaf and mute. Mr Jack Horner announced today that he would be Mr Watson's voice in court. Mr Horner said that he had learned sign language specially to communicate with Mr Watson who is an old family friend.

Rose Suffer the little children to come unto me . . . for of such is the Kingdom of Heaven . . .

Davy *shows the magazine to* **Dolly**.

Vi He's got his photo in the magazine, and there's a write-up . . . She's not herself the day, Davy. Come back the marra and see her, eh? Maybe she'll be a bit brighter.

Davy *signals goodbye. As he leaves he makes a victory sign and then signals again.*

Vi (*to* **Dolly**) He says 'No Pope Here'. (*She shakes her head as* **Davy** *exits.*) No bloody wonder, son. No bloody wonder.

Dolly *stares at the concert hall poster.* **Belle** *sings.*

Belle
 Red brick in the suburbs, white horse on the wall
 Eyetalian marble in the City Hall
 O stranger from England, why stand so aghast?
 May the Lord in His mercy be kind to Belfast.

 This jewel that houses our hopes and our fears
 Was knocked up from the swamp in the last hundred years
 But the last shall be first and the first shall last.
 May the Lord in His mercy be kind to Belfast.

 We swore by King William there'd never be seen
 An all-Irish Parliament at College Green
 So to Stormont we're nailing the flag to the mast
 May the Lord in His mercy be kind to Belfast.

 O the bricks they will bleed and the rain it will weep
 And the damp Lagan fog lull the city to sleep
 It's to hell with the future and live on the past
 May the Lord in His mercy be kind to Belfast.

My Name,
Shall I Tell You My Name?

For my granddaughter, Josie Jennifer Christina Reid

Cast

Andy, *aged 93.*
Andrea, *his granddaughter, aged 24.*
The recorded voice of **Andrea**, *aged two to seven.*

Setting

Simultaneously, Andy in an Old People's Home in Derry,
Northern Ireland. Andrea in Holloway Prison, London. The
year is 1986.

The play was first produced in Belfast for BBC Radio 4 in
1987 with the following cast:

Andy	Louis Roulston
Andrea	Paula Hamilton
Andrea's voice as a child	Siubhan Reid and Trea Duffy

Producer Kathryn Porter

The first stage production was by the Yew Theatre
Company at the Dublin Theatre Festival in 1989, with the
following cast:

Andy	Des Braiden
Andrea	Patricia Doherty
Andrea's voice as a child	Joanne Doherty and Marie Divine

Directed by Pierre Campos
Assistant Director Yvette Campos
Lighting Design Paul Tucker

Andy and **Andrea** onstage. Apart. Remembering their life together when Andrea was a child.

Andy sits in an armchair. He has a walking stick with an ivory top. Beside his chair, on a small table, there is an old tin box and a folded, unread newspaper.

Andrea has a sketchpad and pencil. During the play, she draws her memories.

Their voices are heard reciting a poem, in 1964 when Andrea was aged two and Andy was aged seventy-one.

Andy (*V.O.*) My name, shall I tell you my . . .

Andrea (*V.O.*) Name.

Andy (*V.O.*) It's hard, but I'll . . .

Andrea (*V.O.*) Try.

Andy (*V.O.*) Sometimes I forget it, that's when I'm . . .

Andrea (*V.O.*) Shy.

Andy (*V.O.*) But I have another, I never forget. So . . .

Andrea (*V.O.*) Easy.

Andy (*V.O.*) So . . .

Andrea (*V.O.*) Pretty.

Andy (*V.O.*) And that's . . .

Andrea (*V.O.*) Granda's Pet.

Andy (*V.O.*) You're just perfect. You're my joy. The light of my life. Do you know that? Come on now. Walk. Walk to me. Don't be afraid. You can do it. It's only three little steps. And your old granda would never let you fall.

Andrea It's my earliest memory. Stumbling into his arms, sitting on his knee, mimicking the last word of each line of that poem. The love in his voice, the delight in his face . . . I was wearing a pink dress . . . with white lace, here on the

pocket and the hem . . . and he held out a biscuit to entice me
to walk to him . . . no, not like that . . . between his thumb
and forefinger. This should in truth be two drawings, not
one. I didn't learn to walk and talk all on the same day. But
that's how I remember it. Perhaps because the two events
were joined in his memory. 'I learned you to talk, and I
learned you to walk,' he used to say. 'Your old granda
learned you how to make your way in the world.' Now I talk
to my drawings. To myself. Who does he talk to now, I
wonder? Maybe he just talks. To the wall . . . to the
memories locked away in his old tin box. I wonder if he still
keeps my very first drawing there . . .

During **Andrea**'s *speech* **Andy** *has unlocked the tin box, removed
and unfolded* **Andrea**'s *first drawing.*

Andy She drew me before she drew anything else. God
knows what she's drawin' now . . .

Andrea Draw it out. Work it out. I won't cry. I mustn't
cry . . .

Andy She was always laughin'. Nuthin' daunted her. Brave
an' bright an' beautiful. The cleverest child in the street. And
the best lookin'. Her mother, my Annie, kept her spotless.
Nice wee starched frocks, white socks, shiny patent leather
shoes. The nearest thing Derry'd ever seen to Shirley
Temple, ringlets an' all. A wee beauty, if ever there was
one . . .

Andrea I was a plain child with hair as straight as a rush.
Every night, my mother wound it in cloths to make it curl.
And every morning, I had to sit still and not complain while
she teased and tortured the hair into ringlets. Then she'd tie
it all up like a bunch of sausages in a satin ribbon, and she'd
look at me, and she'd sigh, 'God, child, you must have been
far down the queue when God was handin' out the
glamour . . .'

Andy She was a picture. She must have been right at the
head of the queue when God was handin' out the good looks
. . . and the best behaviour. A chip off the old block, so she

was, just like her mother before her. She was a good child too, my Annie. The best of the bunch. The last of my daughters. It was the wife's idea to call her Annie, after me. 'It's the nearest we'll get to Andy,' she said, 'for I'm havin' no more children.' I didn't blame her. She'd had five, so she'd done her bit. Even if they were all girls . . .

Andrea I was born on his sixty-ninth birthday. His last grandchild. His only granddaughter. To please him, my mother called me Andrea. They say he didn't sober up for three days afterwards.

Andy Sure there's nuthin' to equal a wee girl. And I'm the man would know. Five daughters, and begod if they didn't all produce sons when their time come. Every time another grandson was born, the wife used to laugh an' say to me, 'That'll learn ye to complain about never havin' had no sons, Andy Smith.' An' then Andrea come along. Worth all the grandsons put together. You see, wee lads? They're never at peace. Always runnin' about an' shoutin' an' makin' a nuisance of themselves. No respect. Not like her. She never put a foot wrong. (*Small pause.*) When she was a child.

Andrea I was a right little madam. Not a bit of wonder my brothers and cousins couldn't stand me. They used to taunt me, when he wasn't around. 'Granda's Pet! Granda's Pet! Give us a lick of the Good Ship Lollipop, Shirley!' He walked in one day and caught them at it. Scattered them with his walking stick . . .

Andy Wee hallions! They'd of laughed on the other side of their faces if I'd got the houl of them. I told their mothers, you're far too soft on them boys. A bloody good hidin's what they need. My mother used to beat the livin' daylights outa me if I as much as said a word outa place. Made a man of me. That an' the Army. (*Taking an old photo from the tin box.*) Man, them were the days with the lads in France. Real men. Heroes. Ulster Protestant Orangemen. We'll never see their like again . . . Joseph Sloan, Billy Matchett, Issac Carson, Samuel Thompson, Hugh Montgomery . . .

The shared memory of these names has also come to **Andrea** *as she draws and remembers her childhood. She has been mouthing the names* **Andy** *taught her as he speaks.*

Andrea . . . Hugh Montgomery, Frederick Wilson, James Elliott, John Cunningham, Edward Marshall . . . a Litany of the Glorious Dead. Pale faces in a sepia photograph in his old tin box. Just a handful of the five and a half thousand Ulstermen who died on the first day of the Battle of the Somme. By the time it was all over, the total number of dead, British, French and German, was one-point-two million. My grandfather was one of the two survivors from our road in Derry. He went to hell and back when he was just twenty-three years old.

Andy A Glorious Victory. Their Finest Hour. An inspiration for painters and poets.

Andrea It was the first proper painting I ever saw. It hangs in the City Hall in Belfast. We went there on a train from Derry when I was about seven, to visit his eldest daughter. But his real reason for going, was that he wanted to stand with me in front of that painting . . . and teach me another poem . . .

Andy (*V.O.*) There it is. There they are. I'll read ye the inscription . . .

Andy The Battle of the Somme. Attack by the Ulster Division. First of July 1916. Presented by the Lord Mayor Alderman James Johnston and the Corporation of the City of Belfast as a gift to the citizens from the Ulster Volunteers to commemorate 'one of the greatest feats of arms in the annals of the British Army'.

Andy (*V.O.*) Now, what do ye think of that, eh?

Andrea (*V.O.*) Why is that man wearing short trousers?

Andy (*V.O.*) He's the officer.

Andrea *is drawing the painting.*

Andrea The officer is young, golden, angelic faced. A boy scout leading grown men into battle. 'Fritz' is being taken prisoner . . . top of the painting . . . more to the left . . . and another German soldier lies dying. Not there . . . bottom left . . . An Ulsterman walks away from the dying man . . . he carries a bayonet. Blood-covered. He looks . . . nothing. Blank. His eyes are wide open, but he looks blind. The officer is bathed in a golden light . . .

Andrea (*V.O.*) Why is that man wearing short trousers?

Andrea (*knowing now what she didn't know in 1969*) Because young English officers, barely trained, were posted straight to the Somme from India. They arrived wearing tropical uniforms.

Andy (*V.O.*) Can ye read the poem on the brass plate beneath the paintin'? Have a go. Go on. I'll help ye with the big words.

Andrea (*V.O.*) On Fame's . . .

Andy (*V.O.*) . . . eternal . . .

The past merges with the present. The adult **Andrea** *recites the poem.* **Andy** *interjects with the difficult words ('bivouac' in particular) as he did when the child* **Andrea** *stumbled with the pronunciation.*

Andrea
> On Fame's eternal camping ground
> Their silent tents are spread
> And Glory guards with solemn round
> The bivouac of the dead

Andy *talks as if to the child* **Andrea** *in the past on that day in the City Hall Belfast in 1969.* **Andrea** *remembers the conversation.*

Andy See that soldier there with the bayonet? Spittin' image of Billy Matchett. Poor Billy. I was one of the lucky ones. Got injured minutes after we cleared the trenches, so they found me quick. Operated on the knee before it turned septic. Billy got hit further out on the battlefield. Three days before they found him. They got him back to a hospital in England. But the oul gangrene had set in. A terrible death, they say. Better to get killed outright. Billy was the best Lambeg drummer the road had ever seen. The Orange Lodge paid for his headstone. White marble with a black soldier inset. Done him proud. Billy's son, wee Billy, took over the beatin' of the Lambeg drum when he grew up. Carryin' on the name. Carryin' on the tradition. Which is how it should be. That's what life's about, child. Knowin' who ye are, an' what ye come from. Don't you ever forget that.

Andrea   My name, shall I tell you my name . . .

Andy   And now, young Billy's dead too. Cut off in his prime, like his father before him. Second World War. Dunkirk. Still, *his* son, wee Billy, has stepped into his father's shoes. God's good, and life goes on.

Andy (*V.O.*)   When we get back to Derry, I'll take ye to see Wee Billy Matchett beatin' the Lambeg drum.

Andrea (*V.O.*)   Will he let me beat it?

Andy (*V.O.*)   Beat it? You couldn't even lift it. Sure, the drum's bigger than you are.

Sound of the beating of the Lambeg drum. **Andy** *caught in the memory.*

Andy   Go on, ye boy ye! Yer granda'll never be dead as long as you're alive! Hey, Mrs Matchett, lift our Andrea up on my shoulders so she can see your Billy better!

Andrea   Wee Billy Matchett was a huge, fat, sweaty man. The Lambeg Drum was strapped to his chest. He had been beating the drum for a long time, and his hands were bleeding. The blood trickled over the tattoos on his arms . . . Ulster is British; No Surrender; Remember the Somme/Dunkirk/the Relief of Derry. Billy's little sparrow of a wife kept darting forward with a sponge soaked in whiskey and water to cool his parched mouth and his burning face. She didn't attempt to sponge away the blood on his hands. That was sacred. I was more curious than frightened. I couldn't make sense of why the great fat man was hurting himself like that. And why was his silly little wife so pleased about it? Maybe she had him well insured, and was hoping he'd drop down dead. I was about to ask my grandfather what it was all about, when suddenly he began to sing . . .

Andy (*sings*)
We'll fight for no surrender
We'll come when duty calls
With Heart and Hand and Sword and Shield
We'll guard Old Derry's Walls

Andrea And then I understood that it was about war.

Andy When Wee Billy stopped drummin', he lifted Andrea off my shoulders an' held her up above the cheerin' crowd. I was that proud, I could hardly speak.

The child **Andrea**'*s small voice is heard amid the sound of the cheering crowd.*

Andrea (*V.O.*) Granda! Granda! There's blood on my frock!

Andrea *looks at her present-day clothes, remembering the stain.* **Andy** *smiling, remembering only the pride of the moment.*

Andrea Wee Billy Matchett dropped dead one day when he was beating the big drum before the Twelfth of July Parade. His funeral was nearly as big as the parade itself. The drum was set on the ground alongside the open grave. And Wee Billy's son, ten-year-old Little Billy, solemnly hit the drum three times as soil was sprinkled on the coffin. My grandfather patted Little Billy on the head, and said, 'You carry the name, and one day when you're older, you'll be man enough to carry the drum.' God's good, and death goes on.

A short pause. **Andy** *gets his war medals out of the old tin box.*

Andrea (*V.O.*) Can I put your medals on, granda?

Andrea (*remembering her grandfather's reply*) No, love. Medals is for men.

Andrea (*V.O.*) Why?

Andrea (*remembering the question*) Because that's the way things are, that's why. The men go off to war, and the weemin' and the children stay behind and keep the home fires burnin' till the men get back.

Andrea Since my grandmother's death, my mother had been keeping two home fires burning. For as long as I could remember she'd been running his house as well as her own. Trudging half a mile in all weathers to light his fire, do his shopping, cook his meals, because he'd stubbornly refused to accept help from the council.

Andy Strangers in your house. Pokin' around. Knowin' your business. I'll have none of that carry-on! I have five daughters. They were brought up to know where their duty lies.

Andrea His older daughters were ageing women, and had other duties. Irish husbands. Irish sons. My mother, being the youngest and the fittest, and a widow, fell for it all. She gave up trying to persuade him that he was entitled to a free Home Help and Meals-on-Wheels.

Andy Entitled! That's the trouble with the world the day. People thinkin' they're entitled to charity from the cradle to the grave. An' the ones that do the most complainin' about hard times, wouldn't know what a day's work looked like. On the sick or on the dole. They don't want to work, that's their trouble. From the day that I come back from the Great War, till the day that I retired from the Linen Mill, I never went sick once. Not even when the oul knee was that sore I could hardly walk, let alone work. I never used my war wound as an excuse to lie in my bed and live off the State.

Andrea (*V.O.*) My mammy says it's time you let the State do something for you.

Andy My country give me medals. Honoured me. I never demeaned that by lookin' for a hand-out.

Andy (*V.O.*) Tell me who else got medals. Tell me the names.

Andrea (*V.O.*) Joseph Sloan, Billy Matchett, Issac Carson, Samuel Thompson, Hugh Montgomery, Frederick Wilson, James Elliott, John Cunningham and Edward Marshall.

Andrea And Edward Reilly, the only other survivor with my grandfather. His greatest friend . . . before the war. After the war, Edward sent his medal back. They were together in the middle of the photograph, and he cut Edward out, and stuck it together again. They had their arms around each other's shoulders. Heads together. So to get rid of Edward Reilly, he had to cut himself out too.

Andrea (*V.O.*) Why aren't you in the photo, granda?

Andy (*V.O.*) (*slight hesitation because of the lie*) 'Cause I took it, that's why.

Andy Turned down his medal. Turned traitor. Canvassed for the Labour Party after the war. Made speeches against the government and the monarchy. Betrayed all the brave men who fought and died so that we could be British and free. Turncoats and Communists. Catholic throwbacks, the lot of them. What sort of a name's Reilly for a Protestant family. Intermarried way back to raise themselves out of the gutter. But it never leaves them. Popery. Bad Blood. Nationalism. Communism. Same difference.

Andrea I never knew that Edward Reilly existed until I was nearly sixteen. His grandson, Eddie, was small and dark and fierce, and looked like John Lennon. I was that lovesick, I took to wearing oriental eye make-up. I had some sort of confused notion that if I looked like Yoko Ono, Eddie would automatically fall madly in love with me. Instead, he showed me the original photograph, and told me his grandfather's version of the Battle of the Somme. How the Ulster Divisions were sent in first. High on alcohol and Ulster Protestant Pride. How they wore Orange sashes, and went over the top singing songs about the Battle of the Boyne and the Siege of Derry, as if the Catholic King James had been resurrected and was leading the German Army.

Andy Makin' mock of brave men. Just like his grandfather before him.

Andrea Eddie's grandfather mourned them. They were brave men. His friends. And he loved them. And he lay in the mud for three days, listening to Billy Matchett screaming and sobbing and moaning. He could hear Billy, and he could see him. But he couldn't help him, because his own legs were broken, and he was half-buried in an avalanche of mud and blood and bits of the bodies of Joseph Sloan, Issac Carson, Samuel Thompson, Hugh Montgomery . . .

Andrea (*V.O.*) Hugh Montgomery, Frederick Wilson, James Elliott, John Cunningham, Edward Marshall.

Andrea And Edward Reilly. Who survived and wept every time he told that story to his grandson.

Andy Like an oul woman. Nobody never seen me cry.

Sound off of a metal prison door slamming in the distance.

Andrea I won't cry. I mustn't cry. Give me some of your fierce, proud strength, granda. Did you ever cry, I wonder, when there was nobody there to see? Perhaps you didn't dare, in case you could never stop.

Andy I told her. You keep away from that skite Eddie Reilly. He's a Commie, like his oul granda. No good'll come of it.

Andrea I was dyin' to go to the bad with Eddie Reilly. I increased the oriental eye make-up and powdered my lips white.

Andy You want to have seen the state of her. Like a demented Geisha Girl with a heart disease.

Andrea I don't think Eddie ever noticed what I looked like. His passion was for talk and books. Getting at the truth. His truth, as opposed to my grandfather's. I wanted to talk of love, not war. (*Small pause.*) Nor walking sticks.

Andy 'Who paid for your walkin' stick, granda?!' I knew the minute she asked, who put her up to it.

Andrea (*V.O.*) My granda's walkin' stick has a real ivory top. The man who owned the mill bought it for my granda when he retired.

Andy Done me proud he did. Presented it to me personal.

Andrea Presented it. But didn't pay for it. The mill workers paid for it. They organized a collection, and the mill owner gave a pound towards it.

Andy Sir John was a gentleman. As was his father before him.

Andrea On the day that you retired, young Sir John descended from his carpeted office on high, and delivered a short speech about loyal workers who'd served his father and now served him.

Andy Shook me by the hand, he did. Called me one of the True Blue Breed, and wished me a long and happy retirement.

Andrea You worked your guts out in that mill for over forty years, and he gave a pound towards your retirement present.

Andy Them Reillys were always disturbers. Repeatin' hearsay. Fillin' her head full of daft nonsense.

Andrea Questioning things that mustn't be questioned. 'Who paid for your walking stick, granda?' It was the first time I ever hurt him. He flew into a rage, and then sulked for days. There was more to the story than I realized. His workmates wanted to buy him the best stick in the shop, but they were ten shillings short, so my mother made up the difference. 'He never knew the ins and outs of it,' she said. 'He just assumed Sir John bought it, and nobody never told him no different.' Of course he knew. If Eddie Reilly's granda knew, then so did mine. My mother said it wasn't a question of knowing. It was a question of pride and loyalty, and I was too young to understand the importance of these things. And how I could hurt him like that in defence of a waster like Eddie Reilly, she'd never know.

Andy She soon learned her lesson, trustin' the Reillys.

Andrea It was all over the road, before I heard it. Eddie Reilly had got the girl from the sweetshop pregnant, and they were getting married. I couldn't believe it. Doris Braithwaite was a tall, skinny, blue-eyed blonde. Not a bit

like Yoko Ono. I was that incensed, I gave Eddie back all his
big books and told him he was a rotten traitor, just like his
granda before him. I thought of destroying my John Lennon
records, but couldn't find it in my heart to go that far.
Instead, I settled for scrubbing off the black eyeliner, gave
up Socialism for Art and Drama, and got top grades in my A'
Levels. And hurt my grandfather for the second time, by
opting to go to an English university.

Andy It wasn't that I wasn't proud of her passin' all her
exams. I was the one always knew she had it in her. But I
don't see why our Queen's University in Belfast wasn't good
enough for her.

Andrea There was no Drama course at Queen's.

Andy Drama! What sort of a career's that for a respectable
girl. Floozies an' nancy-boys, the lot of them. I told her, stick
to the sums an' the writin'. Train for a proper job.

Andrea I wanted to design sets for the theatre. I wanted to
be an artist. I am an artist. I get that from you. Nobody else
in our family can draw.

Andy Like my mother said, 'You'll never make a livin'
paintin' pictures.' (*Pause.*) I was thirteen when I won the
scholarship. There was an open competition. The mill
owners set it up. You had to write a composition. Anything
to do with the linen mills. I wrote about my mother. She was
widowed young, an' after my da died, she earned her keep by
ironin' the linen handkerchiefs. An' every time she had a
hundred done, she wrapped them in brown paper, an' I took
them back to the mill an' collected the money. Anyways,
that's what I wrote about. An' I drew pictures to go along
with it. Pictures of her heatin' the irons on the stove, foldin'
the handkerchiefs. She was that neat. The handkerchiefs
looked like a bundle of rags when they come, an' they were
all crisp an' lovely when she'd finished. I loved the smell of
them handkerchiefs. Like bread bakin'. Anyways, I won. I
suppose because I was the only one drew pictures as well as
writin' the composition. There was a bit in the paper about
me. An' my mother got into a terrible state about everybody

knowin' she ironed handkerchiefs at home to make ends meet. I always thought she wrapped them in brown paper to keep them clean. But the real reason was that she didn't want people knowin' her business. She was a proud woman. The prize was a place in one of them posh schools, or ten pounds. My mother took the money. Well, she needed it. And what would I have done among all them fancy children? They give me a job in the mill as well as the ten pounds. An' I worked there till the war started, an' they took me on again when I got back. It's not that I didn't want Andrea to have her chance. It's just that London's no place for a good girl. They're not like us over there . . .

Andrea He paid my plane fare. Wouldn't hear tell of me going by boat like an immigrant. Before I left Derry, he gave me a pep talk on the dangers awaiting me on the Mainland. He seemed to think there were White Slave Traders lurking on every corner. What he didn't say was that he was hurt at me even considering that anything in England could be better than anything in Northern Ireland. It's one of those paradoxes of the Ulster Protestant Mentality – being more British than the British, but at the same time, believing that anybody leaving the Province for the Mainland if they don't have to is letting the side down. Slighting the family. Betraying the cause.

Andy I wanted her to be safe an' looked after proper. With regular meals, an' hot milk on her cornflakes. The English put cold milk on their cereal of a mornin'. God, your heart wouldn't lie in it. I fixed her up with a room at Freda Sloan's. I knew Freda would see her right.

Andrea Walking into Freda's house was like stepping back into his. There they were, framed above the fireplace. Her dead husband's dead father Joseph Sloan and Issac Carson and . . .

Andrea (*V.O.*) Samuel Thompson, Hugh Montgomery, Frederick Wilson, James Elliott, John Cunningham and Edward Marshall.

Andrea And my grandfather. The Sloans hadn't cut their photo, they'd blanked out Edward Reilly's face. Freda and Joe Sloan hadn't left Derry. They'd brought it to London with them. Freda was kind and strict and interfering. Like a well-intentioned warder in an open prison. (*The metal door slams and echoes in the distance again.*) You can run away from an open prison . . .

Andy *has taken a bundle of postcards out of the tin box.*

Andy Dear granda, I'm sorry if I've upset you and Freda by moving out . . .

Andrea (*quoting from the postcard*) I know she was good to me, and I did thank her, but she lives miles away from the university. It was costing me a fortune in tube fares, and making me late for lectures . . .

Andy . . . The house I'm in now is very nice. I share it with five other students . . . we're all doing the same course so we can buy the books between us and save money . . .

Andrea . . . I'm very happy. Don't worry so about me . . .

Andy I know it's natural that they grow up and find their way in the world. But at least if they do it near home, they can visit ye regular. England's awful far away. It's not as if you can put your foot on the bus or the train and come home for an hour or two . . .

Andrea Dear granda. Yes, I'm working hard, and eating properly, and getting plenty of sleep. Thanks for the postal order. Do you mind if I buy a sweatshirt with it, instead of a hat and gloves?

Andy Dear granda, thanks for the letter and the fiver. I bought a book about war poetry. We're doing an . . . improvised play . . . about war through the eyes of the writers of the time . . .

Andrea . . . No, I won't be able to get to the Cenotaph to see the big Armistice Day Parade. I have a lot of essays to write, and it'll take me all weekend . . .

Andy . . . I'll be thinking of you in the Derry Parade. Heaps of love . . .

Andrea I spent the entire weekend in bed with my new landlord. Hanif, Hanif . . . oh my love, are you thinking of me? Remember that first weekend together. Remember. We sat in bed on the Sunday morning, eating chocolate and reading war poetry for the Monday tutorial. Church bells were ringing. And you laughed when I told you that my grandfather, if he knew, would call you a white-slave-trader. The poem was among some stuff you'd photocopied in the British Library . . .

Andrea (*V.O.*)
  On Fame's eternal camping ground
  Their silent tents are spread
  And Glory guards with solemn round
  The bivouac of the dead

Andrea *Poems of American Patriotism.* It's not about the Somme at all. It's about the American war with Mexico. Written in 1847 by Theodora O'Hara to commemorate the bringing home of the bodies of the Kentucky soldiers who fell at Buena Vista, and were buried at Frankfort at the cost of the State. 1847. 1916. I expect it's much the same, no matter what war you die in . . .

Andy Army trainin' keeps you fit. Stands you in good stead for the rest of your days. All my daughters dead and gone, and here's me, ninety-three years old, an' still goin' strong. There's ones in this place only seventy-odd, an' they're never out of their beds. You have to keep on your feet or you get old before your time.

Andrea I went home for my mother's funeral. Afterwards, he told me he'd been offered a place in an Old People's Home nearby. He didn't ask me to stay and look after him. But it was there, unspoken, between us. I felt guilty for not offering. For wanting to be with Hanif more than I wanted to be with him.

Andy I don't mind it here. It's clean an' orderly an' meals regular as clockwork. I'm not sayin' it's like bein' in your own wee house, but sure nuthin' ever is. My grandsons is mostly scattered all over the globe. No jobs, no prospects for them here. The two that did stay in Derry, visit the odd time. Christmas, Easter, that sort of thing. I have great-grandchildren in Canada and Australia that I've never seen at all. All wee lads. No great-granddaughters.

Andrea I went back to visit him once. It was the last time I ever saw him. I went specially to tell him . . . to tell him . . . it was four years ago. 1982. The day after the sinking of the Belgrano.

She walks across to **Andy** *in the old people's home.*

Andy Haven't you picked a grand day to come home. Isn't it great news? Britain rules the waves again. By God, if Maggie'd been Prime Minister when that scum rose up out of the Bogside, the Troubles would have been over in a day. She'd have sailed the big gunboats into Derry the way she did to the Falklands, an' wiped the Fenians off the face of the earth. I admit I was a bit took back when the Tories elected a woman. But Maggie's a good 'un. The equal of any man. What I wouldn't give to be a young man again. Fightin' fit an' rarin' to go. But no matter. Maggie has two of my grandsons, carryin' on the tradition. Carryin' on the name. I'll bet your English friends are real proud of you havin' a brother and a cousin in the Falklands. Have you heard from either of them?

Andrea I went to see them in Southampton before they sailed. They looked so young.

Andy No younger than me, when I went to war. They'll be men when they come back. What about a wee drink to celebrate? (*Takes a quarter-bottle of whiskey out of the tin box.*)

Andrea Not for me, thanks.

Andy It'll put a bit of colour in your cheeks. You're lookin' dwamy. Is there anything wrong with ye?

Andrea I've come home specially to tell you something . . .

Andy Are you in some sort of bother?

Andrea I'm getting married. I'm having a baby. I want . . . I need your blessing . . .

Andy You're only a child yourself.

Andrea I'm twenty. He's twenty-two. I wanted to tell you first, before anybody else in the family. I don't care what my brothers or my cousins think, but I don't want you thinking bad of me . . .

Andy Ach, child, you never had a bad bone in your body. Don't upset yourself on my account.

Andrea I was so afraid you'd be angry. I thought you might disown me. All the way over on the plane, I kept rehearsing what I would say. I didn't intend to blurt it out like that.

Andy Is he a good man? Is he fond of you?

Andrea Yes.

Andy Well then, that's all that matters. An' he must be a decent man, doin' the right thing by you. Though, mind you, he should of come with you. Not sent you to face the music on your own.

Andrea He couldn't come. He's in hospital. He'll be all right soon. He got beaten up, you see. A gang of skinheads broke into the house one night when he was there by himself. He was studying, and he hadn't pulled the curtains. It was dark outside. They could see him, but he didn't see them . . . until they . . .

Andy Why would anybody want to do the like of that?

Andrea They were drunk. They'd been out celebrating the English Fleet sailing from the Falklands.

Andy Rabble! Too cowardly to join up and do some proper fightin'. Was your man badly hurt?

Andrea Yes. Yes he was. But he's over the worst. As soon as he comes home we're getting married.

Andy You'll need money. I've got a wee bit put by. It's left to you. You might as well have it now.

Andrea There's no need. We have a safe roof over our heads. His father owns the house we live in. And one of the other students is moving out soon, so we're going to turn her room into a nursery.

Andy You'll still need cash. Babies cost money. I'll arrange it. It's not a fortune, mind. But it's yours. His father owns the house, you say? And doesn't need to live in it? Must be a well-to-do family.

Andrea His father's an accountant. His mother lectures at the university.

Andy You're movin' up in the world. Don't be forgettin' what ye come from.

Andrea Don't be daft.

Andy It happens.

Andrea They're nice people. Hanif's never been short of a bob or two, but he's no snob . . . Oh God . . .

A pause.

Andy What the hell sort of a name is that?

Andrea I meant to tell you that part of it slowly, too . . . (*Takes a photo out of her pocket.*) Look, this is Hanif. It was taken outside his parents' house. Isn't it lovely? They live in the country . . .

Andy He's an Argy!

Andrea He's British. His father's from Bristol. His mother was born in Pakistan . . .

Andy (*quietly*) Get out of my sight.

Andrea Granda . . .

Andy Get out of my sight!

Andrea Granda . . .

Andy A half-caste! A nig–nog!

Andrea Don't . . .

Andy Get rid of it.

Andrea No . . .

Andy Get rid of it! I'll have none of that carry-on in my family!

Andrea No!

Andy You have a name to upkeep! We are respected in this town!

Andrea Please . . . talk to me. Listen to me . . . don't . . .

Andy Don't you ever come back here. Do you hear me? Get back to England and keep your black bastard there with you!

Andrea (*more in distress than in anger*) You're the black bastard, you stupid, bigoted old man!

Andy *raises his walking stick as if to strike her.* **Andrea** *runs away, back to the London area of the stage. As she runs, sounds of another metal prison door closing. Closer this time.*

Andrea I mustn't cry. I mustn't cry. Don't draw his face. No more of his face. Draw my Annie. Golden and beautiful like her father. What are you doing today, little love? In the country, being spoiled rotten by your doting grandfather. My grandfather will have been awake since daybreak. It's the seventieth anniversary of the Battle of the Somme today. He'll have made his own bed. It's the only domestic thing he ever could do, making his own bed. They taught him that in the Army. He'll be sitting, waiting for the British Legion car to collect him for the parade. Oh God, please let him have this day. Don't let him read the papers. That press photographer was from Derry. He went to school with my brother. He recognized me. I know he did.

Andy *has opened the folded newspaper.*

Andy Derry girl arrested at Greenham Common. Conchie! Trollop! Traitor! If you were here in this room, I would kill you with my own two hands!

Andrea Sometimes I wish they'd killed Hanif outright, and not left me to live with a stranger. I don't really mean that, Annie. I love your father. No . . . I love what he was. Gentle,

tender, easy-going, full of fun. I hate what he has become. I
hate it. I live with a stranger. When he's at home. His injuries
healed. But he didn't. When you were born, the panic
attacks got worse. He put padlocks on the doors and the
windows. He said they were watching the house. He said
they were going to kill us all. There was never anybody there.
I feel guilty every time I have to take him back into that
hospital. Even though I know he's happier there than he is at
home with you and me. He feels safe there, you see. How can
he feel safe with them and not with me!? And how can my
grandfather hate me now, having loved me all those years!?
There's no rhyme nor reason to love, Annie. I never wanted
Hanif to change, and he did. And I hoped my grandfather
would change, and he never will.

Andy I'll go to the Somme Parade the day. Wear my medals
with pride. Hold my head high, despite what she has done.
And well dare anybody mention her name in the same breath
as mine. My loyalty has never been in question. I have always
fought for what is right. I wore these medals the day I joined
Carson's army, after the Great War. We beat the English
Government then, and we'll beat them this time round too.
Anglo-Irish Agreement be damned! Lloyd George couldn't
defeat us in 1920, and Maggie Thatcher won't defeat us in
1986. Carson may be dead, but his spirit, never!

Andrea (*V.O.*) (*sings, to the tune of Yankee Doodle*)
    Sir Edward Carson had a cat
    It sat upon the fender
    And every time it caught a rat
    It shouted no surrender

Andrea Edward Carson. The English lawyer whose
rhetoric rallied the Ulster Protestants to fight the Home Rule
Bill. The English lawyer who prosecuted Oscar Wilde.

Andrea (*V.O.*) My granda cut his thumb with a pocket-
knife and signed the Ulster Covenant with his own blood.

Andrea Maybe I'll sign these drawings, 'The Ballad of
Holloway Gaol'. No, that would be giving myself an
importance I don't deserve. I'm not like the other women

who were arrested at Greenham. I'm not a campaigner, a fighter for what is right. I've never been that brave. I was brought up in a city with armed police and soldiers on the streets, and I never questioned it. I don't remember Derry without barbed wire. Checkpoints. The war was always there, a part of everyday life. Going shopping and getting frisked by Security Forces in Security Zones. For our own protection. An acceptable level of violence. I didn't go to Greenham Common to protest about a lethal Security Zone. Nothing as noble as that. Hanif had gone back into hospital, and his parents had taken Annie down to the country, and I was feeling sorry for myself. And Hanif's sister said, 'Do something positive. Come to Greenham with me for the weekend.' So I did. Because I had nothing better to do. I hated it. Campfires and mud. I've always liked my home comforts. I wandered down to the main gate because I was miserable and bored . . . and curious. And there they were. All those women, sitting in the road in front of a bloody great Army vehicle. And they were singing. I thought it was silly. I even felt a bit embarrassed on their behalf. And then the riot squad moved in. There was no riot till they created it. I just stood there, on the edge of it all, watching. And then this elderly woman sat down beside me. She was carrying a cake. A daft chocolate cake and a box of white candles. And she put three of them on the cake and lit them, and she said, 'One for my nephew crippled in the Falklands. One for my lover killed at Dunkirk. One for my father shellshocked at the Battle of the Somme.' And then she got up, and she walked towards the riot at the main gate. She left the cake and the candles behind. Like a light burning in a window. A policeman dragged her into the back of a wagon. She was at least sixty years old. I lit twelve more candles. Held them in a bunch in my hand, and walked towards the policeman. It was as if we were the only two people in the world. I held out the candles, and I said to him, 'These are for Joseph Sloan and Billy Matchett and Issac Carson and Samuel Thompson and Hugh Montgomery and Frederick Wilson and James Elliott and John Cunningham and Edward Marshall and . . .'

And when he heard my accent, he called me a stupid IRA cunt and threw me into the back of the wagon. The candles were lost in the mud. The other three candles were for Edward Reilly and my grandfather and Hanif. But I didn't get to say their names. (*Sounds off of* **Andrea**'s *cell door being unlocked.*) Perhaps I'll say it in court.

As **Andrea** *looks/moves towards the direction of the cell door, a military band is heard playing at the Somme Commemoration Parade in Derry. Also marching feet and crowds cheering. The band plays 'Marching through Georgia'.* **Andy** *is on his feet. He sings along with the band when it reaches the chorus.*

Andy (*sings*) We are, we are, we are the Billy Boys!
 We are, we are, we are the Billy Boys!

The band music plays on as **Andrea** *shouts at an unseen prison warder.*

Andrea You have no right to do this again! No right! No, it's not normal procedure! It's harrassment! How could I have hidden anything? I was strip-searched when I was brought here. I haven't been anywhere else. What could I have hidden? Don't . . . please, my period's started . . .

Andy (*sings*) We are, we are, we are the Billy Boys!
 We are, we are, we are the Billy Boys!

Andrea (*V.O.*) Granda! Granda! There's blood on my frock!

The noise of the band and the marching feet and the crowds dies away.

Andy *is now back in the old people's home in Derry.* **Andrea** *is back in her prison cell after her court appearance.*

Andrea I didn't cry in court, but I didn't make a heroic defence either. I just told them my name, and refused to promise to be a good little girl and keep the peace. So, I'm a guest of Her Majesty for the next three weeks. It was the chocolate-cake lady's third offence. The magistrate asked why a woman of her age and class persisted in breaking the law. And she said, 'Because I want my grandson to die of old age, that's why.' They've sent her to see a psychiatrist. When we were arrested, she advised me to concentrate on someone

I loved, to give me comfort. To give me strength. I close my eyes and try to picture Annie, or Hanif, or my mother. But my heart and my hands reach out for him, and I draw his face over and over again . . .

Andy *is looking at the drawing of himself that* **Andrea** *did on her first day at school.*

Andy (*V.O.*) What's this?

Andrea (*V.O.*) It's you, granda. It's you.

Andy (*V.O.*) So it is. So it is.

Andrea (*V.O.*) And I said our poem for the teacher, all by myself.

Andy (*V.O.*) You never did.

Andrea (*V.O.*) (*recites without faltering*)
    My name, shall I tell you my name
    It's hard, but I'll try
    Sometimes I forget it
    That's when I'm shy
    But I have another
    I never forget
    So easy
    So pretty
    And that's Granda's Pet.

Andrea For four years now, you haven't answered any of my letters. Do you throw them away unopened? Or do you lock them away with the medals and the photos and the memories in the old tin box? I miss you. I need you. I need to make my peace with you. I love you in a way that I've never loved anyone else. I love you, even though I have grown to loathe everything you believe in. How can I make you understand that, when I don't understand it myself? You must have moments of doubt. You must have. You're stubborn and you're proud, but you're not a fool. Loyalty. Patriotism. Them or Us. You daren't question what all that has done to you, because once you question even a small part of it, you end up questioning it all. And to do that, would be to negate your whole life. Everything you've lived and survived by. I wonder if you're ever afraid. I wonder what you're doing now. I wonder if you ever think of me . . .

Andy Brave an' bright an' beautiful. The cleverest child in the street. A good girl ruined by bad company. Not her fault alone. Sure, a woman's only as good as the bed she lies in, and even the best of women can be led astray by the wrong man. I wonder, did she ever get to design a set for a play? I suppose she draws different pictures now. But she drew me before she drew anything else. And that's somethin' nobody and nuthin' can take away from me.

Andrea They say that one Christmas Day, during the First World War, a group of British and German soldiers called a halt to the fighting, and declared a truce. Just for an hour. There must be an hour, a place, where he and I can meet. A piece of common ground. A no man's land. If it's possible for strangers, then it's possible for us. Or maybe it's easier to declare a truce with someone when you don't bear their name, or their face . . .

Andy I walked in the Somme Parade the day. Done the heroes proud. Held my head high, despite what she has done. The Legion collected and brung me back in a big car. Every year. Regular as clockwork. They always look after their own. An' they're gettin' my picture painted. They're gonna hang it up in the Legion Hall. I'm the only one left from the Great War, and they want to honour me. I used to draw pictures myself. But I never kept it up, an' I lost the way of it. I won a prize once, but it was a long time ago . . . a long time ago . . .

Andrea (*V.O.*) (*sings to the tune of 'Yankee Doodle Dandy'*)
  Sir Edward Carson had a cat
  It sat upon the fender
  And every time it caught a rat
  It shouted no surrender . . .

The child singing merges into the sound of a military flute band playing 'Yankee Doodle Dandy'.

Clowns

A sequel to Joyriders

For Marta and Michael Quinn

Clowns *was first performed in The Room at the Orange Tree, Richmond on 21 March, 1996, with the following cast:*

Arthur	Peter Kenny
Sandra	Caroline Lennon
Maureen	Lesley McGuire
Tommy	Conor Moloney
Iris	Nell Murphy
Johnnie	Justin Oates
Molly	Colette O'Neill

Director Natasha Betteridge
Designer Ruth Wilson
Lighting/Sound Design Fiona Kemp
Choreographer Victoria Buttress

Cast
Sandra, *aged 24/25.*
Maureen, *aged 16/17.*
Arthur, *aged 25/26.*
Tommy, *aged 25/26.*
Johnnie, *aged 20.*
Molly, *aged 56.*
Iris, *aged 24/25.*

Sandra, Maureen, Arthur and Tommy were all characters in the play *Joyriders* (1986). *Clowns* is set in the same location in 1994.

Setting
The Lagan Mill Shopping Centre, Belfast – a conversion of the old linen mill which housed the Youth Training Programme which was the setting for *Joyriders*. Now, eight years on, the mill has been modernized into open-plan shops, offices, etc., facing into central walkways/seating areas.

Onstage
The action takes place in part of the ground floor of the shopping centre. This consists mainly of an open concourse where shoppers can look/walk/sit/snack. There is a romantic statue of a 1930s female mill worker and child. (Ragged,

starving, noble). They stand in a fountain, surrounded by plants which have been arranged to create the colours of a rainbow – red, orange, yellow, green, blue, indigo, violet.

Backstage and stage right: an entrance (open) to THE HARLEQUIN CAFÉ–BAR, and an entrance (shuttered) to THE IRIS GARDEN CENTRE.

Stage left: the base of a (moving?) staircase leading to the unseen upper floors.

A shadowy area where Maureen appears and disappears.

A microphone on a stand at the edge of the stage.

Everything is so new, you can smell the paint drying.

Act One

Belfast: August 1994.

The eve of the IRA cease-fire.

Stage in darkness.

Sound of D:Ream singing 'Things Can Only Get Better'.

As the slow introductory verse ends and the music increases in speed and volume, moving lights illuminate **Johnnie**, *who is dancing.*

Johnnie *is a young hood. He wears a top with a Destroy logo, Levi jeans and Timberland or Caterpillar boots. All very new, very clean. His blond, curly hair is cut short. He has the look of a fallen angel.*

Johnnie *enjoys dancing. He is good at it, and knows it. He performs and mimes some of the words of the song as if he is the singer. There is a sense that he is showing-off at a crowded rave/club, until the lights rise on the set, and we see that he is alone in a shopping mall, dancing to music from a Walkman.*

Simultaneously, the music fades to the barely audible, tinny rhythm escaping from his earphones.

Without sound, **Johnnie**'s *class act now looks ludicrous.*

He dances/sings on, oblivious to the fact that **Arthur** *has entered, has been watching him, and is now creeping up behind him.*

Arthur *is wearing upmarket casual Next or Gap-type clothes.*

As in Joyriders, *he has no hair because of head injuries from an accidental shooting. (His facial scars have faded, and he no longer limps.)*

Arthur *grins and sticks his finger in* **Johnnie**'s *back.*

Arthur Got ye!

Johnnie's *genuine terror quickly turns to humilated anger.*

Johnnie That's not friggin' funny, Arthur!

Arthur You thought it was real.

Johnnie I never.

Arthur You friggin' did.

Johnnie I never! All right?

Arthur All right Johnnie.

Johnnie All right.

Arthur What are ye doin' here . . . apart from kiddin' yerself you're Olivia Newton John?

Johnnie Who?

Arthur We don't open till the weekend.

Johnnie I'm lookin' for Tommy.

Arthur What for?

Johnnie He owes me money.

Arthur Join the queue.

Johnnie You can afford it. I need it now.

A look from **Arthur** *as he picks up on a sense of fear/vulnerability from* **Johnnie**. **Johnnie** *quickly covers his anxiety by putting on a pair of fake Ray-Bans. He walks casually towards the exit.*

Arthur Left the dog an' the white stick at the door, did ye?

Johnnie If you see your friend Tommy, tell him from me his credit's run out.

Arthur If you see your friend Tommy, tell him from me he's fired.

As **Johnnie** *exits,* **Tommy***'s voice is heard from behind the statue.*

Tommy Fine fuckin' friend you are.

He emerges from his hiding place.

Tommy, *the former teenage communist, is now a socialist 'crusty'. He wears non-designer grunge/hippy clothing – layers of old, well-worn clothes in grubby-looking, muddy colours. Everything he is*

*wearing has been borrowed or stolen. Typical outfit: long black or
striped big-knit sweater over sweatshirt with cut-off neck. Black,
baggy, army-type trousers with pockets on the sides. Woolly hat with
Soviet logo. DM boots. Dreadlocks and stubble.*

There is rarely any real anger or malice in the banter between
Tommy *and* **Arthur***. Although they're poles apart in outlook and
temperament, they've been friends/sparring partners since childhood.*

Arthur What are you doin' lurkin' in there?

Tommy Keepin' out of the way of Johnnie the Jig.

Arthur Are you out of your mind or what, buyin' stuff from
that skittery hood?!

Tommy Nuthin' serious. Only a wee bit of dope that
happened to come his way. Johnnie's in bad trouble if he's
havin' to come after me for the few pound I owe him. Drop in
the ocean compared to what he rakes in at the raves. Word
has it he's . . .

Arthur I don't wanta know about it. You see if I catch him
selling them shite pills near me or mine? I'll break every bone
in his body . . .

Tommy What are ye like, Arthur?

Arthur What do ye mean?

Tommy All them years of spoutin' 'Give Peace a Chance'
and here ye are threatenin' Johnnie with grievous bodily
harm on the eve of the fuckin' cease-fire . . .

Arthur You owe me a fiver!

Tommy What?

Arthur You bet me there'd be no cease-fire this century . . .
(*Holds out his hand for the money.*)

Tommy It's not midnight yet. (*Puts on an Ian Paisley voice.*)
And nowhere, in Mr Adams statement, do I hear the word
'permanent'.

Arthur Paisley's gutted. And so are you. Yous both got it wrong, an' Arthur got it right. Keep yer fiver. It's cheap at the price . . . did ye bring the van round?

Tommy Aye.

Arthur Did ye pick up the paintin' on the way?

Tommy *produces a painting from behind the statue. It's a seriously bad amateur attempt at Picasso-style art.*

Tommy Are you sure they framed it the right way up?

Arthur That's a prizewinnin' work of art you're slaggin'. I paid good money for that at the community auction.

Tommy They seen you comin'.

Arthur It's an investment.

Tommy It's a bollocks. I could have painted better myself.

Arthur Ye had your chance. It was an open competition.

Tommy I have better things to do with my time than paint stupid pictures for stupid competitions for the openin' of stupid friggin' supermarkets. You can not be serious about hangin' this in your new caff.

Arthur Continental café–wine bar. And this is not a supermarket, ye ignoramus, it's a hi-tech shopping complex.

Tommy There's nuthin' complex about it, Rockefeller. It's the simplest way in the world for owners like you to con back whatever money you've let workers like me earn in the first place.

Arthur You're not a worker no more. You're fired.

Tommy Frig's sake Arthur, I haven't started yet.

Arthur You should have been here an hour ago.

Tommy Why, what happened? . . . Is there any beer in the fridge? I'm parched. See that paintin'? It weighs ten ton.

Tommy *strolls into the café–bar and out of sight.* **Arthur** *calls after him.*

Arthur And a glass of the Beaujolais for the owner! And don't bother fillin' your pockets with pockets of fegs! They're counted!

Arthur *looks at the painting, no longer sure about his investment. Turns it upside-down and has another look.*

He turns to see **Tommy***'s grinning face peering out from the café–bar.* **Arthur** *makes a rude sign at him. Lifts the painting and carries it into the café–bar.*

As **Arthur** *and* **Tommy** *disappear from view,* **Sandra** *enters.*

She is wearing a long jacket, leggings and biker boots. A bag over her shoulder. She looks around. Reacts with amused disbelief to **Arthur***'s café–bar. Makes mock of the romantic statue, until her amusement is dispelled by a realization about the plant arrangement. She moves along the flowers as if she's counting them.*

Maureen*'s voice is heard, disembodied at first (in* **Sandra***'s head), then for real as she appears.*

Maureen *died in 1986. She is cheerful, solid – not at all ghostly. She is dressed like a romantic servant girl (a village-green version of the statue).*

Maureen Red, orange, yellow, green, blue, indigo, violet.

Sandra All the colours of the rainbow.

Maureen It's lovely, so it is. Is it in memory of me?

Sandra Nice frock, Maureen. What have you come as?

Maureen Whatever's in your head, Sandra.

Sandra Columbine.

Maureen Columbine who?

Sandra Just Columbine.

Maureen Like Madonna?

Sandra You wish.

Maureen What did Columbine do when she was at home?

Sandra She was a clown's girlfriend. They were invisible to mortal eyes.

Maureen The things you've learned since you left Belfast. And here's me thinkin' you'd brought me home as Cinderella . . . or Snow White . . . or Judy Garland . . .

Sandra Be what you want. You never managed it when you were alive.

Maureen It's not up to me. It's up to you . . .

Sandra Give my head peace, you stupid cow.

Maureen Whatever you say, partner . . .

She disappears.

Sandra I'm sorry . . . don't go . . . I'm sorry, Maureen . . . suit yourself.

Sound off of a phone ringing in the café–bar. The ringing stops.
Arthur *comes out talking into a mobile phone. He doesn't see*
Sandra.

Arthur What? . . . What? . . . How much per pound? . . . I don't care if they are hand reared, I'm plannin' to cook them, not adopt them . . . No I don't want frozen. I want what I ordered at the price we agreed, or the deal's off . . . what do you mean, you grow attached to them? They're chickens for frig's sake. Phone me back when you've decided what price you're prepared to wring their necks for! (*He presses the cut-off button, talks to the phone.*) What am I? A chef or a social worker?

Sandra Keep your hair on, Arthur.

A small pause.

Arthur Sandra?

A long look from **Sandra** *at* **Arthur**'s *clothes, his mobile phone, his café–bar.*

Sandra Jeesus, you've fairly landed with your bum in the bucket.

Arthur Same oul Sandra.

Sandra No.

Arthur All them years in London, an' ye haven't lost your accent.

Sandra *affects a pose and an exaggerated* EastEnders *accent.*

Sandra Yew fought I'd come back talking like Michelle Fowler, did ya?

Arthur Our Liam did. And he only worked there for a fortnight. You remember our Liam?

Sandra The one with the squint?

Arthur Naw, the one with the eye-patch, wooden leg, parrot on his shoulder.

Sandra Same oul Arthur.

Arthur Our Liam went back to London last year. To give it another go. He's stoppin' in Kilburn. Did ye ever run into him?

Sandra Arthur, there's more Irish stoppin' in Kilburn than livin' in Ireland.

Arthur Are you stoppin' here long?

Sandra Flyin' visit.

Arthur You said you'd come home when the war was over.

Sandra Did I? I don't remember.

Arthur Eight years is a long time . . . You've been missed.

Sandra Like a hole in the head.

Arthur I'm glad to see ye.

Sandra I'm glad to see you too, Arthur.

Arthur You're the same, only different . . . quieter . . . better spoken . . .

Sandra You mean I don't say fuck so much? Fuck!!

She shouts this and yells with laughter at the sight of **Tommy** *coming out of the café–bar.* **Tommy** *is carrying a tray with a bottle of champagne and three glasses.*

Tommy Welcome home, Sandra.

Arthur That's my best champagne . . .

Sandra Am I not good enough?

Arthur No problem . . . no problem . . . it was my place to do that, Tommy . . .

Tommy *hands him the tray, goes to* **Sandra**.

Tommy Hiya doin'?

Sandra All right.

They hug each other. **Arthur** *looks as if he'd have liked to hug* **Sandra**, *but didn't have the nerve.*

Arthur All right with you if I open this, Tommy?

Sandra *is laughing and touching* **Tommy**'s *hair.*

Sandra Frig! Get you! Did you knit it yourself?

Tommy Go easy there. It took years to create this.

Arthur He looks a right eejit, doesn't he?

Sandra You look brilliant. What happened to Tommy-the-Commie, Man-of-the-People? . . .

Arthur He tripped to Tipp and come back a Socialist Hippy . . .

Sandra I would have passed you in the street . . . what's a Socialist Hippy? . . .

Arthur A Commie who doesn't wash. Tommy thinks Runnin' Water was a Sioux Warrior . . .

Tommy It was smelly affluents like you who destroyed the American Indian . . .

During the conversation, **Arthur** *has opened and poured the champagne.*

Arthur Shut up an' drink up, Tommy! Cheers an' cheers, Sandra!

Tommy Here's to Poverty, Paisley, an' the Pope!

Sandra Slainte.

As they drink, **Maureen** *appears. She has a glass of champagne in her hand. She stands beside the statue, raises her glass.*

Maureen
Health and long life to you
Land without rent to you
The one of your dreams to you
And many children.

Sandra *walks towards her.*

Maureen   Last time we all drunk champagne together, was the day Arthur got the big compensation for gettin' shot.

Tommy *has drained his glass and is refilling it.*

Arthur   Any chance of you earnin' your keep, Geronimo?

Maureen   I didn't get no compensation . . . still, you can't take it with you when you go, can you? Slainte!

Sandra *raises her glass.*

Sandra   Slainte!

Arthur   She's class, isn't she?

Sandra   What?

Arthur   The statue. It's an original.

Tommy   It's an arty-farty fuckin' nonsense. When this was a mill, the women an' children didn't work in fresh-water fountains. They stood in water polluted with lead . . . an' there were no friggin' flowers at their feet neither.

Arthur   It's symbolic of human survival.

Tommy   It's what?

Arthur   That's what the sculptor said at the unveilin'.

Sandra   Did the sculptor arrange the flowers in that order?

Arthur   That was my idea. Good, eh?

Maureen   Ach, Arthur, I'm all touched. There's more to you than meets the eye.

Sandra   Fancy you remembering that, Arthur.

Tommy What?

Sandra When Maureen was a kid, her mother made a rainbow on the windowsill with pot plants.

Maureen It was magic, so it was.

Sandra They'd been to see *The Wizard of Oz* . . . somewhere over the rainbow, bluebirds die . . .

Maureen See you, Sandra? You spoil everything.

Tommy I don't remember none of this . . .

Arthur (*quickly*) Pour Sandra another glass of bubbly, Tommy.

Maureen My mother loved that film. She danced round the kitchen with me an' our Johnnie the day the plants flowered.

She hums 'Somewhere Over the Rainbow' and dances in an old-fashioned way as her mother once did.

Sandra She was singing that stupid song and she said . . .

Maureen 'Don't mind us, Sandra. We're all mad in this family . . .'

Sandra '. . . some day the men in the white coats are gonna come and take us all away . . .'

Tommy *has poured the champagne.* **Arthur** *takes it from him, gives it to* **Sandra**.

Arthur Get that down ye. Remember the good times. An' the devil take the bad.

Sandra Cheers, Arthur.

Maureen Cheers, Arthur.

Tommy Flowers come an' flowers go. There should be somethin' more permanent there to mark the spot where Maureen was shot. She worked here, an' she died here. This buildin' has a bad history.

Arthur An' a great future.

Sandra She died in the street. She was dead even before I lifted her, and carried her in here.

Maureen (*cheerfully*) It wasn't nuthin' like this when it was the YTP. Remember you and me on the knitting machines? You sabotaged yours because you wanted to work on the cars with the boys.

Sandra Can I use your loo, Arthur?

She is on her feet and going into the café–bar before **Arthur** *can reply.* **Maureen** *disappears from sight at the moment* **Sandra** *does.*

Arthur It's at the back . . . What the hell did you want to go bringin' up all that stuff about Maureen for!?

Tommy You two started it! What's all this crap about flowers an' rainbows?

Arthur It's a better memory to hold on to than joyridin' and bullets.

Tommy I stood at the window and watched Maureen die.

Arthur I was in the room with ye. Remember?

Tommy You didn't see it happen. You were too busy bein' the YTP Chef of the Year. Shreddin' lettuce for a buffet lunch for a visitin' English civil servant.

Arthur I was better occupied than the likes of you. Hangin' out the windows. Cheerin' for Johnnie. Eggin' him on . . .

Tommy Nobody thought they would open fire . . . he was only a kid . . .

Arthur In a stolen police car . . .

Tommy They don't shoot at children for joyridin' nowhere else in the British Isles. What gives them the right to think they can do it here?

Arthur He was a twelve-year-old hood then. An' he's a twenty-year-old hood now. Still livin' on the luck that his sister give him that day, when she run between him an' the Army . . . there was a big black slug in the lettuce . . . funny the things ye remember . . .

Tommy I remember her shoes. I remember thinkin' she deserved better than dyin' in cheap plastic shoes . . .

Arthur Trust you to think somethin' like that, ye eejit . . . Did ye collect the glasses an' plates on yer way here?

Tommy They're in the van.

Arthur Any chance of ye unloadin' it before the year two thousand?

Molly *comes in. She is wearing a flashy chain-store coat and high-heeled shoes. She has an air of glamorous confidence.*

Molly God, it would founder ye out there. Do us a wee Pernod and blackcurrant, Tommy.

Tommy No sooner said than done, Molly.

He goes into the café–bar.

Arthur What are ye doin' here, ma?

Molly I thought you might need a hand to set things up for the openin'.

Arthur I can't afford you and Tommy.

Molly I wasn't lookin' payment.

Arthur I was thinkin' more of the drink bill.

Molly It's a poor son can't give his mother the odd drink, and her livin' on a student grant.

Arthur My offer still stands.

Molly Don't start! I told ye, I have to do it under my own steam. I want to be the same as all the other students.

Arthur Cadgin' drinks?

Molly Independent . . . any danger of that Pernod, Tommy?!

Tommy *returns with the drink.*

Tommy I made it a double.

Arthur Feel free.

Molly Peace in our time. Did ye ever think you'd see the day? (*She downs half the drink in one go.*) Aw, that's better. Doesn't this oul damp weather seep right through to your bones? More like autumn than August out there.

Tommy Season of mists and mellow fruitfulness . . .

Molly *raises her glass to* **Arthur** *in mock salute.*

Molly Close bosom friend of the maturing son.

Arthur What?

Molly Conspiring with him, how to load and bless with fruit, the vines that round the thatch-eaves run.

Arthur You two takin' a hand outa me?

Molly You see me an' Tommy an' Keats?

Arthur Who?

Molly John Keats.

Tommy He's a poet.

Arthur An' didn't know it. Van, Tommy!

Tommy I'm goin'! I'm goin'! See him, Molly? He has me worked to a standstill.

He goes.

Molly I hope you're payin' that lad proper.

Arthur How much are you payin' him for them university books he gets you?

Molly Half what they are in the shops. He gets them at cost.

Arthur Cost nuthin'. He steals them.

Molly He does not. He has a wee contact.

Arthur With a big lorry.

Molly There is nothing either good or bad but thinking makes it so.

Arthur See you an' yer quotin' ma? It's friggin' wearin' me out. Could you not study something quieter . . . with a proper job at the end of it?

Molly Don't you make mock of me an' my studies. What's a big joke to you means a lot to me.

Arthur I didn't mean it like that, ma . . . I was only geggin' . . . I think you're a star . . . you know I do . . . I hope you an' your poet pal'll live an' thrive for ever.

Molly Keats died in 1821.

Arthur An' here's me thinkin' you bought that new coat to go out on the town with him.

Molly Top Shop sale. £19.99. I thought I'd treat myself for bein' a genius. I bought a frock as well.

She removes her coat to reveal a dress that wouldn't go amiss on Joan Collins.

Arthur Is that your Hallowe'en outfit?

Molly Don't you be so pass-remarkable. It's a brilliant colour, isn't it?

Arthur It's a blinder.

Molly Dunnes Stores. Marked down.

Arthur *lifts his glass of champagne and clinks it against the remains of* **Molly**'*s Pernod and blackcurrant.*

Arthur To my ma. The Dolly Parton of Adult Education. I'm dead proud of you, you know.

Molly I'm dead proud of me too. You see when I get my degree? I'm gonna travel the world. See all them poetic places I've only ever read about. Fifty-six years old, an' I've never been anywhere exotic.

Arthur Haven't ye been to Donegal an' Sligo?

Molly Under bare Ben Bulban's head, in Drumcliffe Churchyard Yeats is laid. It may have been enough for him . . . but I want more.

Arthur You've lost me, ma.

Molly County Sligo. It's where the poet Yeats is buried.

Arthur They don't have much luck these poets, do they?

Molly Here, is that champagne you're drinkin'?

Arthur You'll never guess who walked in here the night, like she'd never been away.

A short pause.

Molly Sandra.

Arthur Sometimes you scare me, ma.

Molly I knew by the look on your face . . .

Arthur What look . . . ?

Molly Oooh, there'll be Whigs on the Green when your Iris hears she's back.

Arthur Why should Iris mind about Sandra?

Molly *gives him a long look to signify that she knows, and he knows, that* **Iris** *will mind very much indeed.*

Sandra *comes out of the café–bar.*

Molly (*aside to* **Arthur**) That look . . . (*To* **Sandra**.) How're ye doin' love?

Sandra Molly? . . . I hardly knew you . . .

Molly Oh, there's been the rare changes round here since you decamped to the metropolis . . . hasn't my Arthur done quare an' well for himself?

Molly *rattles on, to* **Sandra**'s *amusement and* **Arthur**'s *embarrassment.*

Arthur Ma . . .

Molly He's doin' the caterin' for the big openin' do at the weekend. They're gonna set up tables out here on the concourse, and there's gonna be dancin' and a cabaret. It's by invitation only, but Arthur'll get ye in, won't ye son? Arthur's in the Chamber of Commerce. Imagine. Wait'll you see his runnin' buffet. It's a work of art. It's a crime to eat it. Come on and tell me all your news, while I polish the silver salvers from the Big Nobs of Belfast . . . isn't it great news about the cease-fire? Haven't you picked a grand day to come home?

Molly *steers* **Sandra** *into the café–bar.*

Arthur *sits down beside the statue. Listens for a moment to the sounds of laughter (off) from the women in the café–bar. Talks to the statue/to himself.*

Arthur She says she doesn't remember. Frig, she shouted it loud enough. 'See you when the war's over, Arthur!' She laughed like it was a joke that wasn't funny. She shouted it like she meant she was never comin' back.

I took her to the airport in a taxi. I bought her a return ticket. She smiled an' she said, 'Jeesus Arthur, you're ever hopeful.' An' then she kissed me . . . on the cheek . . . I waited till the plane was well gone, just in case . . . Frig, why would she change her mind for me, when she wouldn't even stay for her seventeenth birthday and it only a week away? I only heard from her the once. Years later. A postcard. It was weird. A nativity scene. Only the Three Wise Men were Ian Paisley and the Pope and God. And the Virgin Mary was Bernadette Devlin. And she was smilin' at the three of them and sayin', 'It's a girl.' On the back, she'd wrote, 'Twenty-one Today. Happy Birthday To Me' . . . no signature, but I knew her handwritin' . . . Only it wasn't Sandra's twenty-first birthday. It was Maureen's. It give me the creeps. I never told nobody before, so it's just between you an' me . . . an' her . . . or maybe she doesn't remember the postcard neither . . .

Johnnie *comes in.*

Johnnie Any sign of Tommy?

Arthur What am I? Missing persons?

Laughter (off) from **Sandra** *and* **Molly** *in the café–bar.* **Johnnie** *moves towards the sound.*

Arthur Go ahead. Make my day . . . That's my ma in there
. . . and Sandra . . .

Johnnie Who?

Arthur Who!

Johnnie Frig! That's all I need! What's she doin' back?

Arthur Ask her yourself.

Johnnie Are ye mad or mental? She's a spacer, her. She
threatened to kill me, the day of our Maureen's funeral.

Arthur It was the best part of a bad day, when Sandra
wiped the pious look off your friggin' face. Walkin' behind
the coffin, lappin' up the glory that was rightly Maureen's!
The propaganda that made you the poor wee innocent
brother cut no ice with us that knew you for what you were.
A local hoodlum become local hero because the British Army
shot his sister.

Johnnie I'm outa here. I've had eight years of this shite. It's
not my problem. It's everybody else's. All right?

Arthur All right. (*As **Johnnie** puts on the Ray-Bans, and moves
towards the exit.*) Johnnie!

Johnnie What?

Arthur If you have any problems . . . of your own . . . of
now . . . that've got outa hand . . . give us a shout . . .

Johnnie What for?

Arthur I'll help ye, if I can.

Johnnie What for?

Arthur For Maureen . . .

Johnnie Fuck Maureen!

*As he walks out, **Sandra** comes out of the café–bar, laughing, and
Maureen reappears, also laughing. (They don't see **Johnnie**.)*

Sandra See your ma? She looks ten years younger. What
happened to her?

Arthur My da died.

Maureen *laughs.* **Sandra** *attempts a proper sympathetic reaction.*

Sandra I'm sorry . . .

Arthur Don't strain yourself. My ma didn't. He dropped down dead in the bookies, an' they sent for her. An' do you know the first thing she done?

Sandra What?

Arthur Remember my da always wore a hat, summer an' winter? My ma takes the oul hat off, an' she pulls back the linin' an' she fishes out a five pound note. His emergency money for the racin'. Transpires she always knew it was there, all their married life, but she never let on, even when she hadn't two pennies to rub together, an' him pleadin' poverty. 'First fiver I ever saved from your clutches,' she said to the bookie. An' then she buried my da in style. An' then she got her hair dyed. An' she's never looked back since . . . what were the two of yous laughin' about?

Sandra This an' that. Why?

Arthur Just wonderin'.

Maureen You used to say Arthur would die wonderin'.

Arthur What you smilin' at?

Sandra Us. The way we were.

Arthur We had good times . . .

Sandra We had shite times . . . no hope, on the dole, sniffin' glue, stealin' cars . . .

Arthur *and* **Maureen** *speak/react together.*

Maureen Speak for yourself . . .

Arthur I never . . .

Sandra . . . you never got caught, Arthur . . . (*To herself.*) and Dilly-day-dream hadn't the nerve . . .

Arthur *touches his head.*

Arthur I got caught . . . for somethin' I didn't do . . .

Maureen *clenches her fists across her abdomen in a protective movement.*

Maureen Tell me about it . . .

Sandra *taps* **Arthur***'s head.*

Sandra How is the oul steel plate?

Arthur Hard as nails, like you.

Maureen Nice one Arthur . . . about time you . . .

Arthur Sorry, I didn't mean . . .

Maureen Call her bluff, Arthur. Just for once . . .

Arthur . . . I never fought ye before, an' I'm not gonna start now.

Maureen . . . You blew it then, an' yer blowin' it again Arthur.

Arthur Yer very quiet . . .

Sandra She does enough spoutin' for both of us . . .

Arthur What?

Sandra Remember the way we used to laugh at Tommy for spoutin' from the political magazines he nicked from the library?

Arthur He's moved on . . . to nickin' big books . . .

Sandra We've all moved on . . .

Maureen One way or another . . .

Arthur What do you do in London?

Sandra All sorts . . .

Maureen Tell him about . . .

Arthur Remember when I said you were dead good at the hairdressin' an' you said fuck that, you wanted to be a racin'-car driver?

Sandra I've done both . . .

Maureen Tell him about your night job . . .

Arthur You got to race cars? That's one in the eye for the Careers Officer . . .

Maureen Poncy git. (*Imitating the Careers Officer.*) I'd advise you to settle for something less fantastic, Sandra . . .

Sandra I only do a bit of chaufferin'. In the summer. Drivin' the idle rich to Wimbledon. I mostly do hairdressin' in the winter . . .

Maureen An' the night job . . . all seasons . . .

Arthur I've got a car.

Sandra Get you. I drive other people's.

Arthur You can wear a peak cap in my jalopy any day, Sandra.

Sandra Your ma tells me you're a married man these days, Arthur.

Arthur You see my ma . . . ?

Sandra Is it a secret?

Arthur No . . . what else did she tell ye . . . ?

Sandra Nuthin'. Why?

Arthur Nuthin'.

Sandra So who did you marry then?'

Arthur *gestures towards the flower shop.*

Arthur Iris.

Maureen That must have been handy when he was doin' my flower arrangement.

Sandra And how long have you been happy-harried?

Arthur Seven years . . . an' a bit . . .

Maureen He didn't pine for long, did he?

Sandra Any kids?

Arthur Four.

Sandra Four!? Jeesus, Arthur! Tie a knot in it!

Arthur Iris was an only child. Adopted. She always wanted a big family. A real family. All her own.

Maureen Frig! He married Iris McMonagle!

Sandra You married Iris McMonagle? That snotty bitch who went to the Grammar School with the flash green uniform?

Maureen Thought herself a cut above the rest of us who went on the YTP.

Sandra The wee lads used to chant after her . . . 'Give us a kiss, Eyriss . . .'

Maureen '. . . Name the hour, Passion Flower.'

Arthur There's nuthin' wrong with her name . . . Iris is a very old name, if you wanta know . . . Iris was the goddess of the rainbow, so she was . . . it was in one of Tommy's books . . .

A look between **Sandra** *and* **Maureen**.

Maureen Ye lyin' hound . . .

Sandra Them flowers aren't for Maureen at all . . .

Arthur I never said they were . . .

Sandra You never said they weren't . . .

Arthur Only because it seemed important to ye that they were. Sorry I bothered. You're well out of order, slaggin' off the mother of my children. I love my kids . . .

Sandra I'm sorry, Arthur . . . I mean it . . . I'm sure Iris is different now . . . we've all changed in the last eight years . . . everybody changes . . .

Maureen Except me . . .

Sandra . . . no offence . . .

Arthur None taken.

Pause. **Maureen** *giggles.* **Sandra** *tries to suppress a smile.*

Sandra Does Iris still have to pluck her eyebrows to stop them meetin' in the middle?

Arthur See you, Sandra? You'll come back as a battery hen.

Maureen *giggles again.*

Sandra Do you think the dead can come back, Arthur?

Arthur Naw, or my da'd be hauntin' my ma for his emergency fiver.

Sandra Your ma's great.

Arthur I know.

Sandra And I'm sure your Iris has improved too . . .

Iris *enters, pushing a pram.*

Maureen There's always an exception.

Arthur Hallo, love . . .

Iris *is an efficient earth mother in a designer tracksuit, trainers, and lots of gold rings, bangles and earrings. She's a bit grand in speech and manner. There is no love lost between her and* **Sandra**. **Arthur** *rattles on nervously, as the two women eye each other.*

. . . you remember Sandra, Iris . . . ? I was just tellin' her all about our kids . . . what you doin' here, love? . . . I thought . . .

Iris You're needed outside, Arthur. Tommy is quoting Karl Marx to the Royal Ulster Constabulary.

Arthur What?

Iris Apparently the tax disc is out of date on the company van.

Arthur I give Tommy the money . . . Bastard! He's pocketed it!

Arthur *rushes out.* **Iris** *smooths the cover on the immaculate pram.*

Iris Your daddy never learns, does he? Too trusting for his own good.

A 'get her' look between **Sandra** *and* **Maureen**. **Sandra** *flashes* **Iris** *an insincere smile.*

Sandra Nice pram, Iris. Is this the youngest?

She peers into the pram at the sleeping baby.

Iris Everybody says he's my Arthur's double.

Sandra Well, he's certainly got your Arthur's hair.

Iris He's only seven weeks old.

Molly *has appeared at the entrance to the café–bar. She watches/ listens to* **Sandra** *and* **Iris** *with amusement. (***Molly** *and* **Iris** *have nothing in common except* **Arthur**.*)*

Sandra Poor Arthur always thought his hair would grow back . . .

Maureen Hair doesn't sprout through a steel plate . . .

Iris There's nothing poor about my Arthur.

Maureen Seventy thousand pounds compensation . . .

Sandra Does he still get the headaches?

Iris Not since he married me.

Maureen She must have moved in like Flynn the minute you left . . .

Sandra Did true love cure his limp as well?

Molly That was the dancin'.

Maureen and **Sandra** Dancin'?!

Iris Hello, Molly. I thought you had a creative writing class this evening?

Molly It was cancelled. The teacher's had a nervous breakdown. Did you manage to find a babysitter?

Iris Brenda Patterson's keeping an eye on the girls.

Her tone implies that this is the equivalent of having Princess Di for a babysitter. A wicked look from **Molly** *to* **Sandra**. **Molly**'s *tone is a slight take-off of* **Iris**'s.

Molly The Pattersons are Iris and Arthur's next-door neighbours. Mr Patterson is a barrister, and Mrs Patterson is the chairperson of the local Oxfam Committee, and wee Brenda is going to Oxford University in October.

Maureen I take it Arthur and Iris don't live round here no more?

Iris Brenda can't manage the baby as well as the girls. Arthur'll just have to do it.

Sandra What's this about Arthur taking up dancing?

Molly He was always a great dancer. So were you. Didn't the pair of ye win a medal for the two-hand reel?

Maureen *does a little Irish dance.*

Maureen Hop, one two three. Hop, skip two three . . .

Iris That was in his primary school days.

Sandra You and Vincent O'Hara came second.

Iris You had the better partner . . . then.

Molly Iris an' Arthur do ballroom dancing now. Done wonders for his leg.

Arthur *storms back in, followed by* **Tommy**. *Both carrying boxes of glasses.*

Arthur You can pay the friggin' fine!

Tommy Take it out of my friggin' holiday pay!

Arthur Your life's a friggin' holiday.

Tommy Not on what you friggin' pay me.

Arthur Cash in hand, no tax, no questions asked . . .

Tommy No stamps, no sick pay, no benefits . . .

They quarrel their way across stage and off into the café–bar.

Iris Nobody else'll employ him, you know. Arthur's always been a soft touch.

Sandra Funny, that's just what I was thinking.

Molly I'll just see if the boys need a hand . . .

She goes into the café–bar. **Iris** *pats the pram.*

Iris I promise not to call you a boy when you're twenty-six, sweetheart . . . Nice to see you again, Sandra. You haven't changed a bit.

Sandra Likewise.

Iris I'll see you later, Arthur!

Arthur *comes out of the café–bar as* **Iris** *moves towards the street exit.*

Arthur Here! Haven't you forgot somethin'?

Iris I don't think so.

Arthur Like wee Art?

Iris He's your son too. See you in an hour or so.

Arthur I'm up to my eyes . . .

Iris And I'm late for my keep-fit class.

Sandra Oh, we do keep-fit as well as ballroom dancing, do we?

Iris Do we lead a full life in London, Sandra? Or are we still signing on?

Maureen We're a turn. We make the English laugh.

As **Iris** *exits,* **Maureen** *walks to the microphone, singing. She has a lovely voice. She sings the song straight.*

> Oh Mary, this London's a wonderful sight
> With the people all working by day and by night
> They don't grow potatoes nor barley nor wheat
> But there's gangs of them digging for gold in the street
> At least when I asked them that's what I was told
> So I just took a hand in this digging for gold
> But for all that I found there I might as well be
> Where the Mountains of Mourne sweep down to the sea.

Sound of a London pub/club audience: a smattering of applause, a few whistles as **Maureen** *walks into the spotlight, singing, lifting the microphone off the stand.*

Arthur *is looking curiously at* **Sandra**, *who is looking at* **Maureen**. *Spotlight on* **Maureen** *as the lights dim.* **Maureen** *talks directly to the theatre audience as if they are the audience in the London pub/club.*

Maureen I learned that song from my da. And he learned it from his da, an' his da before him. They used to sing it with tears in their eyes, even though neither of them had ever seen the Mountains of friggin' Mourne in the whole of their friggin' lives. When they weren't on the dole in Belfast, they were on the Lump right here in London. It's no joke workin' in London if you're Irish. People here think we know nuthin'. The day I arrived, I applied for a job on a buildin' site. And the foreman says, 'We don't employ Paddies. You're all thick. I never met one yet who knew the difference between a joist and a girder.' 'Well, you've met one now,' says I. 'Joyce wrote *Ulysses*. And Goethe wrote *Faust*.' (*Pause.*) *He* didn't get the joke. And *I* didn't get the job. So I thought I'd give this a go. I mean, why should Bernard Manning and Jim Davidson make a living out of slagging off the Irish, when we can do it better ourselves. And with more wit and style. That's the real joke. You forbade us to speak our own language. You forced us to speak yours and we took it and turned it into poetry.

There were these thick Paddies . . . Joyce, Beckett, Behan, Synge, Yeats, O'Casey . . . and then there were the great *English* dramatists . . . Wilde, Shaw, Swift, Sheridan, Congreve, Goldsmith . . .

The stage lightens as **Maureen** *turns away from the audience, towards* **Sandra**.

The jokes weren't so sophisticated when we started out, partner . . .

Sandra Tommy's not the only one capable of reading big books . . .

Maureen I wish you'd never started.

Sandra I wish I'd never started. They're doin' my head in . . .

She has forgotten about **Arthur***, who is staring at her.*

Arthur Sandra?

Sandra What?

Arthur You all right?

Sandra Why shouldn't I be all right?

Maureen I said that to Kate . . . didn't know at the time that it was my dyin' day . . . you never know the minute . . .

Sandra What became of our noble leader?

Arthur Who?

Sandra Kate who ran the YTP. You fancied her rotten.

Arthur No, I never.

Maureen You were dyin' to be Kate's toyboy.

Sandra Did that doctor ever marry her? Or is it still the longest engagement since the War of the Roses?

Arthur She broke it off with him. She never married.

Sandra Oh, so you do keep in touch with her, then? Does your Iris know?

Arthur Kate comes in to my restaurant nigh an' again. With Iris. They're both involved with one of them schemes for young offenders.

Sandra Good old Kate. Still doin' her bit for the undeservin' poor. What does Iris do for the young offenders? Bring them bunches of daffodils and leftovers from your restaurant . . . ?

Maureen Hold your horses . . . What restaurant?

Sandra Excuse me? You have a restaurant as well as this?!

Arthur In the city centre. Talk about a gold mine? I'm opening this with the profits.

Sandra Frig! When I left, you were settin' traps for the vermin in Larry's Caff.

Arthur You said I'd go bust within' a year, puttin' my compensation money into a hole like that. After I bought Larry out, I done the place up nice.

Tommy *has come out of the café–bar.*

Tommy An' then the paramilitaries come in lookin' their cut. Arthur was feeling confident that day. Told them to fuck off. So they redeveloped it again . . . with a petrol bomb.

Arthur They done me a favour. I got more from the government than that oul buildin' was ever gonna be worth. I added it to what I'd left from my other compensation, an' bought the place in the city centre.

Sandra You see you, Arthur? If you fell in the river, you'd come up with a salmon in every pocket.

Tommy He pays the boys their cut now, don't ye Arthur? His posh punters aren't goin' to frequent a restaurant that gets wrecked on a regular basis for the want of a hand-out. The boys'll be lookin' more when this caff opens. If it opens.

Arthur You know somethin' I don't know?

Tommy Everybody knows this place is a prime target. English investment. English offices. English shops. Why cross the Water when they can bomb Debenhams right here in Belfast?

Sandra Because they get more publicity when they bomb Britain, that's why. Headline news, speeches in parliament. Even when nobody gets hurt. Anything short of a massacre here gets mentioned in passing, if it's mentioned at all. Over there, they don't give a damn about what happens here, so long as it's kept this side of the Irish Sea, and doesn't slow down the traffic in the London rush hour.

Tommy And you used to laugh at me when I talked politics.

Sandra You talked shite.

Arthur Yer both talkin' history. It ends at midnight.

Tommy Says one side only. A cease-fire is only a cease-fire if both sides stop firin'.

Arthur It's all over, bar the shoutin' . . .

Tommy It started with shoutin' . . .

Sandra If it ends . . . if, after twenty-five years the British government stop mouthin' and start talkin', it won't be because more than three thousand people have died here. It won't even be because a handful of their own have died over there. It'll be because the IRA have shattered a lot of glass in the City of London and interrupted the business on the Stock Exchange.

Tommy Nice people you live among.

Sandra I'm not talking about English people, I'm talking about English politics. I live among people who don't know where Belfast stops and Dublin begins. It's all Ireland to them.

Tommy They know nuthin' about us, an' they care even less.

Sandra Do you know about them? Do you care about them? Do you lie awake at night worrying about the shite conditions in places like Moss Side and Toxteth? About the thousands of homeless sleeping rough on London's streets?

Tommy There's no armed soldiers on their streets.

Sandra Not yet. Not yet.

Arthur Is it as bad over there as it's made out to be?

Sandra That's what people over there ask me about over here.

Tommy And what do you say?

Maureen She makes a joke of it.

Sandra Did you hear about the Irish paramilitary who was a fundamentalist Moslem. He was so incensed about *The Satanic Verses*, that he decided he would carry out the fatwa and shoot the author. Special Branch in London are still

trying to work out why he's so determined to kill Willy
Rushton . . . think about it . . .

Incomprehension from **Tommy** *and* **Arthur**.

Maureen Willy Rushton . . . Salman Rushdie . . .

Sandra They can't hear you . . .

Maureen Explain it to them . . .

Sandra Life's too short.

Arthur They say talkin' to yourself is the first sign of
madness . . .

Sandra I wasn't talking to myself.

Tommy Who, then?

Maureen Tell them, Sandra. Go on, I dare ye.

Sandra I was talking to . . . the mill worker . . . it's a
movin' statue, praise be to God . . . look, there, she done it
again . . .

Arthur Is that another joke?

Tommy So you weren't talkin' to Maureen, then?

Sandra What?

Arthur Shut it Tommy!

Tommy Joke, Arthur.

Arthur It's not funny.

Sandra What's not funny?

Tommy It happened not long after you left . . .

Arthur Give me one good reason why I should be payin'
you two-fifty an hour for tellin' oul wives tales, an' my ma in
there doin' your work for nuthin'?

Tommy *walks nonchalantly to the café–bar. Singing as he goes.*

Tommy
  As soon as this pub closes
  As soon as this pub closes

As soon as this pub closes
The Revolution starts.

Sandra What happened after I left?

Arthur Nuthin'. They imagined it.

Sandra What?

Arthur Daft nonsense . . .

Sandra What, Arthur?!

Arthur Remember people used to tie bunches of flowers round the lamppost out there, beside where Maureen died?

Maureen Typical. Nobody never bought me flowers when I was alive.

Sandra They always do that for a while, and then they forget. There was one dead rose on the pavement the day I left.

Arthur Just as well people forget. Jeesus, if they went on indefinitely puttin' flowers on all the spots where people died because of the Troubles, the traffic wouldn't be able to move for roses.

Maureen Thanks a bundle.

Sandra Go on.

Arthur An' then these daft wee girls decided that Maureen was a Christian Martyr.

Maureen I love it.

Sandra What wee girls?

Arthur The ecumenical God Squad. The Happy Clappies.

Sandra
Bibles under their arm
Faces like sin . . .

Maureen
Passion killer knickers
With a big safety pin.

Arthur One of them said she saw a vision of Maureen, an'
the papers got hold of the story, an' next thing people are
flockin' to the lamppost an' lightin' candles, an' tyin' flowers
on it, an' claimin' they could see things that weren't there.

Maureen People see what they want to see . . .

Arthur An' then one mornin' it was all vanished. The
flowers, the candles, the notes asking for miracles. It was
stripped bare an' scrubbed clean. Everybody was gettin' the
blame of it. The Army. The RUC. The paramilitaries.
Tommy.

Maureen and **Sandra** Tommy?!

Arthur Wouldn't that glype Tommy steal the decorations
off a hearse? The rumours were flyin' thick an' fast, an' then
Iris took the meals-on-wheels round to mad Mary's
house . . .

Maureen Is Iris ever at home . . . ?

Arthur An' there was oul Mary burnin' the lot in her back
yard, an' talkin' crazy. The Happy Clappies said it was
nonsense, but they never bothered no more after that.

Sandra What did Mad Mary say?

Arthur Oul witch-talk about Maureen's soul bein' trapped
in the lamppost. She said she done it so that Maureen could
fly free.

Maureen There's a wise witch.

Sandra Her soul flew to England . . . and me . . .

Arthur Sandra?

Sandra It's the living who are trapped . . .

Arthur Sandra?

Sandra Would you do something for me?

Arthur What?

Sandra Would you just sit still beside me and hold my
hand . . .

Arthur . . . what's wrong?

Sandra . . . and don't ask for why . . .

He takes her hand. She places her other hand over his.

Sounds of pub/club audience as **Maureen** *walks to the microphone.*

Maureen I flew here. I was dead nervous. I'd never been on
a plane before. The air-hostess said, 'No need to look so
worried, love. God's on this flight.' And I looked up and sure
enough there he was. Ian Paisley. Large as life. And twice as
ugly. And he sits down beside me. And he gives my Celtic
Cross a long look, and I give his 'Ulster is British' badge a
long look, and conversation sort of dies on the spot. It was a
terrible flight. Wind, rain, hail, fog. The plane went way off
course, and we ended up making an emergency landing. In
Transylvania. And me and Ian got separated from the rest of
the passengers, and ended up walking along this dark
country road. Just me, Ian, and the moonlight. And
suddenly, Count Dracula leaps out in front of us, fangs out to
here. And Big Ian dives behind me, and wails, 'You're a
Catholic! Show him your cross! Show him your cross!' So I
did. 'Listen you!' I screams at Dracula. 'Get your hairy arse
back in your coffin, or I'll knock your fuckin' fangs down
your fuckin' throat!'

Sounds of laughter/applause from the pub audience. A smile between
Sandra *and* **Maureen**.

Iris *walks in.* **Arthur** *hastily removes his hand from* **Sandra**'s.

Iris My car's been stolen. They were driving it round and
round the car park, and then they just drove off. Laughing.
Kids! Joyriders!

Maureen Is there no end to it?

Iris If you're not too engrossed in other things Arthur,
maybe you'd like to phone the police.

Iris *pushes the pram into the café–bar, more offended wife than former
car-owner.* **Arthur** *goes after her, resigned to his fate.*

Maureen God decided *He* was going to put an end to it.
And he appeared to Ian Paisley and Gerry Adams in a
dream. And he says to the two of them, 'I've got bad news
and I've got good news. The bad news is, the world is about
to come to an end. The good news is, those of you who are
truly the Children of God will enter the Kingdom of
Heaven.' And the next morning, Gerry Adams announces,
'People of Ireland. I've got bad news, and I've got good
news. The bad news is that the world is about to end. The
good news is that every Irish *Catholic* is guaranteed a place in
the Kingdom of Heaven.' And Big Ian also makes an
announcement. 'Protestants of Ulster. I've got bad news,
and I've got good news . . . and I've got better news. The bad
news is that the world is about to end. The good news is that
every Irish *Protestant* is guaranteed a place in the Kingdom of
Heaven. And the better news is . . . that bastard Gerry
Adams'll never get his United Ireland now.'

Laughter/applause from the London audience.

Maureen *walks to* **Sandra** *who is now standing looking at the
statue of the mill worker and child.*

Molly *and* **Tommy** *have come out of the café–bar.* **Molly** *is
watching* **Sandra**. **Tommy** *is listening to the noises (off) of* **Iris**
and **Arthur** *quarrelling inside the café–bar.*

Arthur How many times do I have to say it, Iris?! I was
worried about her. She had a funny turn!

Iris She's always been a funny turn, that one!

Arthur Will you keep your voice down!

Sounds off of baby Arthur howling.

Iris Now see what you've done!

A door slams (off). Silence.

Sandra *speaks to the statue of the mill worker and child.*

Sandra Your Paddy's had a letter from the Child Support
Agency. They wrote to inform him that they'd decided to
award you a hundred pounds a week. Paddy wrote back, and

said, 'That's very generous of ye. I might even send her a few pound myself when I'm flush.'

Maureen That's a new one. Is it going into the act?

Sandra If you like.

Maureen I like the Shergar joke best . . . Who was born in a stable and became world-famous?

Sandra You just spoilt the punchline.

A look between **Molly** *and* **Tommy**.

Molly Tommy, away to the car park, and check that the van's still there. Take your time.

Tommy *goes*.

Sandra I'm not mad, you know.

Molly I never said you were.

Sandra But you were wonderin'.

Molly I'm worried about ye.

Sandra I'm worried about me.

Molly What is it, love? You're not yourself . . .

Maureen *giggles*.

Sandra Johnnie's joyride killed two people that day . . . Maureen was pregnant . . .

Molly I know.

Sandra She didn't tell nobody but me . . . Kate! Friggin! Kate! Her boyfriend did the *post mortem*. I suppose she told Iris, who told Arthur, who told you. She'd no business tellin' it! It had nothing to do with nobody but Maureen and me!

Molly There must have been a man involved somewhere along the line.

Sandra A fly-by-night. A student. A foreigner.

Maureen He was a gentleman. We done it in the Botanic Gardens. And then we done it again in his flat.

Sandra He was due back in Belfast the day she died. I wonder if he read about it in the papers. I wonder if he even realized it was the same girl he destroyed in the Botanic Gardens.

Maureen Destroyed? It was magic, so it was.

Molly You sound like my da. When me and my sisters were goin' to the dances, he used to warn us. (*Imitates her father's voice.*) 'Come yous back the way yous left. Don't none of yous come home destroyed.' It was his idea of sex education. I've got grandchildren at nursery school who know more about sex than I knew when I got married . . . I was seventeen an' three months gone. You had to get married in them days.

Sandra Did you love him?

Molly Arthur's da was mad, bad, an' dangerous to know. I couldn't wait to be destroyed. An' we're no sooner married than he turns into a wee man from the Falls Road. Oh, to be seventeen again an' know what I know now. Fifty-six an' I've only ever had two men.

Sandra Who was the other one?

Molly You mind your own friggin' business. Have you got a fella?

Sandra I have, and I haven't. I find it hard to . . . nobody is ever gonna hurt me the way Maureen got hurt.

Molly Is it her that's botherin' you so?

Maureen Tell her . . .

Molly It must be hard on you . . . Arthur and Tommy have always had each other to talk to. They mostly agree to disagree about what happened that day, but arguin' about it got them through it . . . talk's a way of gettin' to grips . . . layin' a ghost.

Maureen She's not as green as she's cabbage-lookin' . . .

Molly But you walked away without a word . . . you haven't said what brought you back after all these years . . . talk to me, love . . .

Sandra I'm here for the crack. Arthur doesn't need to wangle me a ticket for the opening at the weekend. I've got my own special invitation.

Molly Who from?

Maureen From Arthur, only he doesn't know it.

Sandra I'm here for the cabaret.

Molly They've run out of entertainment in London?

Sandra I'm not here to watch it. I'm in it. Your Arthur and the Chamber of Commerce hired an agent to set up the comedy spot. I'm one of the stand-up comedians she booked. She'd seen me onstage in a club in London, and she asked me . . . I must have been mad or drunk to agree . . . or just plain stupid . . .

Molly You're a comedian . . . ?

Sandra I'm a clown. I tell tall stories that make the English laugh.

Maureen We make them laugh . . .

Molly God, I'm impressed. Are you famous?

Sandra I'm not a star. I'm the one gets shoved on first.

Molly Even so. I think that's amazin'.

Sandra You're the one who's amazing.

Molly Away on with ye. I couldn't do what you do . . .

Maureen What we do . . .

Molly How did ye get started?

Sandra (*ignoring* **Maureen**'s *steady gaze*) How did *you* get started?

Molly I enrolled in a night class for mature students. An' this oul teacher used to swan in as if she was doin' us a big favour. She was that far up her own arse, nobody could understand a word she was sayin'. So one night, when she was goin' all round the house about Thomas Hardy, I just stood up, an' I said, 'Listen love, if you think the man's a whingey wanker, why don't you just say so?' Later on, in the pub, she raises her glass to me, an' she says, 'Fuck the literary critics, Molly. Write what you really feel. I wish I had when I was a student.' Mind you, I'd introduced her to Pernod an' blackcurrant, an' she was on her fourth. But she was right. I think the examiners keep givin' me Grade A because my essays terrify them. I talk to myself when I'm shit-scared that somebody's gonna call my bluff. What's your excuse?

Sandra I'm shit-scared all the time.

Molly Of what?

Maureen Tell her . . .

Sandra Of what I do.

Maureen Of what we do.

Molly You mean like stage fright?

Sandra It was for her . . .

Maureen It was for yourself . . .

Molly Who?

Sandra What is it they say? You don't have to be mad to survive, but it helps. Ask Brian Keenan.

Molly I don't know Brian Keenan.

Sandra She does.

Maureen *lifts the microphone.*

Maureen You see my da and Brian Keenan? (*Crosses two fingers.*) They're like that. As soon as Brian got back to Belfast from Beirut, he come straight round to our house. An' my da says, 'There's a bottle of malt whiskey in the kitchen, Brian. We'll drink it dry.' And as he's goin' into the kitchen to get the bottle, he says, 'I won't be a minute. Just you make yourself at home there, Brian.' And begod, when my da comes back into the sittin'-room, there's Brian Keenan chained to our radiator.

Sandra Not funny . . .

Maureen You taught me everything I know, partner . . .

Molly Who are you talkin' to, Sandra?

Maureen Tell her . . .

Sandra I'm afraid . . .

Molly Of what?

Sandra If I got locked up, I don't think I could survive it . . .

Molly What is it that's frightening you so?

Maureen Tell her . . .

Sandra Stop haunting me!

Maureen I'm not haunting you, Sandra. You're haunting me.

Tommy *rushes in and runs to the café–bar.*

Tommy If anybody asks, I'm not here!

Johnnie *walks in.*

A pause as he and **Sandra** *recognize each other.*

Arthur *and* **Iris** *come out of the café, happy families again. (***Iris** *is pushing the pram with one hand and holding* **Arthur**'*s hand with the other.)*

Sandra I brought you a wee present from London.

She produces a gun. Points it at **Johnnie**. *Pulls the trigger. The gun squeaks and a white flag with the words 'bang bang' drops from the barrel.* **Sandra** *laughs. It is not a funny laugh. Nobody else is laughing.*

Johnnie Stupid bitch!

He exits.

A short pause.

Sound (off) of a car screeching to a halt and gunfire in the street outside.

Maureen *reacts as if she has been shot. (Crosses her fists across her abdomen as before.)*

Sandra *reacts to* **Maureen**.

Molly *reacts to* **Sandra**.

Arthur *and* **Iris** *react to the sound of the gunfire outside.*

Tommy *comes out of the café–bar.*

Tommy So much for your fuckin' cease-fire, Arthur!

Arthur *runs outside.*

Iris Arthur! Don't you go gettin' yourself killed! Tommy! You go!

Sounds (off) of police sirens. Cars screeching to a halt. Doors slamming.

Iris *and* **Tommy** *run outside. The baby howls.* **Molly** *takes him out of the pram. Comforts him. Watches* **Sandra** *who is staring in horror at* **Maureen**.

Maureen *has removed her hands from her abdomen. They are covered in blood. She looks surprised. She holds out her hands to* **Sandra**, *mouths the word 'No . . .'*

Sandra *screams.*

Sandra No!!!

Maureen *turns to the audience.*

Maureen So, one of the Local Heroes, the Defenders of Our Faith, walks into a Belfast pub and points a gun at me, and says, 'What religion are ye?' And I don't know if this is a Catholic-killer or a Protestant-killer, so I says, 'I'm a Jew.' And the gunman says, 'You're dead.' And I says, 'What for?' And the gunman says, 'Because you crucified Our Lord, that's what for.' And I says, 'You're gonna kill me for something that happened nearly two thousand years ago?' And the gunman says, 'I don't give a fuck when it happened. I only heard about it this mornin'.'

Maureen *shrugs. Picks up a glass of champagne. Raises it to the audience.*

People have died for less.

Act Two

Scene One

A short time later.

Sandra *is sitting,* **Molly***'s coat wrapped round her. Perhaps a glass of brandy in her hand.* **Molly** *is giving a bottle to the baby, but her attention is on* **Sandra***.*

Maureen *is at the microphone. She is wearing a beige linen trouser-suit and high-heeled shoes.*

Maureen When I was four goin' on five, my mother Mary Mahoney gave birth to a darlin' baby boy. There hadn't been a birth like it for nearly two thousand years. There was a star in the sky as bright as the searchlight beam on the Army helicopter. And these three big camp queens, wise men from the university area, arrived at our front door, bearing gifts of gold and two jars of ointment from the Body Shop. Frankincense n' Myrrh Exotic Massage Oils. And there was all this carol-singin' outside. And when I looked out the window, there was a heavenly host on our balcony. Choirs of angels, serenadin' the chancer in the flat next door. That soon stopped him from signin' on the dole as the only unemployed shepherd in West Belfast. My brother, Jesus Mahoney, performed his first miracle before he was out of nappies. There was this weddin'-party on a boat on the River Lagan, and they ran out of booze. And our Jesus just toddled across the water, and the Lagan turned from water into whiskey beneath his feet. Black Bush, Malt. None of yer oul cheap stuff. After that, there wasn't a weddin' in the whole of Ireland that Jesus Mahoney didn't get an invite to.

Our Jesus had a happy childhood. There was only one sorrow in his life, and that was that he couldn't sing, and he wanted to be in the choir with me. They let him join anyway, because he was a special case. An' he used to stand in the back row beside me, and mime the words. (**Maureen** *mimes silent choir singing*.) Jesus Mahoney – the Gerry Adams of the primary school choir. The rest of us were brilliant singers. The choir got that famous, we were invited to Rome to sing for the Pope. And we're all in the Vatican, and this official says, 'As soon as the Holy Father enters, you all stand up and start singing.' Only our Jesus was that overcome by the grandeur of the place, he didn't even notice the Pope comin' in. And when the rest of us stood up and started singin', Jesus just sat there, mesmerized. And the Pope says, (*In a foreign accent.*) 'Hold on a minute, why is that singer at the back not standing up?' And I was that mortified, I blurts out, 'Jesus Mahoney can't sing!' And the Pope says, 'Christ, he can stand up, can't he?!

Maureen *turns to* **Sandra**.

What's with the face like a wet week? The darlin' boy is dead and gone. Gunned down in the street. (*Points an imaginary machine-gun.*) Rat-a-tat-tat. Tit-for-tat. What you wanted. What you wished for . . .

Sandra I didn't want . . .

Maureen You wanted. You wanted revenge so much, it done your head in. Can I rest in peace now? Or do they all have to die – the soldier who aimed at Johnnie and killed me, the officer who gave the order, Tommy for organizing the peaceful protest that turned into a riot, Arthur for bein' so engrossed in his runnin' buffet that he didn't stop me from runnin' out into the street? Every mother's son who happened to be there that day? Does it end this day? Or does it go on and on and on forever?

A fast quarrel between **Sandra** *and* **Maureen** *– more like children than adults.*

Sandra You started it.

Maureen You started it.

Sandra You.

Maureen Please Miss, it wasn't me. School's out. Grow up, wee girl.

Sandra Don't you fuckin' talk to me like that!

Maureen I'll talk to you any fuckin' way I like.

Sandra Sorry?!

Maureen So you should be. The way you've made me, the way you dress me. How would you know what I might have become? You can't even remember proper what I was like before.

Sandra You never looked nuthin' like that.

Maureen I never wore stupid frocks, neither. I wore cheap jeans, and skirts up to my bum, and high-heeled shoes. I'd never heard of friggin' Columbine. And neither had you.

Sandra *turns away from* **Maureen** *towards* **Molly**. *A pause. A quiet look between the two women.* **Sandra** *looks away.* **Molly** *puts the sleeping baby back into the pram. Looks back at* **Sandra**.

Sandra Maureen and me were bottom of the class in our last year at school. She hadn't time to read the books, because she had to look after Johnnie. And I hated the teachers that much, I never read anything they said I had to read, just to annoy them. And then when I went to London, and for the first time in my life there was nobody telling me I had to read this to pass that, I started reading for myself. And everything I learned, I taught to her . . .

Molly How clearly do you see her?

Sandra As clear as you.

Molly All the time?

Sandra I used to decide when and where and how . . . But now . . . she has a mind of her own these days . . .

Maureen
Dilly Daydream's dead and gone
And you're the fool for carryin' on . . .

Sandra A couple of hours before she died, she committed her first and only crime. She stole a suit. A beige linen trouser suit . . .

Maureen . . . with a skirt and a top and shoes to match . . . real leather . . .

Sandra The baby's father was due back in Belfast, and she thought if she looked like somebody who shopped in Marks & Spencer's, he would make an honest woman of her. She was friggin' hopeless at shoplifting.

Maureen I didn't have your experience.

Sandra The suit was two sizes too big, and the heels on the shoes were that high, she looked like a deranged ballet dancer. I made a joke of it, to cheer her up. I said that stealing a jacket that would fit two would come in handy later on when . . . only, there was no later on . . . no baby . . . no Maureen. After they took her body out of here, I found the bag of clothes . . . I wore the suit the first time we appeared on stage.

The lights dim to the sound of a London pub audience.

Spotlight on **Maureen**.

Maureen Do you like the whistle and flute? Irish linen. Handmade. It was made for Ian Paisley. That's why it's a bit big on me. Ian give it to me after I saved him from a fate worse than death in Transylvania. He told me that he gets all his suits made by a wee Free Presbyterian tailor on the Shankill Road, Belfast. And they cost £300. Three hundred pounds! 'Frig, Ian,' says I, 'My da's the best tailor on the Falls Road, and he could make you up that suit for fifty quid, and throw in a spare pair of trousers.' And Ian says, 'How could a Roman Catholic tailor make me a suit for a fraction of the cost of one made by a Good Honest Protestant?' And I says, 'Because tailors charge according to the amount of material they use. And believe me, Mr Paisley, you're not nearly as big a man up the Falls Road as you are on the Shankill.'

As the spotlight fades on **Maureen***, and the stage lights rise, we see that* **Johnnie** *has appeared beside her at the microphone.* **Maureen** *looks at* **Sandra***'s shocked face, follows her gaze, smiles at* **Johnnie***, who stares impassively at* **Sandra***.*

Maureen (*sneers at* **Sandra**) That oul joke went out with the ark. Maybe I need a younger partner, partner . . .

Sandra No . . .

Maureen A free spirit like me. Johnnie and me could tell the real jokes. The ones the Irish tell each other. The ones you never hear on the telly . . . the darlin' boy is dead and gone, but him and me will carry on . . .

Sandra No . . .

Maureen *moves towards* **Sandra**.

Johnnie *leans against a wall. Watches* **Sandra** *as she tries to block/escape from* **Maureen***'s onslaught.* **Molly** *reacts to* **Sandra***'s distress.* **Maureen** *launches a very fast, vicious, ugly joke routine at* **Sandra**.

Maureen Let's do the UVF hit-squad version of the chicken sauce advert. (*Moves her arms like a chicken and dances towards* **Sandra***, singing.*) I feel like Fenian tonight, Fenian tonight, Fenian tonight . . . Or what about the wee man wanderin' down the Falls Road carryin' two buckets of shite? And when the Army ask him why, he says, 'My son's being released from the Maze Prison this weekend. He's been on the Blanket Protest for three years, and I thought a bit of shite on the bedroom walls would make him feel at home.' Irish freedom fighters are thick. I mean, why didn't the hunger strikers escape from the 'H' Blocks when they had the chance? After week three, all they had to do was slide out under the cell door. When Bobby Sands, the first hunger-striker, died, the British Army doctor done a *post mortem*. He didn't bother with an X-ray. He just held Bobby up to the light. We'll never forget you . . . Jimmy Sands . . . Grow your own dope. Plant an Irishman . . . What has Brian Keenan got in common with Cinderella? They've both got Two Ugly Sisters. Knock! Knock! Who's there? Bang-bang-

bang. It's the Royal Ulster Constabulary. We don't shoot to kill. A British Army Squaddie raped an Irish girl. And afterwards he says to her, 'In nine months' time, you'll have a son. You can call him Winston Churchill, if you like.' And the girl says, 'In nine months' time you'll have a rash. You can call it measles, if you like.' What's the difference between Catholic Aids and Protestant Aids? Nuthin'. Either way you die blamin' it on the other side.

Sandra Don't Maureen! Don't! (*Screams at* **Johnnie**.) This is your doing, you wee bastard! Dead or alive you destroy everything you touch! Maureen is my partner! Mine! So you just bog off back to the hell ye've sprung from. Hell must be crawlin' with Irish comedians wonderin' where the joke went wrong!

Molly Sandra, love . . .

She grabs hold of **Sandra** *as she lunges at* **Johnnie**.

Johnnie Is she wired to the friggin' moon or what?

As he is speaking, **Iris** *enters. Yells at* **Johnnie**, *pushes him towards the café–bar. She is so angry, she has reverted to the language and diction of her childhood.*

Iris Right, you wee gobshite! You have a lot of explainin' to do!

Johnnie Hands off!!

Sandra He's alive . . .

Iris I'll give ye hands off, ye skittery ghost! A year ago I spoke up for you in court. I got you probation. So what the hell have you been up to now!?

Johnnie Nuthin' . . .

Iris Get in there!

Arthur *and* **Tommy** *enter as* **Iris** *pushes* **Johnnie** *into the café–bar.*

Johnnie What's it like bein' married to Arnold Schwarzenegger, Arthur?!

Iris Move yourself!

Johnnie All right. All right.

Sandra He's alive . . .

Iris (*voice off*) Sit!

A door slams off.

Molly You can take the girl out of West Belfast, but you can't take West Belfast out of the girl . . .

Sandra He's alive . . .

Tommy 'Course he's alive. Wasn't he always a jammy wee bugger?

Molly What happened out there?

Arthur That's what the police want to know. Johnnie's actin' the innocent as usual, but he knows more than he's sayin'.

Tommy Five minutes with Iris, an' he'll be beggin' for internment without trial . . .

Arthur Whoever took the pot-shot at him missed an' hit the wall. An' run off into that oul derelict buildin' opposite. The police say we're to stay in here till they flush him out, whoever he is, in case he opens fire again.

Tommy There's a big car abandoned outside. A Jaguar. An' the police are surroundin' that buildin' like Al Capone's in there.

Arthur They're bein' very cagey about it all. There's more to this than meets the eye.

Sandra He's alive. The wee bastard's alive . . . I feel . . .

Maureen What?

Sandra not glad . . . but not sorry neither . . . I don't want . . . no more . . . no more blood . . . not even his . . . no more . . .

Maureen *goes to the microphone. The lights dim, etc.*

Maureen An eye for an eye. A tooth for a tooth. That's how Christians always condone killin' each other. I've found a better book than the Bible. It's called *Transcendental Levitation for Beginners*. It's brilliant being a Buddhist. You still get the anger and the guilt . . . but you can rise above it . . .
And I've joined a new Peace and Reconciliation Group. Terrorists Anonymous. And you go to meetings, and you stand up and state your name and say 'I am a terrorist' and accept responsibility for your own actions and stop putting the blame on everybody else. And if you're at home alone, and you feel tempted to mix yourself a wee Molotov Cocktail, you just phone one of the other reformed terrorists in the group. And he comes over to your house and talks you out of it.

As the lights rise on the concourse, **Iris** *is escorting* **Johnnie** *out of the café–bar.*

He affects a defiant, unconcerned attitude towards **Sandra**, **Arthur**, **Tommy** *and* **Molly**, *but* **Iris** *is having none of it. She has recovered her middle-class composure.*

Iris Right now, Jonathon. I want you to tell everybody what you have just told me.

Johnnie Tell them yourself. (*As* **Iris** *moves threateningly towards him.*) All right, all right . . .

Iris Not that I believe a word of it . . .

Johnnie It's the God's honest truth . . .

Arthur Try me . . .

Iris He says the man in the Jaguar car, the one who took the pot-shot, is a police inspector, did you ever hear the like . . . ?

Johnnie I thought I was the one had to tell this tale . . .

Arthur Go on.

Johnnie He's been houndin' me for days . . .

Arthur Why?

Johnnie His daughter goes to the raves. Silly wee bitch. I told her to go easy . . .

Arthur Go on.

Johnnie You see them wee rich girls? They haven't the sense they were born with. She told me it was for a party, an' then she goes home an' she swallows the lot herself, an' washes it down with a bottle of her da's whiskey. I warned her about disco biscuits an' alcohol. Not my fuckin' fault she's in a coma. Her da shouldn't give her so much pocket money . . .

Iris You gave a teenage girl . . .

Johnnie Nuthin' lethal. It was the whiskey that done for her . . .

Molly What are disco biscuits?

Tommy 'E' an' other things. Depends who's sellin' them . . . Frig's sake Johnnie, what did you mix it with?

Johnnie Don't you get snotty with me, dopehead. If you an' everybody else had paid up what they owed me on time, I woulda been out of here days ago, an' that maniac RUC Inspector would never have caught up with me . . .

Sandra The darlin' boy's a dirty dealer. The ultimate joyride. You do the driving, and the passengers get killed.

Johnnie So I'm a cunt for myself. Why don' you tell them who you're a cunt for, Sandra?

Arthur *shoves his clenched fist in* **Johnnie***'s face.*

Arthur You know what this smells of?!

Johnnie What?!

Arthur Intensive care, that's what!

Johnnie Still soft for Sandra after all these years, eh, Arthur? You'd do better defendin' your wife's honour.

Arthur *is about to punch* **Johnnie***, but stops.*

Arthur What's that supposed to mean?

Johnnie Ask her yourself. Ask your snooty wife about Brenda Patterson's da. And the Peace and Reconciliation meetings him and her run . . . that go on so late on a Saturday night . . .

A pause as everybody looks at **Iris** *with varying degrees of interest.* **Iris** *is very flustered.*

Iris This is nothing more than a cheap distraction tactic. Mr Patterson and I are friends . . . neighbours with a common interest . . . in political justice through social reform . . .

Johnnie That's not how Brenda tells it . . .

Iris What would someone of your background know about people like the Pattersons?

Johnnie I know a lot of wee rich girls with more pocket money than sense.

Iris You're a liar!

Johnnie I'm the king of the only scene in Belfast that has nothing to do with religion, class or creed. And I've known wee Brenda Patterson since she was fourteen years old.

Iris My children are being babysat by a junkie!

Johnnie No sweat, Iris. Brenda only takes vitamins at the weekends when her ma's out playin' bridge . . . an' her da's out playin' around . . .

Arthur Tommy, take Iris and the baby home in the van. And tell wee Brenda to fuck off and earn her three quid an hour in somebody else's house.

Tommy Three quid an hour!? Frig, Iris, you coulda had me for two pound fifty!

Iris What about the gunman in the building opposite?

Arthur He's aimin' at Johnnie, and Johnnie's stayin' right here till he explains what he meant about that crack at Sandra.

Iris You should be coming home with me, not staying here because of her!

Arthur Sandra and me are just good friends. Like you and Brenda Patterson's da. All right Iris?

Iris You don't believe . . .

Arthur Take the child, and go home.

Maureen *in the spotlight.*

Maureen The trouble with people when they go up in the world, is that they forget what they come from. My ma's second cousin Andy come home from the United States of America, forty years after he'd left Ireland to seek his fortune. And he goes back to the oul family homestead. A huxtery oul farm on the borders of Fermanagh and Tyrone. And he says to his Great Uncle Joe, 'How many acres do you have?' And Great Uncle Joe says, 'Well, Andy, the oul homestead stretches right across there to the old oak tree that your great-grandfather planted, and goes on for a mile or so to where the ditch divides it from the farm next door.' And all-American Andy, with his high-heel boots and his cowhide stetson, says, 'Back home in Texas, I can get into my car and drive all day, and not reach the end of my ranch.' And Great Uncle Joe says, 'I know the feelin' well. We had an oul car like that once. But we got rid of it.'

Iris *and* **Tommy** *have now left to sort out Brenda Patterson.* **Johnnie** *is grinning at* **Arthur** *and* **Molly.** **Sandra** *is standing apart from the group, near to* **Maureen.**

Johnnie *(sings to the tune of Campdown Races)* I know somethin' yous don't know . . . doo-dah, doo-dah . . .

Arthur Is he coked to the gills on his own friggin' pills or what?

Molly You're the poet and don't know it, son . . .

Sandra Johnnie doesn't take what he sells, do you? He doesn't need Ecstasy to turn him on. Creatin' hell on earth for everybody but himself was always his style. Look at him, Maureen . . . this is what you loved more than life . . .

Arthur Maureen . . . ?

Johnnie (*to* **Arthur**) It didn't click with me what turned her on, till I walked back in here an' she started spoutin' an' screamin' as if our Maureen was standin' here large as life . . . an' then the programme for your poncy cabaret made sense, Arthur . . . you haven't seen it yet, have ye? I had a sneak preview. The printer's a customer of mine. He pointed the name out to me . . . our Maureen's name as one of the stand-up comedians . . . 'So what?' I told him. 'So there's somebody else in the world called Maureen Reilly?' Didn't click with me till now it was you, Sandra . . . frig, look at her. People have been locked up for less.

Molly That's enough, Johnnie.

Arthur Ma?

Molly Leave it, son . . .

Maureen No . . .

Sandra No . . . no more leaving it . . . time to tell the truth . . .

Maureen . . . and shame the devil . . .

Sandra Why did you always love that devil more than me, Maureen?

Maureen Everybody loves their own . . .

Arthur Christ . . .

Sandra (*to* **Molly**) Tell him . . .

Molly She sees her as clear as you and me, son . . .

Johnnie She's a friggin' loony.

Molly I said that's enough, Johnnie.

Sandra Do you ever dream about her?

Johnnie What?

Sandra Do you ever give that day a thought . . . you must have seen it . . . the blood . . . I never knew anybody could have so much blood in them . . . she put her hands . . .

. . (*Distressed/clenching her fists on her abdomen as* **Maureen** *did.*)
. . . and the blood came up and out of her mouth . . . she
looked . . . surprised . . . and I ran and put my arms around
her . . . and I lifted her . . . and I . . . tell them, Arthur . . .
you were there when I . . . tell them . . .

Arthur You carried her in here.

Sandra Tell it all . . . say it!

Arthur . . . you started shakin' her and screamin' and
shoutin' at her for being stupid . . . for being dead . . .

Sandra (*to* **Arthur**) . . . because I loved her. (*To* **Johnnie**.)
I loved her . . . (*To* **Molly**.) Never said it when she was alive.
Not the sort of thing you say to your best mate . . . not when
you're sixteen . . . not here . . . not nowhere . . . not
never . . .

Johnnie *sniggers.*

Johnnie Used to feel each other up in the entry at the back
of the YTP, did yous?

Molly *knocks him out.*

Maureen Don't you just love it when the Peace People get
angry?

Lights down on stage. **Maureen** *walks into the spotlight.*

Maureen God got so angry about the Troubles that he
decided to send a second Great Flood. Not over the whole
world this time. Just Ireland.

And he sent for Ian and Gerry, and he said, 'In three days'
time, the Emerald Isle will be under the sea, and then the
pair of you will have nuthin' left to fight over.' And Ian said,
'I will lead my people out of Ireland to a new Promised
Land.' And Gerry said, 'And me and my people will be right
there behind ye.' Now the last thing God wanted was these
two eejits starting up a Holy War somewhere else. So He
smiled and He said, 'Let your people go. But if you two stay, I
promise to deliver you from the Flood.'

So, while the population of Ireland are packin' up and
movin' out, Ian and Gerry are stood in front of the City Hall,

Belfast, in the pourin' rain. And as the water is lappin' round their ankles, the Ulster Freedom Fighters drive by in a car, and shout, 'Get in, Ian, and we'll take you to Scotland!' And Ian says, 'The Lord has promised to deliver me from the Flood!' And the water keeps risin'. And when it has reached their waists, the IRA come by in a speedboat, and shout, 'Get in, Gerry, and we'll take you to America!' And Gerry says, 'The Lord has promised to deliver me from the Flood!' And the water keeps risin'. And when it has reached their necks, a television crew fly overhead in a helicopter, and throw down a steel ladder, and shout, 'Climb up, and we'll take you both to England!' And Ian and Gerry shout back, 'The Lord has promised to deliver me from the Flood!' And the water keeps risin'. And Ian and Gerry are both drowned. And they arrive in Heaven, soaked to the skin and ragin' with it. And there's God sittin' on his throne, surrounded by angels and archangels. And they're all havin' a job keepin' the laughter in. And Ian and Gerry, united at last, yell at God, 'You promised to deliver us from the Flood!!' And God smiles, and he says, (*In a Jewish voice, with a Jewish shrug.*) 'Mr Paisley, Mr Adams . . . I sent you a car, and a boat, and a helicopter. What more could a poor man do?'

Lights rise on the stage, but this time **Maureen** *is left in a slight shadow (which very gradually deepens as the play continues).*

Arthur *has gone outside.* **Johnnie** *is wiping his bloody nose and looking sullenly at* **Molly** *and* **Sandra**.

Maureen *smiles gently at* **Sandra**.

I'd like to think that somewhere over the rainbow there's a God with a sense of humour. But I'll never know one way or the other if I don't go and find out . . . for myself . . . partner . . .

Arthur *comes back in.*

Arthur (*to* **Johnnie**) They want you outside.

Johnnie No way, Hosé.

Arthur The danger's over. He give himself up.

Johnnie Well, I'll be on my way then.

Arthur They've got a nice big car waitin' outside, just for you . . . how much does Tommy owe you?

Johnnie Twenty quid.

Arthur Ten, more like. Here, here's thirty. And whatever you tell the RUC about your drug dealin', keep Tommy's name out of it, okay?

Johnnie *takes the money. Strolls towards the door.*

Johnnie All the police'll want to hear from me is that I have no idea who fired the gun out there. That way, one of their own won't have to stand trial for attempted murder. (*Grins. Waves the money at* **Arthur**.) But thanks anyway, Arthur.

Exits.

Arthur That wee bastard was born evil.

Molly You're just ragin' 'cause you didn't keep your money in your pocket.

Arthur Don't you be tellin' Tommy about that, or I'll never hear the end of it.

Molly He phoned when you were outside. The kids are fine. Fast asleep in their beds. And wee Brenda sittin' downstairs on the sofa, readin' a big book as if butter wouldn't melt in her mouth. Or she was, until Irish belted her over the head with her big book, and threw her out.

Maureen Jeesus, Iris is mustard when she gets going, isn't she?

The shadows around **Maureen** *have deepened a little more.*

Sandra *walks towards her. Stops. Shows signs of distress.*

Molly *goes to her, brings her back.*

Molly The livin' is this way, love.

Arthur What happened to you, Sandra?

Sandra I sent you a postcard one time, Arthur. You never replied.

Arthur There was no address on it.

Sandra It was Maureen's twenty-first birthday . . . that
was the start of it . . . no . . . no . . . it started here. It started
with dreams. Awful dreams. I left Belfast to make them stop.
And they did, for a while . . . a long while . . . out of sight,
out of mind . . . I was doing all right. Never gave that day a
second thought. Over and done with . . . all in the past . . .
out of sight, out of mind . . . Only the dreams came back. Not
when I was sleeping . . . when I was awake. In broad
daylight when I was on a bus or in a shop and suddenly I
could see it . . . Maureen running towards the car . . . the
look on her face . . . she held out her hands . . . I lifted her up
. . . the blood wouldn't stop . . . over her, over me . . .

Arthur Don't . . .

Molly Let her talk, son.

Sandra It began to happen more and more. I was afraid to
go out. Scared to death I'd end up in a loony-bin, locked
away with the blood and the dreams for the rest of my life.
And then I found a way to make it stop. I stopped looking at
Maureen, I stopped looking at the blood. I looked around
the street, around the room . . . made myself remember the
edges . . . Stupid details . . . Your buffet for the YTP open
day all set out on the table, Arthur. There was a revolting
salad in a green glass bowl . . .

Arthur Celery, date and walnut . . .

Sandra and the ham rolled up with a cocktail stick . . . I
said . . . I said . . .

Arthur You said, 'What for? They're gonna eat it, not take
pictures of it . . .'

Sandra . . . and Tommy's graffiti on the walls. 'Fuck 1690,
we want a rerun.'

Arthur 'Give us a job . . . What's a job?'

Sandra 'Snuff is high-class glue . . .'

Arthur 'No Pope here . . .'

Sandra 'No friggin' wonder.' (*Small pause.*) 'Is there a life before death . . . ?' The more I filled my head with all the daft edges . . . the less I could remember her lying in the middle of it all . . . I couldn't see the blood any more . . . until tonight. I should never have come back . . .

Molly You should never have blocked it out.

Sandra I had to, or go crazy. Frig, I went crazy anyway.

Molly You're not crazy. You were caught in a war. There's a fancy name these days for what happened to you. In my day, it was called shellshock. You carried your best friend in from a battlefield. Don't lock it away no more. You can't go on all your life bein' sixteen and mad with shock and grief and anger . . .

Sandra I missed her . . . I missed her just bein' around . . . talkin' daft . . . makin' daydreams. I was always putting her down, making fun of her. She was stupid and romantic, and sometimes she got on my nerves that much, all I wanted was for her to go away and give my head peace. And then she did go away, and it was like there was only half of me left. I started to imagine her as she might be if she hadn't . . . I began to see her . . . It was only glimpses at first . . . out of the corner of my eye. She'd be getting on a bus, or crossing a road . . . or I'd look in the mirror and for a second I'd see her face instead of mine . . . It wasn't scary, like the dreams. It was nice. She looked happy. I was happy. I started to go out again. And then one night I was in a pub in Kilburn. It was a talent night, and this drunk Irishman was tellin' pathetic jokes. 'How do you know who's the bride and groom at an Irish wedding? She's the one in the white wellies and he's the one in the flared wellies . . .' And we were all yelling at him to get off, and I said I could do better myself. And suddenly Maureen was standing right beside me, large as life, laughing out loud, and she said, 'Put your money where your mouth is, partner.'

Maureen *also says these words.*

She smiles, gestures for **Sandra** *to join her at the microphone.*
Sandra *walks towards her. We see them both on stage together, as*
Sandra *has imagined it all these years.*

Sandra We walked up to the microphone. She was real.
Alive and laughing. There was no stoppin' us. We were
magic. We got invited back. The next time we did our
double-act, it was her twenty-first birthday.

Sandra *looks at* **Maureen**. *The shadows are lengthening around
her. A look/gesture of farewell between them.* **Maureen** *walks away
into the darkness.*

It was never a double act. It was only ever me bouncin' off
the walls, all by myself . . . Dilly Day-dream's dead and gone
. . . it's over . . .

Arthur *moves as if to embrace her, but it's the comfort of* **Molly**'s
embrace she chooses.

Molly It's nearly midnight. A new beginning.

Sandra We'll see.

Arthur We'll see it in. Champagne on the house. Set it up
ma . . . the best bottle, the best glasses . . .

Molly *goes into the café–bar.*

A pause.

Sandra (*quietly*) If you tell Iris about this, I'll stove in your
steel plate, Arthur.

Arthur Tell Iris what? Come on over here a minute. I've
got something to show ye . . . Come on.

He takes **Sandra**'*s hand. Leads her to the statue.*

Arthur She's not just a pretty face, you know. She's the star
of the show on the openin' night. Next to you, of course. After
the speeches and before the posh nosh, I come out of the café–
bar, carryin' a big cake with a key on it. And I walk to the
 ̶ ̶ ̶d Mayor's table, and he takes the key, and he goes to the
 ̶ ̶ ̶ ̶, and as he turns the key, the overhead lights go down,
 ̶ ̶ ̶ ̶ to hell with the Lord Mayor. He never worked nor

lived round here. I'm gonna turn that key first. For you. Just for you. Hold on and I'll get it.

He goes into the café–bar.

Sandra *sits alone for a moment.*

She looks at the dark area where **Maureen** *once was. Then she gets up. Picks up her bag. And walks out.*

Sounds (off) of a clock chiming midnight.

Arthur *comes out of the café–bar with the key. When he sees that* **Sandra** *has gone, he just stands still until the clock stops chiming. Then puts the key in his pocket.*

The stage darkens.

Scene Two.

The following weekend. Very early in the morning.

Arthur *is watching* **Molly** *and* **Tommy** *pinning up a banner proclaiming the grand opening of the Lagan Mill Shopping Centre.*

Arthur Up your end a bit, ma . . .

Molly As the Archbishop said to the actress . . .

Arthur You're wasted in higher education. You should be on TV.

Molly I will be son, I will.

Sandra *walks in. Travel bag on her shoulder.*

Tommy Hiya doin?'?

Sandra I'm doin' all right.

But she looks at **Arthur**, *and he at her.*

Molly Come on, **Tommy**, you and me have bread to collect and fresh vegetables from the market . . .

Tommy (*to* **Sandra**) Arthur still won't cook anything from frozen, you know. I keep tellin' him, people don't know the

difference if you don't let on. Remember that diabolical stew
he used to make for the YTP? Ragout (*He pronounces the 't' at
the end.*) he used to call it. Iris has taught him how to
pronounce the French words proper . . . but it's still friggin'
stew, no matter what way you pronounce it . . .

Molly Today, Tommy!

Tommy *raises his eyes heavenward, heads for the door.*

Tommy (*aside to* **Sandra**) I remember the two of them
when they were nuthin' . . .

He exits. **Molly** *goes to follow him.*

Sandra Molly . . . thanks . . .

Molly You're welcome. See you the night. Wait'll you see
my new frock. Joan Collins eat your heart out.

Molly *exits.*

Sandra *sets her travel bag down.*

Arthur You're not stoppin' for the cabaret, are you?

Sandra Ten points for observation, Arthur.

Arthur It won't be the same without you.

Sandra Away on. Everybody here's a comedian.

Arthur All right if I put your name down for the Christmas
show?

Sandra You branchin' into showbiz in a big way, Arthur?

Arthur This is for you . . . it's a return ticket.

Sandra (*gently*) Jeesus Arthur, you were always ever
hopeful.

Arthur I want somethin' in return this time . . .

Sandra Oh aye?

Arthur I've waited a long time to ask you . . .

Sandra What?

Arthur I suppose you have a fella or two in London, eh?

Sandra I'm not a vestal virgin, Arthur.

Arthur Me neither . . . Have you got . . . anybody serious, like?

Sandra Like what?

Arthur Like, somebody who would be dead jealous if you and me . . .

Sandra What?

Arthur Danced together.

Sandra Danced?

Arthur You think you're the only one with fantastical daydreams? You see, when we won that medal at school . . .

Sandra Hop, one two three, hop skip, two three . . .

Arthur . . . That was the start of my great fantasy . . . you an' me on *Come Dancing*. Only the bullets put a stop to my dancin' days. I don't limp no more.

Sandra It was Iris made you better, not me. All I ever did was make mock of your limp and your scars and your oul steel plate.

Arthur I've never danced with nobody else the way I danced with you.

Sandra I'm sorry . . .

Arthur Don't you go soft on me. I like you the way you are. The way you always were. This is for you, you cheeky cow.

He takes the key out of his pocket. Turns it in a lock on the side of the fountain.

The overhead lights dim. The statue is illuminated with all the colours of the rainbow.

Water sprays. Music plays – the opening instrumental of the Furies singing 'Sweet Sixteen'. Quietly at first.

Sandra (*gently*) Jeesus Arthur, every now and again, you break my heart . . .

Arthur (*gently*) Bollocks . . .

He takes her in his arms. The volume increases.

Arthur *is a very good dancer. He leads* **Sandra**. *Makes her dance with him – a mixture of ballroom-dancing and slow jive.*

Every time she attempts to make a joke of it, he draws her back into the dance.

When the opening instrumental ends and the Furies sing the opening line of the verse 'When first I saw the lovelight in your eyes', **Sandra** *laughs and yells.*

Sandra Jeesus, Arthur! Iris'll kill you!

Arthur Fuck Iris.

They dance on.

She laughs and yells again at the second line of the chorus. 'Since first I saw you on the village green' . . .

Sandra The village green?! In Divis Friggin' Flats?

Arthur *continues to make her stop joking and dance. The dance is tender, loving and good fun. They sing/mime some of the words. Towards the end of the repeat chorus, they are dancing very close to each other. Not passionately – in a relaxed, gentle, loving way. During the second chorus, before the final instrumental plays, they come apart.* **Sandra** *kisses* **Arthur**, *very gently, on the mouth. He smiles at her. Hands her the travel bag. She smiles. Walks away.* **Arthur** *watches her go, then sits down beside the fountain.*

The lights and music from the fountain fade away.

The stage in darkness.

Spotlight on the microphone and **Sandra**. *She has a tinsel garland round her neck. A glass of champagne in her hand. She takes a drink. Raises her glass to the audience.*

It is four months later – December 1994

Sandra The last time I drunk champagne, was back home in Belfast. I've been invited back again for Christmas. I might just go, if only to check out the rumour about the new banner on the front of the City Hall. The old one said, (*Ian Paisley voice.*) 'Ulster says no!' Word has it that the new one says, 'Ulster says Ho! Ho! Ho!' Last time I was there, the IRA declared a cease-fire. And since then, the Loyalists have declared a cease-fire. The dole queues in Northern Ireland are a mile long. All them unemployed builders and glaziers and security guards and undertakers commiseratin' with each other, an' swoppin' sentimental stories about the good old days. 'Say what you like about the paramilitaries, Seaumus, they were a quare boom to the economy.' 'Aye, indeed they were, Billy, indeed they were. And what about our hospital facilities? Wasn't this the best place in the British Isles to have a bad accident?' 'We didn't know we were livin' did we, Seaumas?' 'No indeed, Billy. No indeed.'

They think they have problems? What about us? What about the comedians? The day them clowns in the IRA declared their cease-fire, they killed off half the Irish jokes. Not so much lost, as gone before. And then I thought, 'Well, there's still the other half. The Loyalists. They're always good for a laugh. And I'm no sooner back in London, than they declare a cease-fire as well. You see freedom fighters? They're all the same. They couldn't see green cheese but they'd want a bit. I was gutted. I thought, that's it, the end of a beautiful career. Time to sign on the dotted dole line, Columbine. I thought wrong. You can't keep the Irish down. We're a nation of comedians. The best ones are offstage. On the day the Loyalists declared their own cease-fire, two wee Belfast women were standing at a bus stop. And one turns to the other, and she says, 'Bloody typical, isn't it? You wait twenty-five friggin' years for a cease-fire and then two come along one after the other.'

Ulster says Ho! Ho! Ho!

Sandra *raises her glass.*

Happy Birthday, Jesus Mahoney.